THE **DICTATOR'S** DICTATION

THE

DICTATOR'S
DICTATION

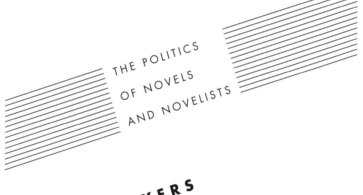

THE POLITICS
OF NOVELS
AND NOVELISTS

ROBERT BOYERS

COLUMBIA UNIVERSITY PRESS   NEW YORK

COLUMBIA UNIVERSITY PRESS

PUBLISHERS SINCE 1893

NEW YORK   CHICHESTER, WEST SUSSEX

COPYRIGHT © 2005 COLUMBIA UNIVERSITY PRESS

LIBRARY OF CONGRESS CATALOGING-IN-PUBLICATION DATA

BOYERS, ROBERT.

   THE DICTATOR'S DICTATION : THE POLITICS OF NOVELS
AND NOVELISTS / ROBERT BOYERS.

     P. CM.

   INCLUDES BIBLIOGRAPHICAL REFERENCES.

   ISBN 0–231–13674–9 (CLOTH : ALK. PAPER) —
ISBN 0–231–51007–1 (ELECTRONIC)

    1. FICTION–20TH CENTURY–HISTORY AND CRITICISM.

    2. POLITICS AND LITERATURE—HISTORY—20TH CENTURY.

    3. POLITICS IN LITERATURE. I. TITLE.

PN3503.B655   2005
809'.39358'0904—DC22   2005048475

COLUMBIA UNIVERSITY PRESS BOOKS ARE PRINTED
  ON PERMANENT AND DURABLE ACID-FREE PAPER.

PRINTED IN THE UNITED STATES OF AMERICA
C 10 9 8 7 6 5 4 3 2 1

DESIGNED BY LISA HAMM

FOR PEG BOYERS

AND FOR

NORMAN AND CELLA MANEA

CONTENTS

THE **DICTATOR'S** DICTATION

INTRODUCTION

THINKING ABOUT POLITICS AND
THE NOVEL

Almost all of the essays in this book were written during the last dozen years. Many were first published in *The New Republic*, where the literary editor, Leon Wieseltier, has often invited me to write about the intersection of politics and the novel. That intersection was once described by Lionel Trilling as a "bloody crossroads," where matters of life and death are taken up and the fate of "society" hangs always in the balance. Often, the bloody crossroads has seemed particularly attractive to writers and critics for whom novels at their best take positions on issues and permit readers to feel virtuous by associating themselves with those positions. By this standard—it is often invoked as a standard—novels resistant to political formulas are sometimes said to be deficient, their authors criticized as "timid" or "dishonest" for willfully refusing to take sides or face up to their "responsibilities."

In my own work, I have tried not to read novels in this way, though it is always tempting to search in novels for confirmation of one's deepest instincts. How often do most of us contrive ways to resist fictions that seem to us "reactionary" or "politically incorrect"? It is no secret that numerous critics have criticized the novels of V. S. Naipaul largely or solely because of their unflattering portraits of African or Caribbean "revolutionaries." Latin American critics often attack the novels of Mario Vargas Llosa because they despise his journalism, which is consistently critical of demagoguery and human-rights abuses in communist Cuba and in other "developing" societies. Vargas Llosa's novel *The Real Life of Alejandro Mayta* is a richly ambiguous, troubling portrait—now severe, now generous—of a Latin American leftist, but it is often read as a one-dimensional tract by readers who think they know what such a novel is supposed to say, and therefore "know" that *Mayta* is a "reactionary" work.

Many optimistic forecasters predicted that, with the fall of the Soviet empire and the close of the ideological cold war fifteen years ago, we would see at last the end of ideology and thus the end of programmatically rigid ideological criticism. But it is obvious that no such end is in view. Everywhere there is ideology. When Philip Roth published *The Human Stain* a few years ago, some deplored his attack on the varieties of political correctness in the American academy, as if his novel had been written principally for a narrow political purpose and had invented out of whole cloth the cruelty and stupidity displayed by a number of his ostensibly enlightened academic characters. Similarly, many were disappointed with Ingeborg Bachmann's great novel *Malina* because of its resistance to aspects of feminist thought and its ambiguous portrayal of a brilliant woman who struggles against her own debilitating sense of herself as a helpless victim. Milan Kundera, once celebrated for his complex portrayal of Czech citizens struggling to preserve some semblance of their identity in the face of Soviet domination, has more recently been condemned by critics on the "left" for his pessimistic view of his countrymen and by critics on the "right" for his failure to sing the praises of Western capitalism and the "open" society. Again and again we see the reduction of literature to doctrine and "views."

Think of Chinua Achebe's famous—or notorious—essay on Conrad's *Heart of Darkness*, an essay that reads Conrad as something of a racist and imperialist writer. Why summon that essay? For one thing, Achebe has long seemed to me a brilliant and sustaining novelist, whose books I teach in several of my courses. At the same time, his essay on Conrad is so wrongheaded that it seems almost to have been written by someone other than the man who wrote *Things Fall Apart* and *No Longer at Ease*. Because I think I understand Achebe, that is, understand how his mind works when he is doing his beautifully refined novelistic work, his essay seems to me a vivid demonstration of the way that ideas or ideology can sometimes immobilize even a first-rate intelligence.

Confronted by Achebe on Conrad, or by some other comparably dispiriting performance, I want to put up a hand before the critic's face and say, gently, calmly, with as much mildness as I can muster: Why not just forget about all of that for a while and give yourself again to the book you wish to discuss? Just go off and be alone with it. Let it do with you what it will. You'll see; it will release you from yourself a little, loosen your attachment to those clever ideas of yours, so that when you turn back to them again at last, as you will, they will seem to you less securely attractive or just, and your own attachment to them will perhaps seem to you less virtuous. Really, you'll see. When you next go out to bear witness to those ideas for the edification of your readers or students or friends, you'll be less sure of yourself, and you'll find it more appealing to make occasional concessions, to let the ideas breathe a little, clutched, as they are bound now to be, a little less fervently to your breast. At the very least, you will know that fiction itself, if it is any good at all, can never be *simply* a weapon of struggle, not, surely, in the way of a political speech or a persuasive essay. As Nadine Gordimer once said, speaking of her own political convictions and the essays she writes to advance them, "nothing I write in such pieces will be as true as my fiction." And nothing, we might add, can make a great work of fiction like *Heart of Darkness* merely an "imperialist" fiction.

3

Of course, it is one thing to think about politics and the novel in this sensible way and quite another to suppose that the politics of novels is invariably incidental or irrelevant. When a critic complains that Michael Ondaatje's *The English Patient* does not sufficiently engage the political issues at the heart of that novel, I say no, that is not a novel *about* politics, and no, the novel has no *necessary* obligation to engage issues in which the author is clearly not invested and that do not significantly affect our sense of his characters or the choices they make. On the other hand, a novel in which politics does clearly play a central role does have an obligation to look carefully at the ideas it has set in motion. When Philip Roth builds his novel *American Pastoral* around the political turmoil of the 1960s, he is obliged to represent that turmoil plausibly and to read its political implications in a way that can satisfy an adult intelligence. It is foolish to assert that Roth's book is merely a novel and that therefore its sole obligation is to be vivid and absorbing and to treat only the important issues—the personal issues—in a richly complex way. As readers, we see what a writer like Roth has purported to do with politics in his novel and, on that basis, we decide whether or not he has been equal to the task he has set himself.

Readers who do not know that authorial intention counts for a great deal in our experience of fiction do not read very well. Though it is surely legitimate to observe that frequently novelists apparently intend one thing, their novels another, that is not a good reason to ignore intention altogether or to propose that readers are free to make of a novel whatever they like. If we understand the significance of politics in a given novel as central, or marginal, that understanding has much to do with our sense that we have been invited to read that novel in a particular way. I cannot read Naipaul's *A Bend in the River* as I read Ondaatje's *The English Patient* because I see that in Naipaul's book, politics determines the fate of characters in a persistent way. Neither can I read *A Bend In The River* as an example of "neocolonialist" fiction simply because its view of African independence movements is relentlessly bleak. To understand the politics of such a novel, I must see whether or not Naipaul has contrived to make the independence movements seem hopeless, and contrived as well to suggest that Western empire had once made something substantially more promising in the Congo. To read such a novel is to attend to everything that its author has set in place and to consider the weight he has accorded to the several contending forces.

Twenty years ago, I published a book on politics and the novel entitled *Atrocity and Amnesia*. It combined close readings of selected texts with an element of "theory." My ambition was to consider books that asked to be read as "political novels," that is, books for which politics was obviously the dominant factor in the lives of characters and in the ideas that apparently mattered most to the authors themselves. This determination seemed clear to me when I was writing about novels by, say, Günter Grass, Aleksandr Solzhenitsyn, and Garcia Marquez, but somewhat more problematic when I turned to Gordimer, Kundera, and Graham Greene, among others. Gordimer, in fact, had once mildly protested against my description of her work as emerging from an essentially political imagination, and though I defended myself by assigning to the epithet "political" a rather more capacious definition than it deserves, I have since been reluctant to assign that very epithet to novels or novelists I admire. I no longer think it useful to speak of "political novels."

The essays assembled here on the politics of novels and novelists are inevitably informed by a wide range of "theoretical" sources, but my ambition has been to keep the theory to a minimum and to allow myself to respond as variously as possible to writers who operate from more than one single motive. There is no overarching theme to this book, no statement defining the nature of novels that deal with politics. Each of the essays grapples with what is most problematic about efforts to negotiate the relation between public and private, society and the individual. Each attempts to get inside the imagination of a writer whose thought has a political dimension but who is also moved to acknowledge that there may well be things in the world more important than politics. Andrew Delbanco has written that the classic American writers "believed in the inviolable rights of the free self" and mostly "wrote in a spirit of hope." About the writers discussed in this book no such general statement may be made. Even the American writers here are troubled by the intractability of dilemmas in the public realm. Others remark on the limitations of language, our inability to say precisely what we mean or to make our meanings and ideas effectual in the world. If, in Gordimer, or Peter Schneider, or Natalia Ginzburg, we find traces of hope, optimism, or political idealism, there is always also a vivid awareness of the constraints within which characters fitfully make their way. The "free self," insofar as it exists at all in the writers I examine, is most often regarded as a product of wishful thinking or, at best, an isolated, exotic instance. If power is by no means what Delbanco calls "the ground of all human relations" for writers like Norman Manea or J. M. Coetzee, neither do they see much promise in the principled recoil from power or the flight into humane privacies. The writers studied here are not much moved either by heaven or hell, and they regard politics, in the main, as an activity not often releasing our better creative energies. The "world more attractive" to which Trotsky once pointed does not tempt these writers, who are as suspicious of utopias and good intentions as they are of ideology.

In fact, it is the relative absence of ideology that differentiates the work of Roth, Manea, Coetzee, and most of the others treated here from the work once called "political fiction." This is in no way to suggest that writers—Koestler, Malraux, Jorge Semprun—whose fictions turn on ideological disputes necessarily adhere to a party line. Such writers, at their best, are no more confined by ideology than Naipaul or Anita Desai. But Koestler and Malraux surely felt that politics had principally to do with the passions invested in ideas as they hardened into ideological positions. When we read *Man's Fate* we are concerned with issues and ideas, though Malraux's characters are by no means entirely reducible to their views, and the novel as a whole is a good deal more than a schematic illustration of ideas. Still, much of the energy of *Man's Fate* or *The First Circle* is invested in debate. Characters believe that reality may be altered, for better or worse, by ideas. By contrast, Roth and Ginzburg, Schneider and Naipaul, Deane and Manea, all of them first-rate intellectuals, all of them gifted critics, nonetheless refuse

THINKING ABOUT POLITICS AND THE NOVEL

to use their novels principally to dramatize ideas or to test or subvert ideological principles.

Very few of the best contemporary writers would seem, then, to be at all attracted to ideology. When they take note of it at all, as Vargas Llosa does in a novel like *Mayta*, they treat it as an unfortunate tendency to which hopelessly credulous or impossibly altruistic people are susceptible. Even where, as in *Mayta* or in some of Gordimer's novels, dignity is conferred upon characters susceptible to ideology, relatively little attention is paid to debate or to the patient working through of ideas as such. Neither do writers like Ginzburg, Roth, or Manea write novels intended to disabuse people of illusions or to promote a commitment to values the authors themselves confidently hold and wish to share. Ginzburg's *All Our Yesterdays*, like *Mayta* or Coetzee's *Waiting for the Barbarians*, as different from one another as they are, all impress us as works in which the writers are feeling their way as they proceed, discovering what they think about questions on which all too many views and ideas are available.

Gordimer is probably the most "committed" of the novelists treated in this book, the author most consistently associated with a stance, but her novels are utterly resistant to orthodoxy, and, as a novelist, she does nothing simply because it is expected of her. If she is more at home in politics than many of the other writers, and more alert than they to the effect of ideology on the consciousness of her characters, she writes, all the same, to contest fixed positions and to engage more intimate and fundamental matters than the word "politics" can encompass. When Breyten Breytenbach wrote, in one of his memoirs, that he looked for an "opening" that might permit him to make "use of all my senses," he might have been speaking as well for Gordimer, who has never been content to use her fiction mainly to propagate ideas.

Of course, there is a danger in fictions resistant to ideas and to ideology. Wars and other great conflicts may be made to look like events that "just happen." Narratives of dispossession or ethnic strife may unfold as spectacle or as reflections of historical patterns that have no specific weight and no possibility of yielding to any conceivable political initiative. Characters may appear to be caught up in events without meaning and for which, therefore, no one may be held responsible. The depiction of such events will sometimes seem poignant and rely very heavily on loss and despair as pervasive, inescapable factors inhering in every significant conflict. But such works may achieve poignancy precisely by refusing to differentiate between one idea and another and, in effect, consigning everything to "fate" or "the irrational in human history." These problems and refusals figure heavily in the chapters of this book devoted to such different writers as Pat Barker and W. G. Sebald.

The very resonance of terms like "fate" or "the irrational" will often disarm political thinking and make politics itself seem thin or trivial. This is unfortunate in narratives that really do have a great deal to do with politics and that cannot be adequately understood without scrupulously developed political ideas. Don DeLillo is a rarity among American novelists by virtue of his appetite for ideas, understanding of ideology, and refusal to allow events to be dissolved in an ether of metaphysics or the unnamable. If politics in DeLillo often has much to do with spectacle, plots, and paranoid elaboration, it is not reduced to those features, and characters who see politics as nothing but spectacle are regarded in novels like *Libra* and *Mao II* as a part of the problem that those books examine.

In an odd way, novels with an interest in politics are most successful when that very attraction is itself made to seem dangerous, or worse. During the long years of the cold war, many writers, in Eastern Europe especially, anatomized the attraction to politics and lamented the relentless politicization of every aspect of the common life. In the West, meanwhile, many writers and intellectuals who deplored the blurring of public and private life in Poland or Czechoslovakia nonetheless came to believe that the word "politics" was applicable to everything and that there was no domain that could be understood without the benefit of political analysis. While Kundera struggled to identify a domain of private experience untouched by politics and not susceptible to translation into the "discourse" of power relations, others insisted that everything from sexual intimacy to childrearing be figured in political terms.

Gender relations especially seemed, to many writers and intellectuals, to invite translation into "politics." Occasionally, as in the work of Doris Lessing and Mary Gordon, this tendency produced sophisticated works with fully autonomous characters moving in plausibly elaborated social and historical contexts. Such writers refused to use the novel to settle ideological scores, though they were not at all averse to dispute or controversy. The chapter of this book devoted to Ingeborg Bachmann considers what may be gained or lost by assigning to a novel a unitary purpose and reading it as if a concept like "patriarchy" might unlock all of its secrets.

THINKING ABOUT POLITICS AND THE NOVEL

The book also includes a chapter on the Swiss writer Fleur Jaeggy. There I resist the temptation to read her work as if it had principally to do with structures of domination. With Jaeggy, someone predisposed to grab at available signs would surely reduce her work to issues of class and gender. But it is the object of the essay on Jaeggy to resist the political reading not on principle, but as a way of honoring what I take to be the intentions inscribed in the work.

The object of criticism, then—so I would argue—is to see the work as it really is, to let it be what it is without imposing upon it what the work does not invite. As the incarnation of a facing consciousness, the work has its own integrity, and I am not permitted to appropriate it as if it belonged to me. Just so, when we think about "reality" in political terms, we are required always to bear in mind that others do not exist simply to bend to our will. We take it as a mark of responsible political imagination that it proceeds from a respect for difference, and we abhor those who would make over the world in their own image and impose their conception of reality on unwilling others. Often, we use words like "arrogance" and "tyranny" to characterize the behavior of politicians who have no respect for others and who are frivolous in supposing that others are less attached to their habits and prejudices than we are. We are rightly appalled when our country blindly wages war on the assumption that those it attacks will approve of us and congratulate us, as if our "enemies" were bound to want for themselves the very things we believe they ought to want.

Of course, we know that analogies are not equations and that arrogance in the sphere of international politics is by no means the same thing as arrogance or tyranny in our willful appropriation of texts. Yet analogies are suggestive, and it is my hope that in coming at novels as I do, I have suggested that politics, properly understood, is best undertaken by people with a healthy respect for reality: that is, for everything in the world and in books that resists us and our wishes. To read as we should—so I believe—is to proceed as if the worst thing we can do is to violate what is not ours to alter or deny. I am pleased, in the work collected in this volume, to take "dictation" from the several creative "dictators" I have chosen to study, though "dictation" must here be understood to entail and to allow for a good deal of resistance, which is to say, criticism.

1

THE INDIGENOUS BERSERK

PHILIP ROTH

In Philip Roth's novel *American Pastoral* (1997), Roth's alter ego Nathan Zuckerman alludes in passing to a once famous writer, now largely forgotten, whose "sense of virtue is too narrow" for contemporary readers. The writer, we suspect, is Bernard Malamud. And what is it that passes for virtue in Malamud? In *The Assistant*, a grim and slender novel, the Jewish groceryman is eulogized as "a man that never stopped working . . . to make a living for his family," a man who "worked so hard and bitter," so that for his family there was "always something to eat." Morris Bober was "a good provider," the rabbi says, and, "besides," he was "honest." He assumed responsibilities. He showed up. He is to be venerated, without exaggeration or ceremony.

It is a narrow sense of virtue, to be sure, and not at all peculiar to Malamud among American Jewish writers. Saul Bellow, too, a provocateur who writes in a racy, unstable idiom and sometimes expresses a venomous antipathy toward the milder emotions, nonetheless swells with admiration for those who show and claim affection, who know, as we used to say, how to behave. "I saw now what I had done," says the narrator in Bellow's novella "Cousins," "treated him with respect, observed his birthdays, extended to him the love I had felt for my own parents. By such actions, I had rejected certain revolutionary developments of the past centuries, the advanced views of the enlightened, the contempt for parents illustrated with such charm and sharpness by Samuel Butler." Susceptible to the allure of subversive ironies and modern ideas, the Bellow protagonist is still responsive to what he calls "the old thoughtfulness."

The narrow virtues have often seemed narrow precisely because they were thought to require little thought. Often they have seemed feeble and gray because they were believed to entail no struggle, no weighing of choices. Habit, it is often felt, is the paralysis of spirit. Ordinariness is the negation of virtue. What is dull, dutiful, and comes more or less naturally is not to be prized. But Malamud and Bellow (and in this they were not altogether alone) hoped to identify in the ordinary activities available to any decent and thoughtful person, in social ritual and mundane interaction, a stay against the inhuman, against the brutality that ensues in the absence of the quotidian ideals and restraints.

Now Philip Roth engages this possibility. In *American Pastoral*, he examines decency, as it is embodied in a good-hearted man whose life seems for a while "*most simple and most ordinary and therefore just great.*" No reader will be surprised to find that such a life turns out to be neither simple nor just great. No one will wonder at Roth's ability to show what can become of "ordinary" when an orderly life takes an unexpected turn, or the repressed rears its head, or the good and measured life seems suddenly tedious and intolerable. Roth has for a long time, through many books, developed a powerful and unanswerable subversion of the rock-solid assurances around which many people attempt to organize their lives. He has taught his readers to hold their noses when confronted by pious reflections on "the human condition." An expert in apostasy and distortion, he has made of his own occasional attraction to moralizing rhetoric an opportunity for savage contradictoriness and wit. His present interest in the ordinary and the virtuous is new in the sense that they now hold him and tempt him, transfixed and bewildered, in a degree not generally discernible in his earlier fiction.

The ordinary man in *American Pastoral* is an assimilated Jew with an unlikely "steep-jawed, insentient Viking mask" and the youthful attributes of a demigod. The young Seymour "Swede" Levov is a star athlete worshiped by everyone in his neighborhood in Newark, a large "household Apollo" of an adolescent who goes on from schoolboy fame to marry a Catholic beauty queen, inherit a thriving business, and move his family to a prosperous farm in rural New Jersey. The Swede is ordinary only in the sense that he shapes his life to the measure of the American dream, aspiring to no more and no less than his share of perfection, which is to say, an existence largely without misgiving or menace.

There is nothing ordinary, of course, about the superb physical grace, the country estate, the ravishingly beautiful wife, or indeed the temperament of a man who can seem both mild and confident, resourceful and contained. But Roth is most taken with his character's desire to be ordinary, at ease in his place, without great ambition, without any desire to tear through appearances or to rage against his own limitations. He draws a character who for all of his success may be easily condescended to as well meaning, naive, blandly idealistic, without force—an average man, disappointing, pleasant, natural, displaying no capacity for irony or wit. Surely such a person—some will feel—deserves whatever can happen to him.

The Nathan Zuckerman who narrates *American Pastoral*, for whom Seymour Levov is an ostensibly remembered person and a character whose life needs to be imagined, is sorely tempted by the prospect of blasting such a life, stripping away every vestige of attractiveness from the character in all of his impeccable generosity and high-mindedness. An early reviewer of Roth's novel describes Seymour as a puppet, "mounted precisely for the purpose of being ripped," a figure who exists "to be punished" for his idealism, his grace, and his credulous embrace of the good life. Not exactly. Zuckerman is more than a little bit in love with this fellow. Recently recovered from prostate surgery, impotent, and in every way more subdued and more thoughtful than we remember him from previous Roth novels, Zuckerman wonders at the Swede the way one wonders at something moving and peculiar, something that defies explanation.

Still, explanations are advanced. Seymour's brother Jerry, a cardiac surgeon in Miami, has no trouble summing him up as a man with "a false image of everything," a man committed to tolerance and decorum, to "appearances" and the pathetic desire "to belong like everybody else to the United States of America." But this diatribe, it is clear, doesn't begin to explain Seymour, and the more he is assaulted by explanations and denunciations and hears himself maligned and diminished, the more securely he remains a wonder, a man astonished to the end at the continuously unfolding spectacle "of wantonness and betrayal and deception, of treachery and disunity" and "cruelty." Zuckerman wants, like the others, to have done with the crummy goodness of this common man, to dismiss him as a man unable "to understand anyone," a man without a shit detector, a fraud. But he remains transfixed, somehow admiring and exasperated. Against his better judgment, he makes the man so much more appealing than anyone else he can invent.

Not until very late in the novel does Swede Levov understand what Roth insists that he grasp. "He'd had it backwards. He had thought most of it was order and only a little of it was disorder." But reality is otherwise. Nothing follows clearly from anything else. Where once there was thought to be cause there is now only chance. A secure home environment can bring forth anything at all. A person blessed with every good fortune may despise her life as surely as a person blasted by fate may remain an optimist. A man with a beautiful wife may be attracted for no apparent reason to a mousy woman deficient in every quality. Those who don't know these things may be virtuous in one degree or another, but they will not know what life is. That is what Zuckerman would have us accept. That is what Roth would seem also to support. But Seymour's capacity to arrive at this knowledge in his own way, his capacity for reluctance and suffering, is a part of what makes him a man we can admire.

But *American Pastoral* is more than an examination of virtue, more than an attack on the delusoriness of liberal good intentions. Roth means it also to be a portrait of America. It moves gracefully from one quintessential American setting to another, from factory floor to rolling hills, from beauty pageant to high-school reunion. Conversations turn on standard American themes, from assimilation to athleticism, from business ethics to sexual fidelity. Characters correspond to familiar American types, including WASP gentry, old-style Jewish liberals, and therapeutic intellectuals armed with fashionably advanced views. Historical markers—World War II, Vietnam, Joseph McCarthy, race riots, the Weathermen, and so on—routinely identify the public landscape within which Americans of the pertinent generations move. The novel is eloquent in its evocation of vanished American neighborhoods such as Jewish Newark, and it allows characters to be sweetly or fiercely defensive about "what this country's all about."

The storyline takes many turns, but in essence it is a fairly simple narrative. Zuckerman remembers the Swede, meets up with him late in life, learns what he can about him, and constructs a narrative of the Swede's life that occupies most of the novel. Seymour is the son of Lou, a prosperous glove manufacturer who looms large in his son's life until his death at the age of ninety-six. Seymour tries to live the good life in an expensive WASP suburb, but he has to contend with Merry, the teenage daughter who develops from elfin companion to tormented stutterer, from antiwar protester to underground terrorist and bomb-throwing killer of innocent civilians.

Merry Levov remains, throughout the novel, a source of enormous agitation and distress for both of her parents. Seymour thinks about her incessantly, rehearsing various episodes in her life and reliving in his imagination all that she does and suffers. He recalls their acrimonious debates and her withering New Left invective. Most especially, he thinks about her setting off a bomb at a local post office and thereby killing an elderly man. He is contacted by a young companion of his daughter, who grotesquely exposes herself to him and offers to lead him to Merry if he will sleep with her. When he learns that Merry has been raped by someone in the terrorist underground, he cannot drive the fact from his mind; he seems almost mad with grieving and pity for his savage little lost girl. Though there are numerous opportunities for the novel to move in for a closer look at the terrorist operation, Roth is satisfied to focus on Merry and her revolting companion, emblems of the ravening ferocity of their kind.

In Merry's final incarnation, she is a fanatic of nonviolence, a Jain who wears a mask over her face to avoid doing damage to delicate microorganisms in the air. Her father cannot bring himself to turn her in when he has the chance, and he torments himself about what has happened to her, about his responsibility for having produced a monster. Though he cannot abandon his attachment to America and all that it has represented to him, he is sorely tried in his relations with his wife, his brother, and his father—particularly his father, a powerful man who periodically erupts in outbursts of colorful invective against degradation and indecency.

The dust jacket of Roth's novel promises a work that will take us back "to the conflicts and violent transitions of the 1960s." It invokes, in Roth's language, "the indigenous American berserk," "the sweep of history," and "the forces of social disorder." It describes, in short, a novel with large ambitions. The narrow virtues celebrated by earlier American Jewish writers were often played out in settings so circumscribed that one could feel the pressure to forget the world and to refine the perspective to a metaphysical essence. But Roth's novel is absorbed in worldly matters, in history. He wants to know how things happen, how places and events leave their mark on people.

There are instances, here and there, of the profligate extravagance that consumes so much of our attention in novels like *Sabbath's Theater* and *Operation Shylock*, with their verbal energy and their compulsive recourse to every variant of shtick and artifice. But *American Pastoral* strives mightily to situate its characters in a more classical manner, to insist that their passions are shaped, constrained, and exacerbated by circumstance. It worries about probability and verisimilitude, and it asks, again and again, how this can be and how that can be when reality so manifestly declares what is and what is not allowable. Questions of virtue and responsibility are complicated in this novel by what Henry James called the "swarming facts." It is not simply that nothing Roth imagines quite adds up; it is that he does not expect the facts to add up, that he supposes reality to lie in the sheer multiplicity of facts, their thickness of texture and their bewildering resistance to dreams of order.

So what is Philip Roth's America? It is a place where some people work and build and thrive while others fail and destroy and suffer. It is a place where everyone is increasingly aware of vast differences in wealth and where those who feel guilty about their own successes are increasingly made to feel foolish and irrelevant. It is a place in which radical ideas about fundamental change are held almost exclusively by lunatics and by intellectuals so divorced from fellow feeling that they can only laugh at deterioration and disaster, "enjoying enormously the assailability, the frailty, the enfeeblement of supposedly robust things."

There is a side of Roth that likewise revels in the tendency of things to fall apart and expose the illusoriness of order and optimism. But he is also susceptible to fellow feeling. Roth appreciates, however reluctantly, the satisfactions that are sometimes generated by those who believe literally in the American dream. When Seymour Levov mourns the Newark destroyed by riots and decay, the Newark "entombed there," its "pyramids . . . huge and dark and hideously impermeable as a great dynasty's burial edifice has every historical right to be," Roth invests with weight and dignity the sense of loss for things hard won and precious. His America, after all, is the place where immigrants not only make fortunes as a result of often despised virtues such as hard work and persistence, but in which those same immigrants often bring forth children endowed with vision and compassion.

It is possible, of course, to suppose that what Roth calls "the indigenous American berserk" has more to tell us about the country than the stories of immigrant success and the building of viable political institutions. Or at least it may tell us what Roth himself regards as fundamental to the American spirit: a propensity to violence, conspiracy, and irrationality. This propensity is not at all times and places obvious. Americans are adept at convincing themselves that it is a limited propensity, that it belongs to lunatic fringes that cannot in the long term threaten our collective commitment to reasonableness and tolerance. Yet Roth seems to believe that violence and irrationality are never very far from the surface of American life, that we deny them at our peril, and that our optimism is purchased in the way the individual purchases tranquility, through repression and willful blindness. The daughter of Seymour Levov is not simply a lunatic. She is to be understood, insofar as we may presume to understand her, as an important expression of our collective unconscious. If this is not easy to accept, any more than we would find it easy to accept, say, that the Bader Meinhof gang in Germany or the Red Brigades in Italy expressed the deeper selves of the societies they terrorized, well, as the novelist would seem to say, there it is.

Merry Levov is Roth's exemplification of our impatience with limits, our hatred of the gradualism and decorum that we profess to prize. As an adolescent growing up in the first days of the Vietnam War, she finds her opinions confirmed by her parents and her grandfather, but she grows impatient with their support. Like other young people involved in antiwar activities in the 1960s, she finds a way to turn the epithet "extreme" against her own family, as in: "No, I think extreme is to continue on with life as usual when this kind of craziness is going on . . . as if nothing is happening." Those who are opposed to America's involvement in Vietnam must bear witness—so she insists—by turning against their own comfortable lives, if necessary by throwing bombs. Just so, those who profess concern for black people going to pieces in urban ghettos must refuse to persist in business as usual, must refuse to insist upon profits, even if their refusal should cause their factories to fail and jobs to disappear. The worst is not to be feared if it may be a prelude to drastic change. The American berserk, as embodied in the figure of Merry Levov, is associated with ideas that were pervasive in the 1960s, and it is in part the burden of *American Pastoral* to suggest that these views really do express an important feature of American life.

The strangest thing about all of this is that Merry Levov never emerges in this novel as anything but a pathetic figure. As a child she is appropriately lovable and childish, but she rapidly grows into a fearful thing, twisted and angry, a caricature of herself. She becomes a type. She is, in fact, precisely the type pilloried by those critics for whom opposition to the Vietnam War and participation in the civil rights movement were mainly psychological expressions, the work of rebellious adolescents acting out their mostly impotent rage against authority. This tendency to reduce the movements of the 1960s to an undifferentiated cartoon of adolescent rebellion is given new life in Roth's novel. By contrast, writers such as James, Conrad, and Vargas Llosa, in their novels of politics

15

PHILIP ROTH

and society, mounted a savage attack on bomb throwers and ideologues while permitting them their misguided idealism and a sometimes adult grasp of power and injustice. To place Vargas Llosa's wild-eyed Alejandro Mayta alongside Merry Levov is to appreciate at once the dignified passion for radical renovation that the Peruvian novelist permits his character and the utter puerility and one-dimensionality of the American novelist's radical figures.

That Merry Levov is depicted as something of a lunatic is not especially objectionable, for it is surely true that there were lunatics and obsessives in the radical movements of the 1960s. But she and her more luridly drawn companion are, in Roth's novel, the primary exponents of oppositionist and critical views. The conditions that aroused so many mature adults to participate in the antiwar and civil rights movements are barely mentioned in a book committed to examining the period. For *American Pastoral*, recent American radicalism is to be associated with irrationality and the unconscious. In fact, it was both more dangerous and less dangerous than that. There is no effort in Roth's novel to link it to the genuine tradition of American radicalism that goes back at least to Emerson and Thoreau and, in this century, to Randolph Bourne, Paul Goodman, and Bayard Rustin. Merry Levov and her companions in extremism are all we need to know, apparently, when we come to consider what blasted the social order.

The failure of Roth's novel, in this respect, is quite considerable, however unmistakably particular passages are the work of a master. If there is such a thing as the indigenous American berserk, then surely it must entail a good deal more than a lunatic fringe largely limited to deranged adolescents acting out fantasies of retributive violence. And if these adolescents, who usually grow up into pinstripes, tweeds, and cappuccino bars, can be so readily dismissed and condescended to by their elders, including Nathan Zuckerman, then how can they be said to represent an enduring and significant feature of American life, a tendency to which even the best of us are regularly susceptible? This novel wants to have it both ways. It wishes to develop an apocalyptic vision of the real America, the underside of our characteristic optimism and bland goodwill, but it wants also to propose that what we refuse to acknowledge in our pusillanimous American selves is pathetic, adolescent, laughable, and decidedly marginal, however terrible the occasional consequences associated with this "other," supposedly truer reality.

Consider Roth's presentation of the facts involved in the destruction of Newark. The dominant perspective belongs, more or less equally, to Zuckerman, to the Swede, and to his father. According to them, there was once a "country-that-used-to-be, when everyone knew his role and took the rules dead seriously, the acculturating back-and-forth that all of us here grew up with." Of course there were conflicts in that once-upon-a-time land, but they were usually manageable, they conformed to something about which you could make some sense. And Newark was very much a part of the "country-that-used-to-be," a place where pastoral visions may not always have been easy to come by, but where "the desperation of the counterpastoral" was also not much in evidence.

In Roth's reasonable Newark of Jewish and other immigrants, there are factories and businesses that produce well-made goods and turn reasonable profits. They employ people "who know what they're doing," who are pleased to do good work, and more or less content with what they are paid. At least they do not complain. They are loyal to their employers, and they may well remember gratefully how things have changed for the better since the bad old times one hundred years earlier, when factories were places "where people . . . lost fingers and arms and got their feet crushed and their faces scalded, where children once labored in the heat and the cold." The factory owners are also apt to have a vivid sense of their own origins, to remember working "day and night" and living in intimate contact with working people at all levels of manufacturing and selling. Their stubborn celebration of everything American has much to do with how well things can go when people believe in the system and rely on one another.

Given this account of reality, it is no wonder that the eruption of civil strife in the 1960s should seem so incredible not only to the Levovs but, apparently, also to Zuckerman. The nostalgia for the "country-that-used-to-be" is so palpable in this novel that it virtually immobilizes the imagination of reality and leaves the reader susceptible to a rhetoric for which the deteriorating urban landscape is a "shadow world of hell" and predatory blacks roaming the Newark streets are part of a "surreal vision." Once not long ago, according to this narrative, everybody had it good, or good enough. But many Americans suddenly went unaccountably crazy, and what "everyone craves" came to pass, "a wanton free-for-all" in which what was released felt "redemptive . . . purifying . . . spiritual and revolutionary." However "gruesome" and "monstrous" what followed, something real happened in Newark, something irresistible and deeply implicated in the American grain.

PHILIP ROTH

So we are to believe. Though the Levovs watched with horror, and deplored what was happening, and most other Americans presumably recoiled as well, we are asked to accept that somehow "America" spoke its deep, revealing truths in the intoxication of riot and mayhem. We are also asked to accept, as befits this pattern, that those who set the cities on fire and who beat on "bongo drums" while their neighbors looted and sniped and left behind a "smoldering rubble" were actually in flight from the good life. We are to accept—so the logic of the novel dictates—that the blacks of the inner city must have been incomprehensibly dissatisfied with their wonderful jobs and turned on by the prospect of liberating something vital and long buried in their otherwise admirable lives.

The problem is, Roth's book offers us no way to think about such a view of things. Its elegy for the dead city and its old ways is affecting, but it is also disconnected from anything like a serious account of what the old ways actually entailed and what were the varied motives and desires of the inner-city residents who were caught up in the destruction of their own communities. To read Roth on the Newark riots is to suppose that just about everyone participated in the looting and the carnage and that no one can have had good, concrete reasons for loathing the conditions in which they lived. To understand the 1960s is, again, to invoke individual and group psychology, to refer to something deep and peculiarly American, to deplore what happened while at the same time suggesting that it had to happen and cannot be accounted for by citing social, political, or economic factors.

Roth's novel is finally not an adequate study of social disorder. It does not tell us what we need to know about America, does not tell us what a novel can tell us about the complex attitudes and allegiances of a time and a place. It laments the denial of reality on the part of middle-class suburbanites such as Seymour Levov while offering as the alternative to illusion "surreal" and "grotesque" eruptions such as few Americans are likely to encounter. It sets up as representative figures of disorder and "reality" people who are mad and whose attachment to disorder is so pathological that they make it impossible for us to consider seriously the actual sources of discontent in American society. When violence breaks out in this novel, it is more like an inexplicable convulsion than an expression of feelings shaped by complicated individuals responding to the actual conditions of their lives.

And yet Roth's interest in an idea of simple virtue is an impressive achievement. For if the world as he understands it is a place of chaos and contradiction, in which order is fragile or even illusory, then virtue, too, may seem like a figment of someone's wishful thinking, a willed fantasy with nothing to sustain it. But Roth finally suggests that it is not. Like the rest of us, he wonders what virtue can be worth when it is rarely effectual in worldly terms. And he refuses to allow goodness to sweeten anything, to distract him from what we are and what we do. Yet his triumph in *American Pastoral* is in the portrayal of people who are unmistakably good and genuine. They understand no better than he does what to make of events that astonish and assault them, but they do not give up on their sense of how to behave.

Seymour Levov is no paragon of perfect virtue, and his father can seem shrill and forbidding in his vehemence. But these are men who continue to display thoughtfulness, however much reason they have to be disappointed and to flee in bitterness from the decencies that make them seem irrelevant to their contemporaries. The father may have absurd ideas about how to deal with disorder—"I say lock the kids in their rooms"—but he is strangely appealing in his insistence that "degrading things should not be taken in their stride." That is right. And the son, who suffers greatly, who does not know enough, who takes "to be good" everyone "who flashed the signs of goodness," retains in Roth's hands the capacity to be appalled—not thrilled, but appalled—by transgression, to be tormented by the spectacle of needless suffering, and to think, ever to think, about "justification" and "what he should do and . . . what he shouldn't do." His humanity is intact. And it is, Roth is saying, the only thing we can rely on.

2

IDENTITY AND DIFFIDENCE

SEAMUS DEANE

Irish history is bad history. So says one character in *Reading in the Dark*, Seamus Deane's first novel, and no other character in the novel seems much inclined to deny it. In a land of "small places," as it is described here, people have too often made "big mistakes." They lie to themselves and to one another. They rely on old certainties when they might better have abandoned them. They carry around "stale" secrets and bitter resentments. Their courage is too often merely a willingness to absorb meaningless defeats and inflict pointless damage. For all their eloquence and their gift for storytelling, they are not, typically, much good at distinguishing truth from fiction, the past from the present. The language of feud and retribution, of shame and fatedness, is on every tongue.

Of course, clear-sighted Irish men and women can also see plenty to be proud of in their past, but all agree that the history of Northern Ireland contains every kind of motive for resentment, rage, and hopelessness. "The whole situation makes men evil," says one of Deane's priests, and "evil men make the whole situation." To live in a place like Derry in the 1940s and 1950s, when Deane's novel is set, is to remember failed rebellions and to confront, day after day, the British policemen one has learned to regard as intolerable, both for their casual brutalities and their unwelcome efforts at commiseration and intimacy. Most of what goes on in such a place has nothing to do with politics, as it happens, but always there is a sense of "the whole situation," and people who might well have seen themselves as the source of present difficulties are embittered and coarsened by the long sense of injustice they have borne. The priests speak, when they can, of "an inner peace nothing can reach" and "no insult can violate," but the Irish refuse to forget the "cruel birth" of their country, and they suffer their history like a perpetual humiliation.

Deane's novel is no polemic. It presents no case for or against his countrymen, no brief for a particular reading of Irish history. It is mainly the story of a boy's coming of age, and it is told mostly in very brief chapters with titles such as "Maths Class," "Crazy Joe," "The Facts of Life," and "Sergeant Burke." The chapters mostly cover minor events: the boy encounters and engages with family members and strangers, with schoolmates, priests, and teachers. He goes to classes, gets in and out of trouble, and generally behaves very much in the way we might expect of a boy in such a time and place. The sequence is strictly chronological, and incidents are often "necessary" only in the sense that they convey the flavor of the narrator's experience.

The novel is haunted by the story of a series of betrayals, a story revealed in bits and pieces picked out of fragmentary confessions and intimations. The betrayals are both personal and political, and though they have the power to corrupt lives in Deane's little world, they never take control of the narrative. The boy at the center of the novel makes what he can of the fragments, understanding dimly, then more clearly, that members of his own family are implicated in the various betrayals. At times he is angry and confused, at other times he is overwhelmed by pity and tenderness. Alert to the deceptions of priests, policemen, and politicians, he is properly skeptical of traditions and myths, but he entertains no serious possibility of reversing deeply rooted customs or assumptions. Blindness, like love or hate, is a condition that persists, no matter the inducements to see or to change.

A reader who comes to Deane's novel without a substantial understanding of "the troubles" of Northern Ireland will learn little from the narrative. It refers vaguely to early struggles and uprisings, but it offers no hard information, and its ideas are rudimentary. Dramatic encounters are briefly recalled. People occasionally refer to protests "at the founding of the new state" or to retaliation for a particular injustice, but the encounters as recalled are not especially important in themselves. The IRA gunmen on a roof are no more comprehensible than the policemen who surround them. Riots are just events that happen, like the death of a child or the infidelity of a husband. If people sometimes behave in particular ways for particular reasons, they are rarely good reasons, and acknowledging them leads nowhere. "There was a belief" in this thing or that, in this cause or that dark necessity, but it does no one any good, apparently, to persist in the belief or to abandon it.

Deane tells the stories of people's lives with a crisp lyricism, though it is not always easy for a reader to remain interested in characters who have few thoughts and little inclination to open themselves to sharp sensory experiences. People are said to live in silence, to feel hopelessly separated from one another, "trapped," desiring routinely "to be free of the immediate pressures." The regret for missed opportunities darkens every consciousness. My Father? "He would have loved. . . . " My Grandfather? He "realized for sure the mistake he had made. . . . " My own life? "Rehearsing conversations I would never have." To make something of lives so committed to the desultory and unconsummated is a challenge, and Deane is not always up to it.

Lacking the will to analyze and the appetite for metaphysics or morals, Deane is content to set things down as if they spoke for themselves. But often they do not say much more than "failure" and "regret." Deane's people are so inured to the facts of their lives that they are almost constitutionally averse to development. To his credit, Deane resists the temptation to claim for these characters qualities that they do not possess, but too often we feel that they are important to him for reasons that he does not know how to share. The work sometimes reads more like a memoir than a novel, in that people and events matter only because they were actually a part of the narrator's experience.

As if alert to the prospect that Deane's book will seem to many readers thin and lacking in ideas and development, Seamus Heaney has praised it as "sudden" and compares it to Isaac Babel. But Deane's book is not "sudden" like a Babel story, and it is without many of the virtues that make a Babel story distinctive. Deane's irony, only occasionally in evidence, is broad, more an irony of circumstance than of voice. We do not find in Deane the internal conflict—as between the physical and spiritual—that seethes everywhere just beneath the surface in Babel. Deane knows and accepts his people and his place as they are; he does not allow what he knows to raise in him the self-doubt that gives such an edge to Babel's laconic fictions.

In Deane's book, we have the material for moral inquiry, but the inquiry is not pursued. Still, there are passages of exceptional vitality. The boy sits through a memorable "facts of life" session with the school's spiritual director and is confounded by unfamiliar words and concepts. ("Ask him, you stupid shit, ask him, that's what you're here for, but I couldn't do anything except stare at him.") The mother suffers a breakdown and begins to communicate long-buried thoughts in a language

23

strangely suggestive and obscure. ("Paradise was not far away when I died.") The voluble police sergeant confesses that he has beaten suspects he knew to be innocent, since not to have done so "would have looked strange." Throughout the novel, often in unlikely places, things come suddenly to life. We remember that these people are more than the sum of their refusals and resignations. The mother, who absorbs several varieties of humiliation, is eloquent in repudiating the "dirty politics" of the British and the routine admonitions directed at those who struggle and resist. The father, hardworking and forlorn, is stubbornly faithful and resilient, and his aversion to posturing is so powerful that he chastises his young sons on their knees in prayer for making "a meal of it" and "trying to look like little saints."

24

Though *Reading in the Dark* is a first novel, Deane has been a literary presence since 1972, when he published the first of several volumes of poems. More recently, he attracted attention as the general editor of *The Field Day Anthology of Irish Writing, 550–1990*, a massive three-volume compendium that presents not only an extraordinary range of literary voices but an abundance of "texts," from incendiary pamphlets to political speeches and historical accounts of public events. The controlling idea of the anthology appears to be that it is futile and misleading, at least in the case of the Irish, to isolate literature from politics. And Irish writers have been more or less unanimous in affirming this sense of their work. Yeats wrote that Irish writers were necessarily "maimed" by the "great hatred" that they carried around with them, and that his own meeting with the Fenian leader John O'Leary was singularly important in bringing "the poet in[to] the presence of his theme." Even those who did not choose to dwell on political themes, such as Joyce, were deeply absorbed with questions of marginality and identity. Deane himself has said that "the dominant public experience of my career has been the political crisis in Northern Ireland."

What is most remarkable about Deane's novel, then, is its refusal to permit the lives of its characters to be wholly swallowed by politics. Desultory their lives may be, but the presumptive causes are more various than any singleminded obsession with "the situation." And of course, the novelist who, like Deane, immerses himself in various lives is always likely to discover occasions for verbal extravagance and merriment. Examples abound in this book. A classroom instructor in mathematics leaves an indelible picture of manic aggression and wit, unleashing a relentless verbal assault on the "brain dead" and "memory-less" among his charges. Is this a reflection of an inveterate Irish inferiority complex that can emerge also as physical brutality and torture? Deane does not instruct us to read it that way. Does the instructor's emphasis on "corruption" and the "evolutionary cul-de-sac" represented by especially recalcitrant students not produce in them a resentment and defensiveness that can be fed and turned to violence by skillful demagogues? Deane charts no such consequence. In place of diagnosis, his chapter on "Maths Class" offers the marvelous and the unaccountable, an expression of verbal playfulness that in spite of his punitive sarcasm requires neither justification nor relevance.

Where the political does take center stage in Deane's novel, moreover, it may well seem indistinguishable from the dissemination of propaganda. In 1956, an Anglican priest in British army uniform visits the boy's school as a part of the "battle for the hearts and minds of men" against the specter of world communism. The battle is represented by the genial priest as "a battle of faithlessness against faith; a battle of subtle wiles against manly freedom; a battle of cold atheism against the genial warmth of that Christian faith that has lit so many Irish hearts down the centuries." In the face of this battle, the disputes that divide Irish men and women are said to be "no more than family quarrels." A "traditional" society, whatever its internal dissensions, will wish to uphold "the eternal verities," says the priest; its people will know what is truly important to its survival and what is, in the long term, incidental.

The boys, of course, are mostly deaf to these appeals. Accustomed to hearing things that they know to be untrue, they rarely pay much attention to the particulars of the case presented to them. What they are likely to hear in the way of political discourse can be readily dismissed. It is encouraging to note how little susceptible to the priest's calculated pieties are the Irish schoolboys. Yet neither are these children on their way to anything approaching a mature grasp of political issues. At least, Deane makes no such claim for them.

The best that can be said for the political intelligence of the adults in Deane's world is that occasionally they feel sorry for the troubles of others and reflect, in a spirit of resigned incomprehension, on the way that events elude their grasp. "It's a strange world," says the boy's father, moved by his own encounter with the father of a British soldier shot dead by an IRA sniper in the course of a street search. "I feel for him. Even if his son was one of those," the father says. No more comes from him on this score; no more is to be expected. His reality does not demand of him complexity or a sustained reconsideration of old positions. The facts are what matter: the curfews, the street barricades, the armored trucks, "the avocado battle-dress of the soldiers," the intermittent gunshots, and the routine humiliations of search, suspicion, and seizure.

Does it matter that the story of these people is told from the perspective of a working-class boy? Deane wrings from the tale very little of the easy charm and naïveté of the usual first-person child's narrative. No effort is made to simulate the familiar headlong rush of infant volubility, the childish locutions or fragmentary reticence intended to evoke innocence or embarrassment. Even where there is an immediacy in the language, in the contrivance of a retrospective present tense, the language belongs to an adult voice: "She would come down with me," he writes of his mother, "her heart jackhammering, and her breath quick . . . her face in a rictus of crying, but without tears."

Likewise, where sequences are organized to make a point, we feel that it is a point elected by the adult novelist, who is at once inside the experience he narrates and well past it. "Was that house really a brothel?" the boy wonders, retreating from an open door and the painted face of "a young woman with tousled hair. . . . What would it be like with her?" he wonders further, later whispering to himself the chastening words of St. Ignatius on the subject of mortal sin. But we stand always a little outside of this confusion, kept deliberately out by the poetic cadence and elevation of the writing, as in the following conclusion to the chapter entitled "Brothel": "And still the vision of that young woman drifted there, vague one moment, the next vivid, reaching for me, unloosing the clasp of her skirt that rustled down as I leapt back and came forward, blurring inwardly, making my election."

More important than the boy's perspective is his working-class background, however little Deane wishes to make it an issue. There are, in this world, few places to hide from the indignities that the boy comes to expect. The occasional beatings or taunts administered by local policemen are matched by the assaults of street gangs and the bruising insults of others alert to every prospect of inflicting abuse. Growing up among unsophisticated people who are nursing their own memories of want and hurt, the boy has little chance of escaping the vindictive parochialism of his community. For Deane, it sometimes seems that the worst thing a decent person can do is to talk to a policeman, as if to do so were to sell one's soul to the devil.

As in other Irish works focused on betrayal, the central term in the lexicon of abuse here is "informer." To inform is to forfeit any semblance of self-respect and to sever irreparably one's ties to the community. Forgivable in principle, the informer is in practice regarded as grotesque and out of bounds. When the father utters about a member of his own family the words "he was an informer," the son can only beg him to unsay them. "Say nothing," he repeats to himself. "Never say. Never say." Members of families thought to have contained an informer are tainted, carry a curse, and may expect at any time to be punished for the unhappiness that has befallen them. To marry into such a family is not only ill-advised, it is a breaking of "sacred laws."

Like everything else in Deane's world, his people may regret certain attitudes and practices regarding informers, but the attitudes are too deeply rooted to deplore or to reform. When the boy finds himself suspected of informing on a few street toughs who had intended to rough him up, he finds no support, even within his own family. It makes no difference that he gave no information to the policemen who questioned him, and that no movement or organization was at stake, no oath violated. "Have you no self-respect, no pride?" screams his mother:

> "Thank God my father's too ill to hear about this—the shame alone would finish him. A grandson of his going to the police!"
>
> "I didn't go to the police. I threw a stone at them."
>
> "Same thing in the circumstances. . . . "

Nor is the usually more generous father more understanding. "Why didn't I take a few punches? Didn't I know what sort of people the police were? Had I no guts, no sense, no savvy, no shame?" Tempted to mark up the entire demand system of the community to "stupidity," the boy concludes that his father and all the others are "right" but "wrong too." To live in such a place, it seems, is to accept that wisdom consists in learning to tolerate what in any case will not change. If it is stupid to be battered for no good reason, and stupid to regard as "informing" what is no such thing, and stupid to live perpetually in fear of disapproval by persons who are ignorant and malicious, it is also stupid to pretend that one can get along in such a place without making substantial concessions to the reigning shibboleths and expectations.

Of course, *Reading in the Dark* is a novel. What would seem contradictory in another genre is here variousness and complexity. Deane need not tell us that he disapproves of much that passes for the facts of life in Derry for us to grasp their awfulness and their sometimes terrible vitality. And for all the stubborn blindness in many of Deane's characters, there is a tenacity that can seem almost wonderful. The situation of Northern Ireland, discernible here only in fragments, allows for a complicated communal life, however crippling its myths. Deane's novel is driven by an impressive power of remembrance and by a conviction that the proper business of the novelist is to make ordinary lives in their own way eventful, so that possibility exists even where fatality reigns.

3

A GENEROUS MIND

NATALIA GINZBURG

Natalia Ginzburg had little patience for pretense or fake civility. Although the Italian writer complained of others who had no love for "the daily current of existence," she was preternaturally poised to criticize. Friends, family members, and colleagues were valued and adored largely, it would seem, for their capacity to avoid sickly sentimentality and self-deception. What she called "the strange gift of motivating and stimulating" she associated with sharp, honest, often harsh truth-telling. "I realized," she declares in one of several 1990 interviews collected in *It's Hard to Talk About Yourself:*

> That this son of mine . . . is an interlocutor for me . . . I offer him what I've written, he reads it and immediately responds with a stream of insults and abusive remarks . . . a savage and amused bullishness. Laughter and happiness pour out of his coal-black eyes, from his wild, black, hairy head. I think that insulting me is one of the pleasures of his life. Listening to his insults is certainly one of the pleasures of mine.

The pleasure is obvious as well when Ginzburg speaks almost gleefully of the scorn directed at her plays and essays by her novelist friend Elsa Morante, or when she savagely criticizes a novel by another friend, Alberto Moravia. "Perhaps there is something cruel in Natalia's art," wrote Eugenio Montale. So clear was it that Ginzburg could be counted upon to hold nothing back that even those on the receiving end of her toughest criticism tended to be forgiving. After all, they felt, she was hard on everyone, not least on herself and her own fictional characters.

Ginzburg was ever alert to dishonesty and hated self-deception as if it were a mortal sin. Typically, it was not the lies of smiling public men or tyrants she wrote about. She despised imprecision and mistrusted language itself, especially in the hands of skilled writers who knew how to "cheat" more effectively than others. "There is the danger," Ginzburg wrote in an essay entitled "My Vocation," "of cheating with words that do not really exist within us"—by which, presumably, she intended to target varieties of rank inauthenticity: the nobler-than-thou posturing of the oh-so-committed dissident intellectual, the self-righteous accent of the moralist determined to challenge evil and remain untainted, the plaintive bleat of the vulnerable, forever victimized innocent kept down by "patriarchy" or by other conspiratorial forces. Everywhere in Ginzburg's writing, the recoil from posturing of any kind is unmistakable. She listens intently, we feel, for the slightest falsity, and pounces upon it before it can establish a foothold in her sentences. When admirers use words like "naked" and "pure" to describe her prose, they are referring to that quality of scruple in the writing, that refusal or inability ever to be entirely forgiving, pleasant, pious, or accommodating.

Although Ginzburg, who was born in Palermo in 1916 and died in Rome in 1991, was a leading figure in Italian literary and public life, she was never quite regarded as a major writer. Even in the United States, where her books have long been admired and available, she is not as widely read as Cesare Pavese, Italo Calvino, Primo Levi, or other contemporaries. Some critics speculate that because Italians tend to admire principally a rich, sonorous, literary prose, they could never quite believe a relatively "plain" writer like Ginzburg could be anything but lucid and elementary. Others suggest that she was narrowly regarded as an artist with a constrained, "womanly" perspective because she tended most often to write in the first person and usually limited herself—at least in her novels—to interpersonal and domestic issues. There is nothing remotely "feminine" about Ginzburg's style, which often calls to mind the muscular cadences of Hemingway's prose (with which it has absolutely nothing else in common), but she seemed to many readers an "occasional" writer, inspired by the quotidian, a recorder of impressions and fitfully entertained ideas.

None of this is to suggest that Ginzburg was an obscure figure or unappreciated. Her life has long been well known and widely discussed in Italy, where for many years she wrote a regular newspaper column for *La Stampa* and served in the Italian Parliament. In 1938, she married Leone Ginzburg, a young man of letters and an antifascist militant (who would be tortured and executed in 1944), and was at once drawn into a circle that was soon to become central to Italian intellectual life. That circle included the publisher Giulio Einaudi, whose press published many of the best writers in postwar Italy and employed as editors Pavese, Calvino, and Ginzburg herself. Ginzburg's first novel appeared in 1942, and it was followed by an ample succession of fiction and nonfiction books right up to the time of her death. For some of these volumes she was awarded the major Italian literary prizes, and by the mid-1960s, Italian schoolchildren of various ages were inevitably confronted by textbook excerpts from her novels and essays. *It's Hard to Talk About Yourself* is a testament to Ginzburg's stature in her own country, where the 1990 interviews were originally broadcast on Italian radio on four consecutive Sunday evenings. The interviews are routinely punctuated by guest appearances, in the course of which several leading Italian critics speak with Ginzburg about her role in the culture.

In Italy it was her memoiristic "fiction" *The Things We Used To Say* that brought her fame in 1963, when the book won the Strega Prize. It is, without question, one of her best and most characteristic works—a combination of sardonic humor and intimate reminiscence, of swift, efficient narrative and harsh yet also affectionate portraiture. Although here and there Ginzburg pauses for reflection, for the long, considered view ("After the war, the world appeared vast and unknowable and without boundaries"), much of the book has the feel of improvisation. The writer wishes to share everything that comes to mind, to tell her stories one after another, and does so with a pungency that seems to us natural, without affectation, and we see at once that the shaping imagination is very much in control of the onrushing narrative.

Conspicuous throughout is an urgency that reflects not merely the biographical or memoiristic impulse but also the need to discover patterns of meaning in what would otherwise seem eccentric and fragmentary. The rages of Ginzburg's father, for example, are vividly evoked, not merely for their own sake but to identify one plausible source for her attraction to the cleansing properties derived from speaking one's mind. If, in Ginzburg's formative years, fascism held sway, creating a climate "in which it had seemed that the world had been paralysed and struck dumb," and even writers were limited in the words "they were permitted to use," it was essential that she had always before her the example of household familiars who would not hold their tongues. For all of the melancholy that emanates from some of Ginzburg's pages, there is as well an alternating current of defiant, sometimes even joyous, truth

NATALIA GINZBURG

telling. And for all of her interest in anatomizing the cultural "paralysis," "nausea," and "ennui" that gripped her contemporaries, particularly during the war years, Ginzburg wrings from her experience stabs of ironic observation; sharp, often paradoxical insights; abrupt, almost casually blunt declarations that stick in the mind, provoking and exhilarating in almost equal measure.

It is characteristic of Ginzburg, in all of her work, to evoke a perfectly singular mixture of affection and admiration on the one hand with anger and disappointment on the other. When she remembers the death of Cesare Pavese or that of another figure, it is neither theories about suicide she wishes to offer nor formal disquisitions on intelligence or calculation: she is thinking, as she always does, about varieties of the human. Ginzburg seems, now and again, to draw conclusions; but they are, all of them, provisional. They emerge from a particular set of experiences, and although they tempt us to invest in them as if they constituted reliable truths, they become, in Ginzburg's hands, at most a temporary resting place, a pause before the next foray into confusion, anecdote, trifle, and the darkly consequential. Everything matters for Ginzburg, not just the "important" figures like Pavese and the big things like fascism and the resistance to fascism but also whatever stirs her to feeling, judgment, misgiving, and back again to a new round of anecdote and reflection.

Ginzburg never determines to be entertaining or edifying. She entertains and edifies because she is alert to every prospect of amusement or paradox in her material. When she writes that her father, a professor of anatomy, "wanted to treat people, but only on condition that they didn't ask him to treat them," she inadvertently offers a key to her own temperament. She wants to amuse, to chasten and instruct, but only on condition that she can do so without feeling that she is answering someone else's call or fulfilling a requirement.

She knows that there is some virtue in consistency, but won't demand it of herself or of anyone else simply because it is responsible for rational people to insist upon it. "My father smoked like a chimney," Ginzburg writes, "but he didn't approve of other people smoking." From this, many different conclusions might be drawn, and at selected moments, Ginzburg is not averse to trying them on. Typically, though, she is as resistant to the definitive and the portentous as she is to the ceremonious and the bathetic. In place of theory or platitude she gives us astringent play of mind. She is always ready to reconsider—if not quite to take back—everything she says.

Of course, the emphasis on astringency and disinfatuation may suggest that Ginzburg was not naturally a generous person, that her instincts were invariably critical. You read one almost matter-of-fact account of the death of her husband and you feel, at least at first, that this is a person ill at ease with emotion who will not allow herself to be vulnerable. Elsewhere, as in certain pages devoted to the death of a friend, occasional sentiments of loss will be subordinated to expressions of anger, reproach, or clear-eyed criticism. Ginzburg is not always quick to swallow her bile or to forgive what she takes to be an inexcusable self-indulgence in a friend or in herself.

Yet she places enormous emphasis upon generosity, regarding it as a spiritual achievement that deserves to be ranked above all others. In "The Little Virtues," perhaps her most famous essay, Ginzburg declares that children should be taught "not the little virtues but the great ones," identifying "generosity" as essential. But "generosity" in Ginzburg does not always resemble what is usually associated with the term and is, moreover, by no means merely the opposite of "thrift" or "stinginess." "The great virtues," Ginzburg writes, "well up from an instinct in which reason does not speak." Generosity is close to "frankness," "a love of truth," and "a contempt for danger." If to be reasonable is to be tactful and to protect oneself from censure or ridicule, to be generous is to worry not at all about seeming impossibly altruistic or impulsive or embarrassingly frank. There is generosity, Ginzburg argues, in refusing to tell lies, even to children, who "should know from infancy that good is not [always] rewarded and that evil [often] goes unpunished." To love goodness and hate evil is not to pretend that the world is something other than what it is. Quite the contrary: we are generous and good and loving in spite of the fact that there is no "logical explanation" for such things. For Ginzburg, goodness is at the furthest possible remove from the chic irony and the mock-serious detachment that have long passed for sophistication among the enlightened classes, for whom virtue itself is a word invariably set within quotation marks.

Many of Ginzburg's contemporaries also thought hard about the distinction between the moderate and the expansive, the tactful and the frank, trimming and truth-telling. Doris Lessing, for one, identified in the British what she called "a smallness, a tameness, a deep, instinctive, perennial refusal to admit danger," and believed that this was manifested in characteristically "small, circumscribed novels." Ginzburg, however, saw no reason why smallness of spirit should be associated with "small,

33

circumscribed novels." Her own circumscribed fictions are alert to a great range of dangers, shocks, and betrayals, and often one feels that, in works whose characters are entirely without generosity of spirit, this very impoverishment is the primary phenomenon Ginzburg wishes to examine.

In her 1984 novel *The City and the House*, Ginzburg limits herself entirely to epistolary exchanges among a varied cast of characters. There are no passages of description, no breaks of lyricism or literary language, no signs of an authorial voice or surrogate perspective. Where feelings are expressed they are often skeletal, fragmentary, occasionally enigmatic, even when the letter writer intends some sort of explanation. As readers, we are moved to follow the shifts and feints of this weirdly associative discourse, which can be grimly comical and improbably affecting. If there is generosity at all in the precincts of Ginzburg's novel, it has mainly to do with the willingness of her characters to tell one another what they think and how they feel.

Yet the characters do not have any idea that they are being frank or open or generous. They have no inhibitions about telling their limited "truths" simply because they have no scruples or sense of shame or privacy to inhibit them. People who can say everything to one another may in fact do so because they have nothing inside to hide. Bluntness here is not a sign of virtue or strength but of people who are all surface, however feverish their efforts to achieve a semblance of connection and gratification.

Often the candor in *The City and the House* is so extreme as to bring us to laughter. One character tells a friend that she is marrying Nino Mazzetta "for the following reasons," and goes on to list them, including in her litany "To please my father" and "Because no one's ever thought of marrying me." Our concern, as we read through her "confessional" letter, is to observe how even the most intimate revelations here tell us only that there is not much to recommend these characters. Ginzburg allows them to be as they are and to express what they are so as not to have to say, in so many words, what she thinks of them. But we know what she thinks of them and we are grateful to be allowed to decide for ourselves that these people are really as disappointing as they must seem to their author.

If authentic generosity is rarely in evidence in Ginzburg's minor figures, it is not often discernible in her important ones either. *The City and the House* gives us leading characters who are compulsively open about themselves. They tell one another that they were always failures as fathers, that they betrayed their husbands or loved ones because they fell "in love easily," or that they made momentous decisions—to marry or to leave family and friends—simply because they were bored or in need of change. "I am coming to America," Giuseppe, the central character, writes to his brother, "like someone who has decided to throw himself into the sea and hopes he will emerge either dead or new and changed." The apparent desperation underlying the assertion is more than a little misleading, however, and reflects mainly the character's inability to think seriously about the implications of his own avowal. He cares not at all about the brother who must now take care of him in America or about the fact—which he blithely confesses in more than one subsequent letter—that as a middle-aged man he remains a child.

It is not that Ginzburg is stubbornly committed to a disenchanted view of human beings. In each of her books she allows for exceptions, which are quite properly represented as exceptional. Giuseppe's homosexual son in *The City and the House* displays a redemptive attachment to an adopted child and a capacity for forgiveness that make him a plausibly generous person; a cousin named Roberta does her best to keep family members in touch with one another and dispenses helpful advice to people in need. But these instances, however sharply represented, clearly have no prospect of turning any tide or effectively altering the picture Ginzburg draws. The facts of life are unmistakably facts, and if Ginzburg is not moved to make speeches about moral obscenity, preferring instead to dwell quietly on what is all too human, that is because in her outlook she is at one with the Tolstoy who wrote, of his own Ivan Illych, that his life was "most simple and most ordinary and therefore most terrible." No need, surely, for any worked-up melodrama to underscore that simple, fatal vision of the way most of us are.

In *It's Hard to Talk About Yourself*, Ginzburg is reminded again and again that she has always been a pessimist. "It always seems," an interviewer tells her, "as if there is something that at a certain point tramples on your sensitivity or provokes your indignation." This indignation, this sense of being somehow violated or revolted by events in the world, surely inspired much of her best work. Having lived through the passage of Mussolini's race laws in 1938 and the years of her husband's detention, imprisonment, and murder, Ginzburg might have been expected to reserve her indignation for comparably convulsive developments. But it is often the smallest of things that exercises her; nothing is so minor that it can escape her notice or fail to provoke her wrath or judgment.

NATALIA GINZBURG

There is no impulse to self-dramatization in the recoil and response of Ginzburg's writing. She does not admire or insist upon her own principled fault-finding. Her pessimism is never overmastering. She writes, it would seem, to discover what she thinks, and if she proceeds, inevitably, from a certain predisposition, there is nothing like an inveterate prejudice to distort her understanding. She accepts that certain things are more likely to be true than others, but she does not hold her characters to an iron fate or refuse to be surprised by what she observes.

American readers confronting Ginzburg for the first time may well think of homegrown writers such as Raymond Carver, whose characters invariably make bad choices and have lives that add up to very little. Typically, the fictions devoted to such figures evoke lives with no prospect of satisfactory resolution or significant shape. The "realism" of American, so-called minimalist writing comes out of the sense that nothing can be done and that there is little or no meaning in the lives of people who are largely vacant and adrift. By contrast, where Ginzburg is bleakest and her characters most clueless or pathetic is where she is persistently intent upon penetrating to the roots of the pervasive ennui and disaffection. There is an informing urgency that makes the uneventfulness and grayness of the lives she examines not merely disappointing but deeply symptomatic. Although it is not explanation as such that she is after, she does wish us to see that what we are looking at is not to be taken for "reality" pure and simple. What seems to us intolerable or disheartening in the lives we observe is felt to be so because Ginzburg intimates that there might be something better. The vision informing American minimalist fiction often seems pinched and programmatically narrow; Ginzburg, however, refuses ever to write out of lowered expectations or grim determinism.

The Austrian writer Robert Musil once wrote, "Irony has to contain an element of suffering in it. (Otherwise it is the attitude of a know-it-all.)" Ginzburg is a relentless ironist, but her irony is never presumptuous or defensive. She criticizes or exposes not to air a grievance or to shore up a position. Even when her tone is angry, her sentences betray an awareness of that anger and an openness to correction. A blunt indictment in Ginzburg never seems to come easily to her, as she herself notes in an essayistic self-portrait: "Compared to telling the truth, inventing was like playing with a litter of kittens. Telling the truth is like moving through a pack of tigers." To be savagely ironic at the expense of an idea or person necessarily entails assuming responsibility for the cogency and effect of that indictment. The ironist needs to suffer for the portion of the truth or reality not adequately encompassed by her irony. Ginzburg had, in a very high degree, what others have called "a conscience in intellectual matters." There is no tranquility in her, no instinct to self-approval. Emerging from her own troubled relation to reality, irony was for Ginzburg a means to an end, an instrument of thought, never an end in itself or an expression of self-regard.

Of course, the word "irony" does not begin to suggest the range of Ginzburg's biting portraiture and commentary, but it nicely captures her distaste for rhetoric and her preference for what one reader calls "comic incongruity" and "a low angle of observation." When Ginzburg turned to politics, she knew that matters of life and death might well be involved. But she also thought a good deal about the silliness and posturing that are so much a part of politics as usual. A woman of the left, Ginzburg was sympathetic to progressive ideas but caustic about movements and the ideologues they attracted. Was she a "feminist"? If she was, she regarded her ties to the "cause"—to any cause—as "obscure, subterranean, visceral." Should women have the right to choose abortion? No doubt they should, she believed, so long as they did not delude themselves about the moral clarity of the issue or try to talk themselves out of their own ambivalence.

When the advantages associated with a choice seemed most obvious and compelling, Ginzburg was most moved to resist. She hated not only slogans but also the pretense that a policy could be adopted without any thought of consequence. Abortion might seem a reasonable option for some women some of the time, but it had to involve "tearing from one's own being forever a definite but unknown living possibility." Feminists who adopted a "position" on abortion without acknowledging the darker aspects opened up by their choice seemed to Ginzburg unserious, and she occasionally directed at them a withering scorn. "I share all the practical goals of the feminist movement," Ginzburg wrote, but she had to admit that she did not "love feminism" and did not trust what she called its "spiritual attitude," which was too often triumphalist.

Just so, she was often troubled by revolutionary fervor and political idealism when espoused by people whom she took to be credulous or immature. In an early episode of her greatest book, the long novel entitled *All Our Yesterdays* (1952), Ginzburg observes what revolution can mean to a young woman drawn to it by her infatuation with other young people in the antifascist resistance. The woman's head is filled

NATALIA GINZBURG

with romantic images of mounted barricades, gunshots sounding in the night sky, people's tribunals, and foolish promises ("and they would give the soap factory to the poor"). Remote from any genuine political reality, she is intermittently exhilarated by her own enthusiastic radicalism: "These thoughts blossomed joyous and arrogant within her," Ginzburg writes. The irony is unmistakable, the criticism more than implicit, directed not at radicalism but at the arrogance and self-deception that are often constitutive features of political radicalism. Again, it is the "spiritual attitude" that concerns Ginzburg—that is, the failure, even on the part of good people, to hold ideas or commit to actions with a determination to see things as they are and to acknowledge misgivings.

That determination is beautifully embodied in Cenzo Rena, the most "positive" of all the major characters in Ginzburg's fiction. A man who mounts no barricades and fires no shots, he is sublimely free of cant and highmindedness. Living in the fascist era that dominates *All Our Yesterdays*, he is at once furious at the stupidity and greed of most people and moved to do what he can to help them. Sympathetic to the resistance and willing to risk everything if absolutely necessary, he is principally a "radical" by virtue of his untiring efforts on behalf of ordinary people, working to assist them in the most unromantic of ways. "All the time making himself a nuisance," Ginzburg writes, Cenzo Rena spends his days "digging out old crumbling records from the bottoms of drawers" in municipal offices, berating incompetent schoolteachers, and urging pharmacists to supply remedies needed by the peasants in his village. He loathes above all things useless make-believe, which is to say, lies, inertia, idle fantasy. "He did not pretend," Ginzburg says of him. He is what he purports to be: friend, protector, scourge. By no means a saint or impossibly wise, he is, all the same, refreshingly blunt and in every way genuine, unapologetically defiant in his resistance to dreamy sublimity. Although Ginzburg was, by her own account, more than a little susceptible to drift and dream, she admired at least this one utterly down-to-earth character whose gift for truth-telling matched her own.

At one point in the novel, and then again several times later on, Cenzo Rena tells Anna—the young woman, pregnant with another man's baby, whom he eventually marries and cares for—that she has lived her life "like an insect. An insect that knows nothing beyond the leaf upon which it hangs." Others too are judged in this way, though the word "insect" is principally and most memorably addressed to Anna.

Occasionally, Rena says "that she had not had quite so much of an insect face recently," but such "praise" is rare.

More than one critic notes that the abuse directed at Anna is inexcusable, issuing as it does from the mouth of an older man attacking a younger and clearly more vulnerable woman. But there is no pattern of gender-coded abuse in Ginzburg's work. She is, as we have seen, critical of everyone, men and women, and Rena is no less tolerant of male "insects" than he is of Anna. If Rena did not do his best to love his wife, treat her well, or encourage her to behave more responsibly and thereby to think better of herself, he would not seem to us admirable. When he says "like an insect," he intends criticism not simply of his wife's behavior but of the attitude informing everything she does. There is, he believes, something cheerless and passively accepting in his wife's stance. She has allowed herself to become someone for whom things are done and to whom things merely happen. This passivity Rena finds almost unforgivable. He sees something frail and blanched in this person, who has seemingly resigned herself to the idea that she has nothing to give and therefore little capacity to say no to what others would make of her. What Ginzburg demanded of herself in an autobiographical essay— "She would be assiduous and generous in bestowing her wealth"—Rena demands, in effect, of his wife. She is an "insect" because she does not wish sufficiently to be anything else. It is not confusion or reluctance that Ginzburg dislikes but the absence of will, which is here another word for generosity or fullness of being. Rena's virtues—impulsiveness, decisiveness, and the combination of impatience and tolerance, anger and affection—obviously seemed to Ginzburg the essential alternatives to insecthood. Rena doesn't abdicate from life: that is the best that can be said for him, and it says a great deal.

Ginzburg was a great writer in part because she never allowed herself or any of her characters to get away with an investment in false horizons. She loved—or honored—reality enough to believe that it could somehow be enough. Although she was impatient with delusion, she had a gift for the unfathomable and never met a contradiction that didn't at least tempt her. Rarely afraid of being a bore, she was faithful to her own insights and never wrote a lax or boring sentence. She knew she would "never be cured" of the "evil" she encountered during the war, but she rightly speculated that there was "one good" that came out of those years: "We cannot lie in books and we cannot lie in anything else we do. We have a toughness and a strength that those who came before

NATALIA GINZBURG

us have never known." Young words, those, written just after the war by a young writer. And in many respects Ginzburg was right, at least where she herself was concerned. She couldn't lie, and if she was to the end of her life "bound to this our anguish," she wrote as one who was "glad, at heart, of our destiny as human beings" and committed to the idea that "our destiny" was hers to make and unmake and remake as the spirit moved her.

4

CLEAR LIGHT AND SHADOW

ANITA DESAI

The novels of Anita Desai resist enchantment. Quietly, defiantly secular, they are skeptical about the quest for mystery and unimpressed by the wisdom of sages or swamis. Compassionate, occasionally tender, they are, much of the time, unforgiving toward the deluded and the vacant. If they seem, as some have said, Chekhovian in their attention to "the sad humor of provincial lives," they can also be savage in their repudiation of provinciality and innocent self-approval. Apparently remote from political intentions, the novels are yet alert to history and refuse to submit to the formulaic reductions of postcolonial literary theory. Enchantment—so Desai's work insistently suggests—comes in a great many forms, not the least of which is the effort to construct neat oppositions between East and West, backward and advanced, authentic and inauthentic, free and unfree. By dwelling on the petty destinies of men and women shadowed by great events, the novels anatomize the mythmaking propensities of most human beings while insisting, in ever so many ways, that there can be no release from the world, from heterogeneity, from the impossible combination of meaning and meaninglessness that is "reality."

Of course, Desai's work has inspired comparisons with other Indian writers, particularly with those of mixed heritage or affiliation who write principally of India, but in English. Is she "more at home" with the work of R. K. Narayan than with the work of Salman Rushdie? Is she a "student" of V. S. Naipaul? Does she belong, with Ruth Prawer Jhabvala, to a "school" or "movement"? Questions worth asking, perhaps, though the range of Desai's fiction is such as to make sustained comparison with such writers difficult if not impossible.

More helpful, perhaps, for our purposes, is the example of E. M. Forster in *A Passage to India*, where the issue of enchantment is engaged in ways that are, at least, instructive. For it is the business of Forster's novel to suggest that there is something more "out there" than the standard Western vision can encompass. India itself, in its variousness, is one version of that "something more," so that Forster's narrator can exclaim at one point: "How can the mind take hold of such a country?" But it is Forster's character Mrs. Moore who more suggestively points the way toward the something more, embodying in her progress toward transcendence that rejection of the merely rational and legal that has long seemed a hallmark feature of the East's challenge to the West, its "romance," as it were, with enchantment. Though Mrs. Moore arrives in India a Christian, her experience in the Marabar Caves alienates her from "poor little talkative Christianity," and if she does not achieve any final illumination, she is yet decidedly cut off from any possible further recourse to ordinary Western standards of judgment. She is, so it might be said, open to exaltation, however modest and diffident her demeanor. We also recall that Forster's humane, thoughtful, liberal intellectual Gabriel Fielding grows progressively dissatisfied with his own spiritual limitations. Merely "sensible, honest, even subtle," Fielding is "wistful" about what he lacks, and summarizes that deficiency when he says of himself and Miss Quested that they "are, roughly speaking, not after anything." To be limited to a life built "on advanced European lines" is to be forever cut off—so Fielding suspects, so Forster confirms—from a vital "something else" he might instead "have been working at . . . he didn't know at what, never would know, never could know."

But then Desai would surely say that anyone might reasonably, at some point in a life devoted to doing modest good, grow disappointed and begin to think of "something else" without necessarily supposing that "it" entailed "an infinite goal behind the stars." That very language, Forster's language, would be found to release in Desai an adversary impulse, a steady focused recoil. For the language is, after all, vague, and no amount of wanting it to be other than vague will change that. And truth be told, there is nothing in Forster's novel to indicate that he knew any better than Fielding what to make of the spiritual powers associated with his ostensibly superior "spiritual" beings. He can celebrate them for their instinct to say "no" to elementary legalism and garden-variety pragmatism, but he does not know what else they may be good for, and surely Desai, on the evidence of her novels, would not be inclined to help him.

In fact, in Desai's novel *Baumgartner's Bombay*, there is a response to Forster's Marabar Caves passage, with Baumgartner cast as the antithesis to Mrs. Moore. When Desai's character enters a cave, he hears not a repeating pregnant echo but silence. For a moment Baumgartner fears that he will be clawed by birds or bats, and even briefly speculates that he is entering the cave of an idol. "Could it be," he wonders, "that black-engorged penis he had seen in roadside shrines, or an oxen hump, placid and bovine, some swollen udder of blood? . . . Something was blocking the chamber, emanating a stench and watching *him* . . . " But, in a dense passage that extends over two pages, Desai insists upon the absence of "the slightest sound or motion," so that Baumgartner's efforts to see and hear are hopeless in the pitch darkness of the cave, and his sense that "the chamber seemed to hold a secret" is understandable only as the speculation of a man fearfully trying to navigate with "no priest, no pilgrim" to help him and "no voice, no song, not even a dim inscription" to ratify his quest. Moved to think that perhaps "he had arrived at a final barrier," a temple occupied, perhaps, "by death," the scene, conceivably, "of some hideous human sacrifice," Baumgartner lets himself go, gives himself up to wildly frantic images of decapitation, "crimson stuff," watering "this immutable black blob of God-spit, God-sputum," a sign really of "death piled up, as casually as dogs' turds, saying to Baumgartner—the end, no more."

But of course this is Desai, not Forster, and her Baumgartner, quite as we would expect, "would not have its no," would find himself, and declare himself in the end "indigestible, inedible." Confronted with some sign, indecipherable, suggestive, opaque, of ultimacy, Baumgartner necessarily recoils and learns that in fact "the Gods had spat him out. *Raus*, Baumgartner, out. Not fit for consumption, German or Hindu, human or divine." Nor is this evacuation much of a disappointment, really, however hastily Desai's man will retreat bewildered from the spot, for he will be—how can he not be?—"laughing in humiliation and mortification," expelled "from some royal presence" or whatever it might have been, not "found fit," after all, merely a "shabby" and "unwanted" man, a mere foreigner in a strange land: "*Raus*," the appropriate word to summarily dispatch such a creature, order him definitively out.

But it is not Baumgartner alone who is "unfit" for the mysteries. Often in Desai the mysteries are bogus, the missionary spirit cruel, conversion a fraud, so that to turn away "unfit" is not necessarily to be deficient but honest, steeled or resigned to randomness or bleakness, willing to live in doubt or despair, unfit merely to invest in chimera. In Desai, the willingness to live with things as they are may be more honor-

ANITA DESAI

able than insisting that things be other than they are or might be. She delights in exposing the conformities and banalities of mystical poseurs, and if she would surely accord all honor to the difficult and searching Mrs. Moore, she would hardly be inclined to recommend to others that they renounce their own commitment to seeing clearly in order to pant after an idea of transcendence that is not authentically theirs. Desai's Baumgartner is a damaged man unfit for many things, but his refusal to have the "no" he seems to have been offered is not as he supposes the mark of a diminished being but the reflex of a man who cannot submit to something that is not reliably real to him. In this he is like many other characters in Desai's novels who otherwise do not resemble Baumgartner at all.

Desai's response to Forster—she referred to it as such at a public reading one night in 1989, shortly after the publication of *Baumgartner's Bombay*—is by no means intended as a dismissive rejoinder. There are, after all, things to fear in the world, and we often do fear what we cannot see or understand. But Baumgartner's crisis in the cave suggests that it is perhaps a good thing not to capitulate to an imagined or imaginary horror, not to take a presumptive "no" for a definitive "no." There is, Desai would seem to suggest, in our substantial humanity something truly "indigestible," a physical-sensual-moral reality that cannot be consumed or wished away by our yielding to large, inchoate desires. To belong to the world is not for Desai a fault, and to be averse to spiritual reflection as such is not—not always or inevitably—to be without any capacity for devotion. Desai knows, as her characters sometimes know, that to belong to the world is not to be fatally *of* the world. Her best characters are unworldly even as they resist any slightest flirtation with transcendence or, indeed, with magic or mystery. They are attractive or admirable so long as they refuse to be entirely comfortable in the world they inhabit.

Baumgartner's Bombay may be, in some respects, the best of Desai's novels in its perfect blending of activity and isolation, meanness and tender fellow feeling, violence and surrender, worldliness and withdrawal. The alternation of retrospection and seething forward momentum ("the starting gun was fired and the horses released like pellets from their barrels") makes the entire novel active and unstable in a fully gratifying way. There is no sense anywhere of "figures in an etching or a tapestry," as Desai herself once put it in her novel *Journey to Ithaca*, no sense of what Pico Iyer once called the "slow, detailed . . . Merchant-Ivory aesthetic" favored by Jhabvala, which is "sometimes more concerned with décor and textures than with drama."

But it is *Clear Light of Day* that more sharply and characteristically reveals what is fresh and original in Desai. Like others who praise this novel, Iyer describes it as "poised" and "slightly housebound." He links it with other Desai novels (*Fire on the Mountain* and *In Custody*) which are, "for the most part, centered on people seeking refuge from the world or some sanctuary in the imagination," people "oddly solitary" and, again, "without much contact with the world around them." This is a view of Desai that stresses what one critic calls her gift for "mood painting," her "unfaltering hand," so that she may be condescended to as merely delicate and refined and, more than a bit like her characters, inclined to be "seeking refuge from the world or some painted, tapestried sanctuary in the imagination."

In fact, nothing could be more misleading than this take on Desai. For one thing, her writing is often geared to tearing apart what she calls the "taut membrane of reservation." For another, Desai is extravagantly good at evoking "the stained, soiled, discolored and odorous rags" of her characters' lives. She is not at all averse to dwelling in obscenity, drunkenness, and ineptitude. If there is poise and measure in her writing, those virtues are not purchased by an exclusive investment in silken phrases or edifying examples. If there is nothing like hysteria in her work, there is often panic and farce. *Clear Light of Day* has none of the comic extravagance of *In Custody*, none of that brilliant novel's zaniness or manic propulsion. But in its more apparently subdued manner, it is a comic work and a satire that aims at a great many targets. It is, moreover, in the very best sense, an exemplary novel—exemplary without sacrificing one wit of particularity.

Clear Light of Day likes to play with and tempt us with categorical oppositions: modern and traditional, backward and forward looking, responsible and irresponsible. After all, these are the terms in which most of us "know" things. There is this and there is that. The one who goes away is adventurous; the one who stays at home is afraid. The one who marries is open to risk; the one who fails to marry is weak, frail, inhibited, immature. For an Indian woman to go to the United States is to confront modernity; for her sister to spend her life in her family home in Old Delhi is to remain locked in the grip of tradition. Desai's novels often tempt us to these oppositions by exposing us to characters for whom they seem all but irresistible. In *Clear Light of Day* the oppositions are central to the work, its principal characters drawn to them even as they sense that they are deceptively easy and misleading.

In this novel, even the distinction between enchantment and disenchantment is found to be obviously false and irrelevant. After all, there is nothing remotely enchanting about the would-be enchanters in *Clear Light of Day*, so that what might otherwise be extolled as disenchantment is here simply a straightforward response to nullity. Without a compelling seduction, mystery, or excess to measure itself against, a "realistic" response to experience is merely plausible. The absence of melodrama or irrationality is not a corrective when nothing cries out for principled correction.

At the heart of Desai's novel is a patent opposition between two sisters, Tara and Bim. Tara is the wife of a successful cosmopolitan diplomat who has taken her to the United States and thereby released her from the world of her childhood. Presiding over the family home is Bim, a middle-aged spinster, "gray and heavy now," glimpsed "in a curious shapeless hand-made garment that Tara could see she had fashioned out of an old cotton sari by sewing it up at both sides." Tara has come home with her husband for a visit and notes, again and again, "how everything goes on and on here, and never changes," so that her sister too seems somehow "exactly the same," a prisoner, as Bim herself only half-playfully suggests, to "all that dullness, boredom, waiting." At every turn, in virtually every exchange, Desai has her characters express the standard opposition, the sense of irrevocable choices made, one thing rather than another, this not that. "Anyone who isn't dull and gray goes away," Bim says, provoking her sister to confirm or deny, though Bim knows what she thinks and hardly requires Tara to confirm or instruct her. " 'Oh, to going on—to growing up—' Bim declaims, teasing, provoking, testing, 'leaving—going away—into the world—something wider, freer—brighter,' Bim laughed. 'Brighter! Brighter!' she called, shading her eyes against the brightness." The irony here is broad, but there is no denying the force of the speaker's assault—playful, bitter, practiced—upon the standard notion that to go out into the world is to be worthy and free and new and bright.

Desai very deliberately sets up Bim in such a way as to make everything she says an apparent reflection of her own unhappy condition. For she has not only stayed at home and assumed the role of official family guardian, but she has also for the most part renounced any prospect of marriage and agreed to watch over her retarded brother. When

she utters the standard formulas about leaving and freedom and brightness, she would seem to be speaking out of her own failure to make for
herself "a life." But it is the brilliance of Desai's novel to make Bim not
simply a dim, disappointed, embittered woman, but a brilliant woman
whose "failure" must be measured against her unmistakable distinction.
Tara does not fail to note the oddity of the situation, and neither does
her husband Bakul, who is mercilessly ridiculed by Bim but has to acknowledge her superiority, "for all her plainness and brusqueness." To
be sure, Bakul notes, Bim has "that rather coarse laugh and way of sitting with her legs up," though she does impress him and everyone else
with her "firmness," "resolve," and wit. It is not surprising in the face
of her wit and her sharp, satiric laughter that Bakul should realize, as
so often before, that "he never liked Bim when she spoke in this manner. He liked nothing abrupt, staccato." And of course he also realizes
that his own dear wife, in her way really too passive and disappointed,
is after all—anyone could see it—a great deal "gentler, more tender." A
more suitable wife, surely, however "deplorably" without those other
admirable qualities.

   The internal debate regarding the relative merits of the two sisters
is some of the time brought into the open in their own exchanges, but
the differences are most effectively expressed in the reveries and thought
patterns of each sister. Trying at one point to think admiringly of her
husband, Tara recalls that "gradually he had trained her and made her
into an active, organized woman," though rapidly the thought brings
her around to the idea that it had therefore become her habit "to retire
to her room at night, tired with the triumphant tiredness of the virtuous and the dutiful." We are struck, here as elsewhere, by how steadily
Tara manages to arrive at the truth of her condition, her development,
however well "trained" she is to think positively and to avoid reflections ostensibly beyond her. Desai's willingness not only to enter the
consciousness of her characters but to let them provide for themselves
precisely the language they need to uncover what they know and feel is
an important aspect of her distinction as a novelist. The novelist does
not begrudge her characters their bursts of insight. Their limitations do
not fatally define for her what they are. She watches them and listens to
them, as it were, not to catch them out but to let them be. Tara's damaged integrity—it is an integrity—is caught perfectly in the informed
contradictoriness of those words: "triumphant tiredness of the virtuous and the dutiful." For who would wish to be "triumphant" if that

ANITA DESAI

entailed merely a life consecrated to virtue and duty as defined by one's own resident trainer? Even the words "active" and "organized" assume, in this context, something less than the robustly efficient character typically associated with them. Tara is forgiven her dutifulness and passivity precisely because she is without the bland self-confidence of her husband.

With Bim, the level of internal conflict is even greater, and the virility of mood and utterance often at odds with the accent of sour defeat that Bim does not always resist. Tara is often the lens through which Bim is observed, and though she finds it difficult to be "objective," her vision often "obscured and screened by too much of the past," she does sharply register the contradictions that mark her sister. Was Bim always "competent"? Had she always the "rough, strong, sure grasp" of reality she seems to have, or is that grasp even now not really secure? Does she not, in fact, "stampede through the house like a disheveled storm, creating more havoc than order"? When Bim speaks she is typically firm and unambivalent, though open to currents of memory and reflection, "Thinking. Wondering," not always brusque or hard. When, often, she strikes a sour note, she does so for the sake of her interlocutor, seeing things at least for the moment as she supposes they must appear to someone not herself. Will their brother Raja, long absent, not be "thrilled," as Tara puts it, to come home at last for a visit? "Oh yes, *thrilled*," Bim replies, with "a sour face." And who, she asks, could possibly be thrilled to come back to "'this dead old house? . . . anyone would be horrified to return to it. Weren't you horrified?' she demanded. 'To see it so dead and stale—just as it's always been?'"

Again, it is not—so we observe—that these words accurately express all that Bim feels about her situation. Speaking of it in this way, she sees it as it would inevitably be seen by somebody like Tara who had left it behind. And of course there is a sense in which it should be so observed. It is true to say that one who had chosen to remain in such a place, not to venture out, would likely be herself rather too comfortable with the "dead and stale." But of course there is that familiar edge in everything Bim says. Her formulation—"anyone would be horrified"—effectively challenges others to stand by such a view of the house and the lives it contains, to regard it as a just and sufficient assessment rather than the expression of a prejudice. For is it not—so the novel encourages us to ask—a peculiarly provincial notion to suppose that what is old is inevitably stale? There are unmistakable signs of staleness and deterioration in the family home, such as an old damaged phonograph record played by the retarded brother. But it is simply not possible to regard Bim herself as "dead and stale," and as she is the final embodiment of the family home, there is more to it than is expressed in her own caustic formulation.

Desai's characters are typically caught on their way from one thought or sentiment to another. Though we feel we know them, they never seem to us reducible to a single emotion. We pay very close attention to them because they promise to surprise us or at least to unsettle what we had prematurely concluded about them. The movement of consciousness in a work like *Clear Light of Day* is at once disclosing and steadily gesturing at what is not quite available to expression. The thoughts of characters are not harshly fractured in the way they would be in a standard modernist work, but there clings even to apparently finished thoughts and statements a suggestive incompleteness. We care about Desai's characters because we feel there is always more to them than we have been given, though we have quite enough.

With the portrait of Bim this quality of incompleteness is really quite remarkable. She says, after all, a great deal. She is, moreover, impressively articulate, willing to come out with or to signal what is on her mind. Desai never exaggerates any quality in her, never exaggerates what she would be apt to say or what she might conceivably think, but she wants very much to grant her every allowable expressive opportunity. We never sense that Desai is holding her character back, determining to withhold from us what we would like to know, so that the shadow of incompleteness stirs like the breath of a reticent unease.

Consider a passage in chapter 2 of the novel, a chapter that begins: "The city was in flames that summer." It is the time of the partition riots, when it sometimes seemed that in India no peace would come, as the brother Raja says, until "every Muslim has had his throat cut." In the family home much goes on as before, in spite of the encroaching menace that intermittently flickers. Bakul has been courting young Tara and a Dr. Biswas is attempting to court Bim. We are well acquainted with the sisters by the time we reach this chapter, but we are unprepared for Bim's disdainful responses to the good, mild, earnest doctor, who craves rather "little attention" and is yet accorded less than little. He has, as all acknowledge, a great deal to do in the house, with several family members ill, so that he is needed and has reason to expect gratitude, courtesy, "encouragement." Of course, Desai sets up the encounter against the inescapable "sound of [the retarded brother] Baba's records grinding out on the gramophone one cabaret tune after the other, relentlessly gay, unquenchably merry," so that we can only be certain that Bim will be irritable, as she would have to be, confronted with anything "relentlessly" or "unquenchably" gay. Bim is, in the circumstances, not only "too tired to explain" what she feels, but in the throes of feelings that go too deep for expression. When Dr. Biswas pleads with her, "seriously," to "care for music," and declares that "music is one of the greatest joys we can have on earth," we must expect that Bim will be moved to squash him, laugh at him, or, just possibly, pity him. She will not, surely, like or respect him, "as he stood there, dark and awkward, his bag in one hand, smelling like a pharmacy." But he does not see what he is doing, and so blunders ahead, inviting his companion to a Sunday concert, "a performance of Brahms and Schubert" given by persons who are "not professionals" but "amateurs" though "not bad," so that in the presence of their music "one forgets everything—everything."

Bim, of course, forgets nothing, ignores nothing. Even when she is driven by compulsions she cannot name she is very much on their track, relentlessly alert to her own turbulent feelings. She is not—or not quite—the victim of wounds that cannot heal, but she is susceptible to wounds, large and small. She smolders but refuses to give way to depression. When she reels she is apt to quietly rage or deal a blow. There is steel in the iron circuit of her irritability. She cannot refuse to be irritated by the doctor's earnestness any more than she can ignore the relentless gaiety of the gramophone record. This practiced susceptibility may be disappointing in a person we might hope to like or to know better, but it is, in its way, essential to all that we admire in Bim. She is not complacent. She accepts nothing. If she seems the victim of the situation she has agreed to call her own, she is not a willing victim, and whatever self-hatred there may be in her posture, it is fully balanced by a savage recoil from all that would drag her down.

And thus it is that we take pleasure in Bim's repudiation of the good, earnest, awkward, solicitous doctor. For how would she not be revolted by the easy way in which he asks her to settle, in the course of this invitation, for a performance "not bad," for "beautiful sounds" whose merit is that they make it possible to forget "everything—everything"? This is, after all, a woman whose virtue—for us, for herself, for Desai surely—is that she does not forget, does not blandly forgive or guilelessly renounce. How, after all, would such a woman not find bitterly absurd, if also "immensely funny," the tiny spectacle of "the doctor inviting her to a concert of nineteenth-century music in the riot-torn city—so that she began to laugh and laugh . . . and rang like a bell with laughter, quite uncontrollably," with the result that the little man must only "smile uneasily . . . and slide off sideways in a hurry."

"You find life amusing, Bim, do you?" Bakul asks her shortly afterwards. "'Amusing isn't exactly the word,' she responds, 'but interesting, interesting enough.'" Small, that correction, but essential, for Bim has none of the patrician detachment that can make the foibles of others seem amusing. Her intelligence is too exacting to be merely amused, and her laughter is characteristically robust, the expression of something only provisionally mastered, placed, the sign of an exertion finally, if casually, brought to a close. There is gratification in Bim's laughter, the flexing of intellectual muscle. In its way this gratification is not unlike the related sense of mastery we hear when Bim notes how hard it was to deal with the hopes and delusion of youth, "with that first terrible flood of life." She is a woman who does not wish to be swept along—"one just goes under." She prefers to "stand up to it, make a stand against it." There is, to be sure, something terrible in Bim's pronouncement, "I would never be young again for anything," but of course we understand entirely what she means, and approve entirely of her determination not to feel victimized by anything. To be young seems to her not "to know how to cope," and there is nothing she so despises. Nothing, that is, except the proposition that to cope is to accept what is dealt, to agree not to be irritated, enraged, or offended by stupidity, mendacity, banality, passivity, or the incorrigible mediocrity she discerns in Dr. Biswas.

Desai paints her character with an irrepressible spikiness of spirit. Bim lacks elementary cheerfulness. The task of the novelist throughout is to make her at once compelling and more than a bit intimidating. We must be made not merely to admire Bim's intelligence but to like the absence in her of tender-heartedness and forgiveness. Of course, she is occasionally forgiving, and she can occasionally be tender, but these must not be made to seem in her essential virtues. They are, at most, marks of her humanity, her vulnerability, though Bim is not a woman for whom vulnerability is a strength. Desai knows that her reader will be much inclined to like in a character—particularly a female character—sentiments not much in evidence in Bim, and so her novel is deliberately constructed to go against the grain of our standard expectations. Bim resists sighing falls and soft swoons, and Desai's novel likewise does not

51

yield, even where it is most melancholy and wistful, to any trace of easy nostalgia or highmindedness.

We had begun by speaking of Desai's resistance to enchantment and of her tendency to subvert familiar oppositions. But we would not wish to suggest that Desai writes consistently out of a cool or delicious irony. Often in this novel, as in others by Desai, the irony is troubled. It spares no one. Disenchantment itself is almost as ripe a target for Desai as the susceptibility to romance or fraudulent mysticism. Bim's refusal to be impressed by the Urdu poetry her brother Raja proudly recites to his young sister is "uncomprehending," lazy, ungenerous. "It was always," she thinks, "as far as she could make out, the cup, the wine, the star, the lamp, ashes and roses—always the same," though to her brother "each couplet was a new-cut gem." To be sure, Bim's take on the poetry is refreshingly blunt. There is something hard and unyielding in her intelligence that we admire, and her ironic refusal to be impressed by what seems to her mere verbiage is a characteristic strength.

But then Desai will not permit us to be too comfortable with Bim. She insists that much of the time there is in her a tendency to rely rather too heavily on mood or reflex. Her aversions are not always reliable. She can be cruel, and where she is "uncomprehending" she is typically a little quick to dismiss or shut down. Desai's irony in this novel cuts deepest when it is associated with Bim's characteristic view of things, but the novelist is careful not to settle too easily into an identification with Bim. The novel's voice does not belong to her. Desai's irony, if we may differentiate it from Bim's, is more tolerant and less definite. Her subversions of hazy rhetoric and lofty sentiment, patiently developed over the course of an entire compact novel, carry with them an undercurrent of wistfulness. How she wishes, we feel, that we might get along without the cleansing ironies of Bim's intelligence. How good it would be—would it not?—if we could go through the world without, like Bim, wanting frequently "to stamp on it and stamp it out, rudely and roughly," to clear away the "filthy" and "pathetic" and delusional and cowardly.

Philip Fisher's recent book *The Vehement Passions* studies, among other things, the close linkage between anger and mourning. Desai would seem, in *Clear Light of Day* more than in any other of her books, to be writing toward that linkage. If she withholds full approval from Bim, that is perhaps because Bim does not sufficiently cultivate in herself that capacity for mourning. The intensity of her anger at those who are delusional or soft prevents her from registering sufficiently her own mournful relation to the past. Desai's novel, on the other hand, is clearly a work of mourning, even as it directs a withering criticism at those who will not let go of the past.

For what exactly does the novel mourn? For the sense, surely, that life itself might in fact be better than it is. Nowhere in this novel is that sense sustainable, though here and there, briefly, the prospect of another, better life is entertained. Raja's absorption into a Muslim family—eventually he marries the daughter of his Muslim mentor—suggests one hopeful overcoming of insularity and ethnic parochialism, though in time the hatreds and fanaticisms sweep away any notion that mildness and cosmopolitanism will win the day. It is not the business of this novel to dwell on politics or to register a particular failure as if it might have been avoided. It mourns what was not to be principally by noting what had to be. Tara would perhaps have been more pleased with her life had she not, still a girl, fled from her bleak family setting into the arms of a man who would take her away. To mourn for her in this novel is to permit her to note that by escaping she managed not to receive an education and not to get beyond a life of mellow, protected restraint. Bim, in this context, provides the anger, the pervasive scorn for those who allow themselves to be small, compliant, and defeated. But the mourning is built into the novel. We hear it in the accent of regret that sounds in ever so many ways, often smothered, diffident, rarely expansive, but unmistakable. If only the sisters had Raja's vitality. If only they could, all of them, hold on to "the pure and elemental joy that [occasionally] shot up and stood straight and bright above the surrounding dreariness" of their lives. If only they were not, all of them, susceptible to "the sense of dullness and hopelessness that reigned over their house." If only they did not find themselves given over chiefly to "waiting." There is mournfulness in those melancholy reflections, so much so that were it not for the steady current of anger that boils and chastens, the novel would sink under the weight of its intermittent, insinuating regretfulness.

But surely Desai understood that it would not be enough for her novel merely to complicate, subvert, and mourn. She needed, clearly, to install in her book some sense that, however intractable the conditions of life, there is some possibility of consequence beyond the parameters of the given. This has nothing or little to do with hopefulness. It has, rather, to do with an evolving sense that even where things refuse to change there is change. Consequence exists where there is some dis-

ANITA DESAI

cernible prospect of an effect beyond the kinetic flash produced by an expression of anger or ironic agitation.

Again, Bim is clearly the primary vehicle for this evolving sense. To be sure, there is around her a "little sensual quiver in the air," a quiver associated with both the sensation of irritability and the intellectual force that emanates from her. But there must be more than sensation if we are to speak of consequence. We note that on more than one occasion Bim sets herself against the entire arrangement of things in her culture. She is not, to be sure, a radical or even a reformer. She has no apparent wish to bring anything down or to be effectual in some focused way. But she is in her own way not merely impatient with things as they have long been, but quietly determined not to lend herself to their perpetuation. The resistance she demonstrates is anything but passive, though it is not easy to say what in fact it is.

At one point the sisters, in their youth, are at the neighboring Misra house for a party, and Bim directs characteristically "dark looks" at the boys "standing about on straddled legs, shouting orders and abuse in their lordly, uncivilized way." The dark looks are much like those she later directs at Tara's husband when he speaks with "calculated ease" and "that bland oil of self-confidence" that had once "made Tara gaze at him with maidenly admiration." But Bim's displeasure with the Misra boys is rapidly redirected to their sisters. "I don't know how those two girls are going to study and pass their finals with all this going on," she says to Tara, who replies, more or less as one would expect: "I don't think it matters to them . . . they are getting married afterwards anyway." And thus the occasion provokes an exchange more than a page in length, on why young women are "in such a hurry to get married" and are not intent on becoming "*educated.*" In this exchange, Bim sounds very much like the earnest provocateur, and Tara like the fumbling, skeptical, mildly "rebellious" sister who wishes plainly to remove herself from argument, her rebellion merely a motion to join the "embroidered" revelers "flocking" to "platters of sweetmeats."

In this exchange the reader will undoubtedly be drawn to Bim's sentiments. She speaks with the authority of her conviction that uneducated young women will soon discover that "marriage isn't enough to last them the whole of their lives." She can think "'of hundreds of things to do instead . . . so many things to do—when we are grown up—when all this is over,' and she swept an arm out over the garden party, dismissing it. 'When we are grown up at last—then—then—' But she couldn't finish for emotion . . . " It is, to be sure, a loaded statement Desai gives to Bim, for it contains among other things not merely the reflection about "so many things to do" but the assertion "I won't marry" and also "I shall work . . . I shall earn my own living—and look after Mira-*masi* and Baba and—and be independent." It is, in many ways, a standard declaration of emancipation. What begins in a reflex of irritation and becomes a reflection on young women who are in too great a rush to marry soon becomes a much more comprehensive and yet personal statement. We hear in it not only the declaration of independence but the deep, instinctual recoil from marriage itself. She *will* care for her aunt and her brother, *will* assume full responsibility for the family that belongs to her, but she *will* not perpetuate the system that has produced that family with all of its smoldering conflicts and balked desires and escapist impulses.

In what way, then, is Bim's way not merely a form of passive resistance? In what way does she do more than simply say "no"? Is it not the case that, as Bim intends, to opt out of the existing system—marriage and subordination and child rearing—is to leave things in the culture where they were? Again, Bim's is not a political revolt, and Desai in no way pretends that her character bears the seeds of some future revolution in her angry, determined hands.

And yet there is some sense of possible consequence in Bim's posture as Desai describes it. For Bim, after all, is a teacher. Yes, of course, we know, we know, teachers are servants of the established fact. And we also know that nothing Bim says about her teaching—she says very little, in fact—suggests that we are to look there for encouragement. And yet she does go on now and then about her students. *Hers.* Desai even has her say that "she is always trying to teach them, *train* them to be different from what we were at their age—to be a new kind of woman," though, "if they knew how badly handicapped" their teacher "still is" they would surely laugh. It is an affecting and thoroughly believable confession. Here we feel is Bim at her best. Desai clearly likes her this way, sees in her for a moment at least the propulsion, however modest, toward "a new kind of woman." And if that propulsion should be grounded in a felt sense of deficiency and inadequacy, so much the better, for then the obstacles to be overcome would at least have to be acknowledged by those who might wish to sign on to the project. Better to know what might be required than to suppose that the only thing required to create "a new kind of woman" is the untutored will.

ANITA DESAI

That is the nature of "consequence" as we come to understand it in Desai. It is an aspect of what was once called "seriousness." The novel in her hands is an instrument of memory and transfiguration. It proceeds from the assumption that we cannot simply get free of what has shaped us. "Nothing's *over*, ever," Tara says late in the novel, and "nothing's over," Bim agrees, "ever." To move forward, to make change possible, is to remember and imagine what might perhaps be possible *on the basis of* what is remembered. The inculpation of established fact in *Clear Light of Day* is effected in such a way as to remind us that it *is* established fact and that its power has much to do with what we are. We, too, in our way, are established facts. We feel things as such creatures do and are limited as such beings are bound to be. To imagine that there might be "a new kind of woman" is one of our inalienable strengths, but it is not in Desai to be trumpeted as if, for every advance, there might not be a price to pay, losses we would rather not consider, though the prospect of loss can never be something we should wish to conceal from ourselves. The very thought of liberation from the established fact is, in Desai, compelling but not exhilarating, for her imagination is at least half in love with the textures and rhythms of reality and with the moral authority that can only come from a felt investment in the actual lives of ordinary human beings.

The novel concludes with the scene of a musical performance, the featured singer an "elderly guru . . . [who] seemed to be having trouble with his teeth which were false and did not fit." Bim hears in the "small, ancient voice . . . a tinge of snuff, of crimson betel spittle, of phlegm. Also of conflict, failure and disappointment." Desai sets up these final pages with the combination of attributes she does not know how to do without, the physical and the moral together with equally affecting immediacy, the facts, inexorable, of age and frailty very much to the fore. And yet Bim is "suddenly overcome with the memory of reading, in [her brother] Raja's well-thumbed copy of Eliot's *Four Quartets*, the line: '*Time the destroyer is time the preserver*.'" And she sees "with her inner eye" that "her own house and its particular history linked and contained her as well as her whole family with all their separate histories . . . giving them the soil in which to send down their roots, and food to make them grow and spread . . . that soil contained all time, past and future."

The words, with their consoling, conclusive accent, are not unearned. They are a fitting culmination, paid for, as it were, by the painful struggle of the novel's principal characters to work through their grievances.

That time past and time future belong to the same soil aptly consolidates, however provisionally, the view of things Desai patiently develops throughout her novel. The discovery is not, of course, promulgated. It doesn't come at us carrying with it an explicit freight of political or social implication, however much Desai might have used it to undermine stock oppositions, as between tradition and modernity, responsibility and liberation. It is right that a novel of steady, subtle disenchantment should end with the rapturous reception of a performance—the old singer's words rising "in an upward spiral of passion and pain"—whose central burden is that we are, all of us, "subjected and constrained." Human, all too human, but not fatally without the faculty of imagination and the prospect, therefore, of genuine if modest transfiguration.

57

ANITA DESAI

5

BULLETS OF MILK

JOHN UPDIKE

John Updike's novel *Toward the End of Time* is set in the year 2020, not long after a brief but devastating war in which millions of American and Chinese citizens were killed. We see none of this killing, and we are told nothing of the causes that led to the war or that brought it to a close. Occasional references are made to the war's aftermath, to a collapsed national economy and deteriorating office buildings, to a "depopulated" Midwest and abandoned neighborhoods, but we do not tour those neighborhoods or feel in any way the effects of the reported disaster. A passing reference to Chinese missiles or to Mexico as a golden land of opportunity will remind us that something consequential has happened, that the world out there is a place different in many ways from the world of today. But in virtually every respect the local world in which Updike immerses us is our—or rather, his—familiar world. It is not at all surprising to the reader of this novel that for Updike's eloquent alter ego, Ben Turnbull, "the collapse of civilization" amounts to little more than an inspiring rise in "the quality of young women who are becoming whores."

A retired investment counselor with a large extended family living nearby in the Boston area, Turnbull is neither an idiot nor a monster. He is sixty-six, and his depravities are practiced on a modest scale. He is as susceptible as the next man to twinges of remorse and pity, or so we are to believe. If the collapse of civilization seems to him remote, it is in part because his routine preoccupations and his immediate prospects have been little affected by the conflagration. When he casually speaks of "rapacity, competition, desperation, death to other living things" as "the forces that make the world go around," he is repeating a settled conviction that took root in him long before the recent disastrous events.

He did not need reports of "the plains [as] a radioactive dust bowl" to instruct him on "the forces that make the world go around."

It matters to Ben very little, so far as we can tell, that the dollar is worthless, for in its place he spends a "scrip" issued by "corporations, states and hotel chains," and he can apparently buy whatever he wants, from private security guards to gardening supplies, from gasoline to Federal Express service. When he is ill, he drives to Boston from his suburban home to see a doctor, and he receives first-rate treatment at a hospital. He visits his grandchildren, attends parties, and carves turkeys precisely as he would have done if no apocalypse had occurred. For such a person, war and change are things that happen to other people. None of his children are said to have been lost or threatened by the nuclear exchange, and his eleven grandchildren would seem to face only the garden varieties of rapacity and desperation that fall to each of us.

Updike betrays no anxiety about the glaring inadequacy of his novel as an account of drastic political and social upheaval. He places his narrative in the hands and in the voice of a man who sees what Updike usually sees. Turnbull is a bright man who can be counted on to say bright things in a language so precise and fluent that he often reminds us of his creator. And he, too, has the habit of lingering for a time in the ample forests of his own prose. He reads books and entertains theories and argues with himself about the status of virtue and the Nietzschean notion of *ressentiment*. He has little patience for actual politics, and he likes to retreat efficiently from troubling questions to manageable problems. These are tendencies of his temperament that Updike has no wish to condemn.

Ben Turnbull is a guide to nothing but the vagaries of his own frequently compelling intelligence. He acknowledges the facts of political reality much in the way that he examines more proximate facts, with a cool empathy, an almost aesthetic detachment. He is more than a little dreamy, eager to lose himself in "cosmic feeling" and to ride the surfaces of life for their "transcendent sparkle." He is more comfortable speaking about entropy than about hope or action. When he recites the facts—this happened, then that, then that—he is already pulling back from the thicknesses of history, drawing around himself a circle of certainty within which existence proceeds as it must, without the possibility that events in the great world will drastically disrupt his security and his routine.

He knows, of course, that events do sometimes disrupt, and that lives have been destroyed or ended as a result of particular conflicts. He registers changes in society, but for all his acute powers of observation, he has little sense of society as a contention of forces in which individual will and intelligence may often play a significant role. He knows how to hurt and how to flatter, how to give and how to resist, how to get on in the world; but he feels that he can no more control the local, small-scale forces impinging on his life than he can control the forces governing the nuclear exchange between China and the United States. He is a very observant quietist, whose passivity is the condition of his acuity. Amused that anyone would presume to learn or to grow by studying the world, he swells with a cruel satisfaction, as when he tells his young hooker-mistress "that I don't much care what happens in the world. What Spin and Phil and the kids from Lynn do with the world is up to them. I just want to buy a little peace, day by day."

61

In the course of his retirement on a small but comfortable property not far from Boston, Turnbull is visited by a bunch of sleazy racketeers offering to sell him protection. Collectors for "local crime overlords," they are likened to "old-style" movie actors, and Updike is so in thrall to their banal cinematic features—one "rolls around in his mouth" a trademark toothpick, another issues sick threats "with a quick hitch in his shoulders"—that he is unable to invest them with even a trace of genuine malice or menace. The federal government can no longer protect its citizens, and the local police are without the resources to do much. How this can have happened we are not permitted to ask. It just happened. And in the same way, we must accept that the predators can be kept more or less out of one's way, so long as they are paid. They may fight among themselves, but they represent no direct threat to Turnbull's well-being. Suspicious and a little put out at first, he learns quickly to accept what is a necessary evil, and becomes increasingly curious about his protectors. Ben accepts that people do what they must do to get along, extortionists no less than homeowners. What we call social order is an arrangement we would do well not to look at too closely. Curiosity about this element or that is perfectly acceptable, so long as it is not underwritten by a nagging interest in social justice.

Ben's relations with these thugs resemble his relations with most other people. He never gets too close to anyone, though he is curious about selected aspects of wives, children, lovers, and clients. His present wife Gloria seems to him now and then a killer, eager for his death or his disappearance, though she sometimes ministers to him with a puzzling ardor. A former wife, Perdita, "loyal if unenraptured," with her "thick and rounded" soles and "little toes," sometimes seems less a person than a pretext for recalling odd potencies and transgressions. His prostitute-mistress Deirdre, a thief and a preternaturally avid sex toy with "silken rivers of dark body hair," betrays now and again, "as in every woman," "the hormones of nest-building." In all, Ben doubts most things, including his own unstable view of these women. He wants from life nothing more than the same old paltry satisfactions that he derides. Now and then he wonders at "the mysteries of overplenteous life," or (somewhat less sublimely) at "the miraculous knit of the jockey underpants stretched across [his] knees" as he sits on the toilet, but these epiphanies rarely prevent him from feeling "dull" and unresponsive.

The action of the novel is very limited. Ben stays close to home, only occasionally venturing out to the office to do a bit of work, finding few colleagues who miss him. He golfs, reads, visits his grandchildren. When his wife is away, he shares his bed with Deirdre, who stirs him up and eventually leaves him for a more exciting criminal companion. He reaches out, at first reluctantly and then more eagerly, to the band of adolescent racketeers living in a makeshift shed on the outskirts of his modest property, offering them advice on extortion and, in the end, mildly mourning their demise. His thoughts range from "the vibrant magenta of crabapple" to marriage as "a mental game of thrust and parry played on the edge of the grave." He remembers his many failures and his frequent derelictions, but consigns almost everything in his experience to "Sisyphean repetitiveness" and "triviality." By far the most important event in his account of himself is his bout with prostate cancer, his struggle "in a narrow wedge of space-time beneath the obliterating imminence of winter." He issues resonant utterances about meaning and meaninglessness, about change and entropy, but he barely moves from the place he has settled in, and his special gift is to avoid "any thought that will tip [him] into depression."

What action there is in the novel is provided by Ben's rarely sluggish imagination. His journal entries move from one sensation to another, from the smell of a crotch to the dread of humiliation, from the springy hair on the head of a half-black grandchild to the "muffled thrumming" sounding through an open storm window. Often the impressions of the visible world are mild, picturesque, reassuring: "sunlight reflected from the granite outcropping warms the earth." A robin startled into flight, "a stuffy bird, faintly pompous in its portly movements, spoiled by the too many songs and poems unaccountably devoted to him," is a quaint emblem, familiar, comforting, literary. Calmly attentive to every little thing, Updike's narrator is especially alert to "repositories"—"in garages and basements and closets and attics"—that "pledge our faith in eternal return," though he is all too aware of an encroaching entropy, "when there is not a whisper, a subatomic stir, of surge."

Still, Ben is subject to powerful surges, to panics and nostalgias and seizures of fervor. He lurches uncontrollably from one time plane to another, trying on identities with a promiscuous, relaxed abandon. His journal entries allow for several varieties of free association: a narrative of Egyptian grave robbers, a fragment from the life of Saint Mark, the reverie of an early Christian monk, the brutal churnings of a uniformed Nazi, a so-called "good German recruited to guard an extermination camp." What the primary narrative lacks in tension and variety, these fragmentary narratives, with their air of peremptoriness and incompletion, of bluff yet authoritative improvisation, would seem to provide.

Yet it is Updike's sureness of touch that is generally sacrificed in these interpolations. The music of the prose remains intact, the full voice of a confident and exacting speaker recognizable even where, as in the musings of the early Christian monk, the language becomes slightly arch, the sentence structures noticeably more symmetrical, the perspective strained to accommodate "our Lord's birth of a meek virgin" and a "Providence in its miraculous patience [lending] scope so as to accumulate ungainsayable proofs toward the eternal damnation of their souls." It is exhilarating to move without transition from "one busy summer day" on which "it fell to [Ben] to fuck three women" to the reflections of a monk in sackcloth about to be put to the sword, but though we are disposed to applaud the sackcloth theater, we must wonder what purpose is served by these showy fragments.

We do not require conventional transitions, which in any case Updike occasionally provides, as when the sight of a Jewish doctor naked in a locker room suddenly stirs Ben to contrive the sequence in the Third Reich. But the fragments do not exfoliate. They tell us nothing about Ben except that, like any literate person, he can identify briefly with people about whom he has read in books. The sequences have no urgency in the design of the novel. Updike sticks with each of them just long enough to satisfy a modest aesthetic imperative. These fragments are shapely, clever, deftly edged, and intermittently poignant, but they amount in the end to discrete triumphs of superfluity.

JOHN UPDIKE

Of course, the fragments belong to Ben Turnbull, and their telling us so little about him leads us to ask what instead they may reveal about the novelist. Is "antiquity" a key to Updike's vision in a way we had not previously suspected? Probably not. No more do the words "early Christian church" or "Holocaust" provide a critical lead. If the interpolations tell us little about Ben, they tell us little about the novelist, or little that we did not know before. It is hard not to see in Ben many of the standard views and obsessions that the novelist has expressed in many other writings. Ben is by turns wise and foolish, refined and coarse, playful and tendentious. He has an eye for color, line, and form, and also a predilection for philosophical or scientific speculation. Occasionally guilty or dissatisfied, he mostly gets on with his instincts and his appetites, and he is rarely restrained by the higher moralities. He displays a sometimes disarming affection for small things, for mannerisms and foibles. Like other Updike narrators, he is good at taxonomy and elegy, and though he finds little cause for optimism, he is frequently consoled by the comely surfaces of simple things. Saddened by the theft of a fine living room rug, he brightens when "its absence exposed a maple parquet whose beauty had been long obscured."

But Ben is most recognizably a standard Updike male in his sexual obsessions. He rightly describes himself as "like some horn-brained buck." Ben's erotic fantasies include a decidedly sadistic component: he is turned on by thoughts of desecration and enslavement. He is regularly aroused by the exposed shoulders of a stepdaughter or a glimpse of a daughter-in-law's thigh. He cannot comprehend his married son's "patently monogamous affection" for his wife; fidelity seems to him peculiar, an atavism associated with a time before the disappearance of the gods. He is perpetually in search of erotic intoxication, of inflammation and submission. The "flesh-knot" of the anus is to him a recurrent temptation, and he likes the thought that the woman who "serves [him] with a cold, slick expertise" is also a teasing, "money-grubbing cunt" who can be screwed "until she squealed for mercy."

All of this, as Ben knows, is cast in the language of standard sexual fare, "constructed mainly of images from popular culture." Now, for a certain kind of writer—Don DeLillo or Robert Coover—these susceptibilities and influences would be an irresistible opportunity to probe the spread and effects of mass culture, to consider its pernicious invasion of our dreams and our desires. But Updike, who no doubt sees as clearly as anyone else what has become of us, has no wish whatever to explore this aspect of American fate. The brief observation about "popular culture" has no significant relation to anything else in the novel, and in effect serves merely to indicate that Updike himself is too clever to be entirely taken in by the language that he has given to his character. To allow Ben to follow up on his observation would be to violate an essential complacency.

To note, in passing, the origin of erotically charged language is to be smart; but to ask further questions about it might suggest that something ought to be done to liberate us from or to make us critical of an unfortunate susceptibility. But that would be the sort of wishful thinking in which no self-respecting realist can indulge. This satisfied sense of the dominant reality is nicely revealed in the following passage:

> There is a warmth in the proximity of a man who has fucked the same woman you have. It is as if she took off her clothes as a piece of electric news she wished him to bring to you. He has heard the same soft cries, smelled the same stirred-up scent, felt the same compliant slickness, seen the same moonlit swellings and crevices and tufts—it was all in Phil's circuitry, if I could but unload it. . . . My sexual memories had become epics of a lost heroic age, when I was not impotent and could shoot semen into a woman's wincing face like bullets of milk. Deirdre's flanks in memory had acquired the golden immensity of temple walls rising to a cloudless sky and warmed by an Egyptian sun. Whore though he thought her, a nimbus of her holy heat clung to Phil—his oily black pubic curls had tangled with hers.

We learn from this passage much of what is real to Updike's character. Potency is real, and the loss of potency. Scent and touch and soft cries are real, and an intimacy based upon shared physical sensation. The young man whose "pubic curls had tangled with [Deirdre's]" feels "indignant" when he realizes that "he mattered to [Ben] only as an emanation of our shared cunt," but Ben has no recourse to indignation. For all his thinking, for all his reading, he is only appetite and tropism. Words such as "sacred" and "holy" and "nimbus" are to him an oil to lubricate the passage of sexual energy. His postoperative impotence is affecting because we feel that he is lost without the faculties that are most real and important to him, but Updike does not permit us to forget who and what this man is. A dark, voluptuous, obscene electric charge is carried by the erotically loaded sentences that Ben constructs. We are stirred but also repelled by his efforts "to drag with [his] tongue the sweet secret of [a woman's] name out of the granular dark of [his] memory cells." And we wonder at Updike's reluctance to build into the novel any figure who might offer some resistance to Ben, who might be repelled by him as we are repelled.

But the character is most fully revealed in the way he confuses realms, swings wildly between celestial and obscene, worships "the little flesh-knot between the glassy-smooth buttocks visible in moonlight . . . at just the right celestial angle." All the intermittent talk of celestial angles and tempting white church collars and "the risen Jesus" serves mainly to reveal the speaker's baffled desire for something other than what he knows and has. His is a rhetoric of disappointed love, of an obscuring, unsubstantiated ambivalence. Ben desires epiphany but he subsists on shame. He cultivates a barren, hopelessly repetitive eroticism. ("She was a choice cut of meat and I hoped she held out for a fair price.") Absorbed by the glamours and the corrosions of the flesh, he has not the strength to think through his confusion. Like everything else, it is a given fact of his condition. And Updike has no wish to think it through, either.

What excites Ben Turnbull is not, apparently, a subject fit for moral or psychological criticism. Updike is content to give us creatureliness without ethical dimension. His character refers now and again to trans-gression or trespass, but he is fundamentally a complacent man, for-giving himself everything, pitying his frailty and his fate, extracting a sensual enjoyment even from his occasional self-lacerations. He counsels the thugs on his property on the ways of the world, advising them to "mention casually" to prospective clients "that [they] would hate to see any of their children kidnapped" and that "if they don't pay up [protec-tion money]" the boys "might think about killing one of their cats." Nor does he beat himself up about his relations with the fourteen-year-old girl of the gang, whom he visits when the others are away. There are traces of tenderness in their carefully delimited transactions. "She was cool to the touch, surprisingly, and clean-smelling," Ben notes. "Her breasts smelled powdery, like a baby's skull, and her nipples were spheri-cal, like paler, smokier versions of honeysuckle berries." There is nothing in this of Nabokovian decadence or play. The man is merely not a bad guy, and he has no reason not to be tender to a young girl who allows him to place his tongue where he likes.

"She graciously offered to touch me, where I jutted," he goes on, but he had earlier promised the boys "no penetration," and the "hand-job" offered by the sweet young thing "would penetrate my soul." This is as close as we come in this novel to "renunciation." But the lapse into soul-fear is without conviction. Ben fears only exposure by his wife, the possible loss of "the island of repetitive safety [he] had carved from the world." His little intoxications are pathetic things, as he well knows. Not for him a full-fledged Dionysian rebellion, any more than a crisis of conscience. In the suburbs this *homme moyen sensuel* can savor the acid taste of teenage honeysuckle on his tongue while daydreaming through the sumptuously appointed living room, "a breezy, translucent person, a debonair proprietor."

Toward the End of Time will call to mind earlier novels by Updike, especially *Rabbit at Rest*, with its self-destructive, relentlessly unappetizing protagonist Harry Angstrom. Like Ben Turnbull, Rabbit regards few things as "his problem," and accepts that he "never was that great" as father or husband. Both characters are unapologetic womanizers. In part an emblem of his society, Rabbit sees that in his America—as in the America of 2020—"everything [is] falling apart," and though, like Ben Turnbull, he is at least mildly interested in many things, from science to history, he is resolutely unamenable to improvement or edification. Rabbit, like Ben, wins a modest claim on our sympathy principally by confronting premonitions of death, by acknowledging "something more ominous and intimately his: his own death." Ben is a more articulate person than Rabbit and less of a slob, but Updike grants him no "greater portion of grace," and discovers in his failings fewer occasions for satire or merriment.

Toward the End of Time is a simpler and less attractive book than *Rabbit at Rest*. For it is defiantly not a book about anything remediable, or about the way we live now. For all of its technical beauties, its proficiencies of diction and syntax, Updike's new novel is especially disheartening in its specious and halfhearted attempt to situate its private malaise in the aftermath of a terrible historical catastrophe. The book is not only indifferent to history, it exploits history. It uses the moral and historical grandeur of a world war to promote its cranky local obsessions to a level of universality and interest that they do not deserve. The near-destruction of the world notwithstanding, *Toward the End of Time* is just the familiar Updikean dystopia. The war in this book is an empty device, and spiritual exhaustion is written all over its pages.

There is in Ben Turnbull, as also in Updike's other characters here, no possibility of growth, and what passes for redemption is at most an activity of consciousness for which genuine advance is reducible to mechanical invention. The novel's easy acceptance of a long cosmic view—the "silently clamorous, imperiously silver and pure" rotation of the stars—merely flattens every prospect of judgment, penance, reconciliation, and change, and reduces it to triviality and illusion. In Updike, the words "transcendent," "trust," and "virtue" have never before seemed so frivolous. The book seems a reflex of frustration and bitterness. To mistake one's own spiritual condition for the final measure of reality—to confuse one's own aggrieved, attenuated shadow on the wall with being itself in all its variety—is to offer a terribly impoverished version of experience. The wonder of it is that Updike, brilliant as ever in evoking the profusion of surface life, in making palpable what he once called "the skin of a living present," seeks here only to distract us from the essential demoralization, the sense of nullity that holds even the novel's most vivid particulars firmly in its grip.

6

POLITICS AND POSTMODERNISM

MARIO VARGAS LLOSA

In the novel *The Real Life of Alejandro Mayta* by Peruvian writer Mario Vargas Llosa, there is an arresting sequence in which the protagonist and his revolutionary comrades stop at the ancient mountain community of Quero. They rest there for two hours before continuing their flight from government troops that have been sent to bring them back to be punished for revolutionary crimes against the state. What is striking in the handful of pages devoted to Quero is not the quality of the political ideas brought forward or the revelation of character facilitated by the protagonist's reflections. What emerges so forcefully, rather, is a powerful sentiment of disgust focused not only on the trappings of the place but on its inhabitants. That disgust is accompanied neither by qualification nor apology. "All the houses in Quero had to be like that," we read: "no light, no running water, no drainage, and no bath. Flies, lice, and a thousand other bugs must be part of the poor furniture." But if this is a sorry spectacle, we are admonished, consider the people who live in this filth: "If they had to pee at night, they probably wouldn't feel like getting up and going outside. They pee right here, next to the bed where they sleep and the stove where they cook. . . . And if at midnight they had to shit? Would they have enough energy to go out into the darkness and the cold, the wind and the rain? They'd shit right here, between the stove and the bed."

This is not an isolated passage in Vargas Llosa's novel. Still in Quero, he wants us to note that the lady of the house probably sleeps with her animals, that she has no doubt been wearing the same skirt for many years, and that it has probably been many years "since she had washed herself." Elsewhere in the book there are many references to the mountains of garbage threatening to overwhelm the city of Lima, and to middle-class citizens who grow so accustomed to it that they no longer notice what has become of their neighborhoods. Poorer citizens are described as "resigned," not only to the garbage, which they routinely throw out of their houses, but to such emblems of crime and disorder as "a decapitated body" lying ignored in the street.

Some will speak of all this as part of the author's apocalyptic vision, reading the signs as a warning of the disaster that is about to befall Peru as it has already befallen other countries in the region. But more than a prediction of political or social disorder is at issue in the imagery that so pervades this novel. To be confronted so steadily with filth and wretchedness is in fact to suspect that political categories are inadequate to comprehend what is happening in places like Peru. Tempted like the rest of us to come at problems of poverty, inequality, and tyranny with the vocabulary of revolution, reaction, and reform, the novelist also seems more than a little tempted by the thought that politics inevitably misses the point. If, as his narrator has it, "Peru's going down the drain," mightn't it be the case that there's no help for it, or worse, that the people almost deserve what they've got? No such awful conclusion is drawn in this novel, but it is hard not to feel that the novelistic intelligence shaping the material has barely managed to resist it.

Ostensibly, Vargas Llosa has written a political novel. The setting alternates between the Peru of the late 1950s and the Peru of the near future. The central figure is an old-line Trotskyist disappointed in the merely theoretic communism he's pursued for twenty years. A member of a splinter party with seven members, Alejandro Mayta has had reason to feel disappointed. His one attempt to break out of the sterile round of ideological disputation and ineffectual pamphleteering was a minor revolutionary action that had no real chance of succeeding and that cost Mayta all the political friends he'd had. Vargas Llosa's narrator, who closely resembles the novelist himself, reconstructs the story of the long-forgotten Mayta and his abortive insurrection by means of interviews with those who knew Mayta in the 1950s. By the end of the novel we see Mayta as a sixty-five-year-old man whose chief desire is to keep himself and his family afloat and whose principal dream is of escape to another country. He lives in an already dilapidated "new town" in the shadow of the prison in which he spent many years of his adult life. Obviously, there are grounds for despair in this narrative outline; and in the detail Vargas Llosa relentlessly supplies, there is more than reason for disgust.

Mayta himself may not inspire revulsion, but the spectacle of his failure and the humiliation of his hope is rarely edifying.

It is legitimate to wonder precisely what Vargas Llosa hoped to accomplish in this novel, indeed, to wonder whether Vargas Llosa knew quite what he was after in a work that is full of misleading details and false starts. If he wished to say, simply, that there is no hope for improvement in countries like Peru, he certainly could have examined the consequences of that observation more rigorously than he chose to. If he wished to inquire, as he did in the earlier novel *Conversation in The Cathedral*, "When did Peru get fucked over?" he could certainly have provided a more ample historical perspective, going back before the 1950s to discover what made revolutionary agitation seem attractive to so many people in his country. However, if he wished simply to settle old scores with a Latin American left that has often seemed not to know what it was doing, he could surely have made things easier for himself by creating a less likeable protagonist than Mayta and by portraying the conditions of life in Peru as requiring something less than total renovation. As things stand in Vargas Llosa's novel, it is hard not to feel that we have been given contradictory signals: on the one hand, a situation that is ripe for revolution; on the other hand, a portrayal of revolutionary ambition that makes it seem alternately cynical or childish, and always futile. If the carefully deposited signs of filth and degradation do not finally add up as we expect them to, neither do the indications that the book is to be read as a political or historical inquiry.

A number of reviewers have described *The Real Life of Alejandro Mayta* as a more-or-less standard postmodern novel, one which creates narrative obstacles only for the pleasure involved in overcoming them. In such a work, some reviewers have said, we are necessarily reminded "that art is as arbitrary as truth is relative" and that "life itself is a moment by moment invention." The author of such a work insists on his own duplicity so as to assert, in Vargas Llosa's words, the author's "enormous deicidal will for the destruction and reconstruction of reality." In these terms, Vargas Llosa may be said to make common cause with those who read him as if he were a contemporary Latin American follower of Vladimir Nabokov, measuring his success by his willingness to use "to the hilt" the narrative instruments he elects. No doubt, as John Updike has aptly noted, "the intelligence of Mario Vargas Llosa plays above the sad realities and unrealities with a coolness that should be distinguished from Nabokov's hermetically aesthetic ardor." But it is the novelist as

MARIO VARGAS LLOSA

gamesman and master strategist who most frequently emerges from accounts of the present work.

There is much to be said for such an approach. The novel reads like a postmodern work, moving rapidly and often without transition from one time plane to another, mingling past and present so dexterously as to subdue them to a single, almost undifferentiated texture. What happened, what might have happened, and what is likely to happen are accorded equivalent status, and the author-narrator's desire to get at the truth is explicitly confounded with the need for a plausible basis on which to fabulate and embellish. Though the apparent subject of the book is Mayta and the unsuccessful uprising in which he participated, we are so often reminded of Mayta's fictional status and of the author-narrator's literary exertions that we might well think it chiefly important to concern ourselves with the creative impulse itself. The advantage of such an approach—apart from the fact that it may answer directly to Vargas Llosa's intentions—is that it forces us to treat the novel as a novel, that it dismisses as trivial or irrelevant questions of historical accuracy that may only confuse our responses as readers. If there is a vision at work in this novel—so we may want to feel—it is the vision of a novelist. The views of Vargas Llosa as expressed in his latest journalistic contribution to the *New York Times Sunday Magazine* may interest us in various ways, but they can have little to do with the vision of the novelist, whose business is to ask questions rather than to promote a position. If *The Real Life of Alejandro Mayta* is a novel of politics, it is also a work that refuses to endorse any programmatic reading of its material.

The narrator in Vargas Llosa's novel is a writer who is clearly intended to remind us of the public figure Vargas Llosa has become. Like other thoughtful people, he is interested in the fate of his country and knows a good deal about its history. He is also attracted to a wide range of ideas. We know relatively little about him, but we have reason to believe that he is not a frivolous man. Though he is something of a "possibilitarian"—Robert Musil's word describes a person who cannot forget that things can easily have been other than they are—his words have a gravity about them that belies the seeming arbitrariness of his novelistic invention. He may play tricks on us, carefully establishing a character's identity only to reveal at last that we were misled, but we feel all the same that his games have a purpose, even if we cannot always say with certainty what it is. Kierkegaard's fear—that if everything is possible and every "fact" subject to sudden contradiction, then nothing is true—does not do justice to our sense of this work. So intent is our narrator upon his inquiry into Mayta and, more especially, into Mayta's abortive revolutionary gesture, that we cannot but feel he believes in the truth his exertions will uncover. In no way reducible to a disembodied voice speaking arbitrary words, he seems everywhere to feel that things have weight, that there is such a thing as a necessity to which even the most playful imagination is responsible. If we are occasionally irritated by the liberties he takes and puzzled by his desire to sabotage his own credibility, we are nonetheless confident that for him certain things are real, that the desire to know what they are is genuine and, in its way, admirable.

The notion that for such a narrator, as for Vargas Llosa himself, the traditional idea of character has been abandoned is at once plausible and misleading. Obviously the absence of linear narrative will entitle the reader to feel to some extent like a participant in the piecing together of the story. So too will the reader feel that he or she chooses from among conflicting possibilities so as to create characters whose identity will nonetheless remain ambiguous. But it is one thing to project possibility without motive or consequence, and another to insist that there are always motives and consequences, however difficult they may be to assemble. Character in this novel is always a primary concern, the key to what may be said about the validity of an enterprise. When we think of the narrator himself, we consider not only his duplicities and stratagems but his character. We try to determine what matters to him, and we conclude at last that we know enough about him to reject certain possibilities and to emphasize others. His absorption in Mayta of course tells us more about him than anything else, quite in the way that Mayta's obsessions largely define his identity. To conclude that Mayta has no identity, no character, simply because there are unanswerable questions associated with his conduct, is to ignore how much is revealed. Vargas Llosa here affirms a traditional conception of character by forcing us to acknowledge that we know these people, indeed, that we can judge them by considering motive, circumstance, and consequence, quite as we would if we were working with a more conventional narrative.

Does this mean that Vargas Llosa's narrative procedures are merely a smokescreen designed to conceal the conventionality of his purpose? Those who would draw such a conclusion would then have to feel that for Vargas Llosa there is a plain truth that the novel is after, that underlying all the complex authorial derring-do there is a simple narrative of naive revolutionary aspiration and inevitable disappointment. But so obviously is there no such plain truth, no such schematic narrative program in this novel that one cannot but concede the futility of attempting to formulate conclusions in a neatly edifying or chastening way. Our attention to character and to its elusive relation with politics will rather lead us to ask whether the novel adds up, whether its devices have something to do with its purpose.

To say that a book of a certain kind adds up is usually only to say that its various parts cohere and collectively underwrite an overarching purpose. With the Latin American novel that purpose is usually taken to include the setting out of a political conflict. Vargas Llosa's novel deals with an incident that actually occurred in Peru in 1962, though he sets the events in 1958, before the consolidation of Castro's revolution in Cuba, so as to make more palpable the audacity of Mayta's insurrection. No attempt is made to justify the insurrection by providing a detailed account of Peruvian politics in the 1950s. Neither does Vargas Llosa at all go over the failure of democracy in Peru in the late 1960s or the coming to power of the military "revolutionary experiment" at that time. The atmosphere of Peru in the near future of the novel makes us feel that all manner of awfulness has occurred. But issues of the sort that Vargas Llosa will debate in public meetings or in newspaper articles are not a part of the texture of the novel. As we read the novel, "we know" that politics in Peru has everything to do with ill health, malnutrition, terrorism, corruption, military dictatorship, and the relationship between various despots and the U.S. Marines. But the novel furnishes no way to talk about these issues. They are part of an undifferentiated given, the more or less unarguable facts of life. In the face of such facts, which are never really subject to rational discussion, the activist impulses of Mayta can only seem misguided (which is to say, without reasonable hope of success) or inevitable (a necessary expression of a desire for drastic change which cannot be impugned by recalling that it had no reasonable expectation of success). It is the special purpose of Vargas Llosa's novel to make the impulses of Mayta seem both misguided and inevitable. Insofar as his motives seem to us idealistic and he proceeds to act without any taint of self-importance, he will also seem to us an embodiment of an inevitable and largely attractive will to change. Insofar as his thinking is revealed as inadequate to the magnitude of the forces arrayed against him, he will seem disappointing. For the reader of Vargas Llosa's novel there is no way to ask whether Mayta might have gone about the business of changing his society in another way, say, by embracing some form of parliamentary democracy and strenuously working toward that ideal. As readers, we are only in a position to consider the motives of the character and the palpable consequences of projects like the one he undertakes.

Evaluated simply in terms of consequence, Mayta is undeniably a failure, his revolutionary aspirations clearly hopeless. The insurrection he leads is rapidly broken up, his chief cohort is shot and killed, and Mayta spends many years in prison. What is worse, this first Peruvian Marxist uprising and subsequent small- or large-scale insurrections inspire nothing but a further cycle of repression and brutality. The Peru of the near future is, if anything, in worse shape than the Peru of Mayta's youth. The evidence, in other words, suggests not only that Mayta was unable to foresee the consequences of his actions, but that motives in isolation from the capacity to think clearly and consequentially are not to be judged as good motives at all. This is not to suggest that the only good motives are those that lead more or less inevitably to the accomplishment of reasonable ends. But Vargas Llosa would seem to suggest that idealism and utopianism ought to be susceptible to judgment in the way that more ordinary and pragmatic approaches to reality have been.

As we try to get a definitive fix on Mayta, we discover that such judgments are not easy to arrive at or to trust. Early in the novel, he emerges as a genuine priest of revolution, an ascetic with a vocation, obsessed with the sufferings of the poor and "capable of reacting with the same indignation to any injustice." Nothing we hear about him in the various interviews conducted by the author-narrator can quite dislodge from our minds that initial, powerful image of the man. None of his homosexual exploits, for example, can at all tarnish the image of the somewhat juvenile idealist, and it matters little to our ultimate sense of Mayta that the vivid accounts of him as a practicing homosexual are later repudiated. Neither is our sense of his somewhat sophomoric enthusiasm diminished by those passages in which he reflects with a grave sobriety on revolution as "a long act of patience . . . a thousand and one vile deeds," and so on. For if Mayta is at forty still a *naif*, he never seems to us a fool or without the capacity to surprise us. If as the novel progresses he seems less and less the intellectual we had perhaps taken him for, he remains in important respects the person we thought we admired earlier and might still admire at novel's end.

MARIO VARGAS LLOSA

What continually complicates our view of Mayta is what we take to be the inconclusiveness of Vargas Llosa's feelings and intentions. The conflicting accounts of Mayta offered by this or that person we can explain by speaking of their particular needs or their limited perspectives. But the author-narrator has a perspective that by definition cannot be limited in the same way, encompassing as it does the full range of sentiments and motives expressed in the novel. If we say that he maintains—through all of the changes Mayta's portrait is made to undergo—a consistent affection for Mayta, and that this affection is more than the novelist's love of a creation upon whom he can project anything he likes, then we have still to say what it is he admires. Perhaps it is Mayta's capacity to hope, to defy reality. Perhaps it is the absence of cynicism, the inexplicable intensity of resolution. Is this what the narrator wants us to admire when he gives us Mayta imagining the aftermath of his little insurrection: "the working class would shake off its lethargy, all the reformist deceptions, all its corrupt leaders, all those illusions of being able to coexist with the sell-outs, and would join the struggle."?

But even in this passage, we suspect that Vargas Llosa wants to admire Mayta's optimism more than he can bring himself to do, and that the impulse to caricature is as strong as the impulse to celebrate. Eighty pages later, when we read, "He saw them multiplying like the loaves of bread in the Bible, every day recruiting scores of boys as poor and self-denying as themselves," or "the assault on heaven, I thought. We shall bring heaven down from heaven, establish it on earth," we cannot but feel that the gap between Mayta's optimism and the reality he confronts is an essential component of the portrait. What may have seemed simply a portrait of the revolutionary as idealist is also the portrait of a dreamer dangerously yielding to a vision that has taken possession of him utterly. As we confront the futility of Mayta's enterprise and its delusional component, we are left with an uneasy sense of not knowing quite what we feel or why we have been taken through Mayta's adventures.

Does it clarify matters to recall that Mayta's delusions are explored again and again in the novel, that the narrator is routinely at pains to remind us that Mayta "let his imagination run wild" and that Mayta's optimism strikes most of his acquaintances as incomprehensible or ludicrous? But this doesn't alter the fact that Mayta remains in many respects an appealing person. Compare him with alternative figures who lucidly criticize his naïveté and his gift for defeat. Even those who are most sensible and sophisticated, like the intellectual in charge of a progressive development center, have little to offer apart from a knowing disdain for visionary intensity and a capacity to thread their way between partisans of the left and the right. It is Mayta's naïveté, after all, that permits him to conclude in his one year at the university "that the professors had lost their love of teaching somewhere along the line"; and it is that same naïveté that permits him to summon something like the old intensity when, at age sixty-five, he tells our narrator about the food kiosk he ran with a friend amidst the squalor of the unspeakable Lurigancho prison:

> "We created a genuine revolution," he assures me with pride. "We won the respect of the whole place. We boiled the water for making fruit juice, for coffee, for everything. We washed the knives, forks, and spoons, the glasses, and the plates before and after they were used. Hygiene, above all. A revolution, you bet. . . . We even set up a kind of bank, because a lot of cons gave us their money for safekeeping."

Perhaps naïveté is not the word with which to describe the quality of character involved in these passages. One way or the other, is the feeling evoked merely pathetic? Here I think we must answer that it is not. If the mountains of garbage swallowing the landscape of Vargas Llosa's Peru have something to tell us about his vision of the country and its people, then surely Mayta's revolutionary pride cannot be dismissed so easily. It may not provide the key to the political vision of the novel, but it does suggest the kind of thing to which the novel most warmly responds. In fact, as already intimated, it is difficult to say that there is a politics in this novel beyond the elaboration of attitudes that in another work might have informed a more focused vision. After all, late in the novel Mayta remarks not only that he is no longer involved in politics but that "politics gave me up." Is this intended to suggest that he is too good for politics, or, more broadly, that politics cannot finally address what is most real in our lives? Again, it is hard to be sure precisely what Vargas Llosa would want us to feel about this. But he would seem to suggest that those who cannot do justice to Mayta will not know how to think about politics or the future.

If this seems doubtful, a passage near the end of the novel may help to clarify what may be taken to be a proper attitude to Mayta:

> Later, when there were outbreaks of guerrilla fighting in the mountains and the jungle in 1963, 1964, 1965, and 1966—all inspired by the

Cuban Revolution—no newspaper remembered that the forerunner of those attempts to raise up the people in armed struggle to establish socialism in Peru had been that minor episode, rendered ghostlike by the years, which had taken place in Jauja province. Today no one remembers who took part in it.

Here, beyond the prestidigitations of Vargas Llosa's postmodern narrative procedures, is some semblance of the sentiment that unites the author-narrator with his protagonist. For all of the novelist's oft-repeated insistence that "all fictions are lies" and that we can never know anything with certainty, he cannot but affirm that there is something in Mayta which continues to compel and attract. The impulse to honor—with whatever misgivings—whatever is authentic in Mayta's passion for social justice is the center of Vargas Llosa's novel and the substance of the meaning that abides.

7

IN EXILE FROM EXILE

NORMAN MANEA

"To learn that we have said or done a foolish thing, that is nothing," wrote Montaigne. "We must learn that we are nothing but fools, a far broader and more important lesson." It is a lesson that many an autobiographer has been all too ready to embrace. In the staging of dramas in which frailty and foolishness are relentlessly depicted, the lighting tends to be very carefully arranged. The assumption informing autobiography has long been that it is at once a constructed narrative and a "truthful" engagement with a nature or a disposition more or less equally compounded of darkness and light. In the telling of life stories, it is assumed, resistances will be overcome, and there will be at least some therapeutic benefit in the uncovering of material previously suppressed, forgotten, or ignored. The opportunities for self-congratulation afforded by the construction of life stories are considerable, and rare are the memoirists who can resist them.

Exiles, whose life stories have to do with the experience of migration and loss, are perhaps more susceptible than others to the varieties of self-approval opened up by memoir writing. Such people have been so numerous in the last hundred years as almost to seem commonplace today. No one who reads can fail to be familiar with the works of writers who have reflected on the subject of exile, though often it is exile as a "metaphysical condition" or a noble effort to compensate for what has been "lost in translation" that is front and center, rather than exile as occasion for posturing or delusion. Joseph Brodsky recommended that the writer in exile wholeheartedly embrace "the metaphysical dimension," for "to ignore it or dodge it is to cheat yourself out of the meaning of what has happened to you . . . to ossify into an uncomprehending victim." At the same time, he warned that because he has suffered, usually at the hands of a political tyranny, the writer in exile is apt to regard himself as a "certified martyr" "unchecked by anyone," whose potential insignificance in the place to which he has emigrated can only be countered by the steady assertion of his privileged status as exemplary sufferer and witness.

Since the writer in exile will usually feel marginal in his new place of residence, he is likely, Brodsky argues, to become "a retrospective and retroactive being," ignoring, for the most part, his present reality, recycling "the familiar material of his past" and gravitating to the elegiac. The dangers here are obvious. They include what Brodsky calls "the repetitiveness of nostalgia," the slowing down of the writer's "stylistic evolution," and even an insidious cynicism. "The good old stuff served him well at least once: it earned him exile. And exile, after all, is a kind of success. . . . Why not push the good old stuff around a bit more?"

No memoirist would seem to understand more sharply than Norman Manea the dangers anatomized by Brodsky. Again and again in *The Hooligan's Return*, Manea recoils from flattery, from sympathy, from praise. Persistently he sniffs around in his own sentences for traces of cliché, illusion, self-promotion. For every modest self-assertion there are numerous passages of caustic self-mockery. Everywhere Manea interrogates his own tendency to become what he despises: an emblem, an embodiment, a "marketable" victim-figure or avenger. He knows how seductive it is to push the good old stuff around, to collude in the cozy mythmaking that trivializes suffering. No witness to the several barbarisms of the past century has so persistently instructed his reader in the process by which "Thursday's atrocities have become grist for the mottoes on Friday's T-shirts." Does he cultivate, now and again, what he calls "the Judaic taste for catastrophe"? Is he addicted, just a little, to the extremity that helps a man to seem interesting to himself? If so, there is also a pronounced distaste for the "whinings and jeremiads of the victim" and a sly contempt for the "fatigue of being oneself."

Norman Manea was born in a small Romanian market town in Bukovina in 1936. His father was a baker's son, his mother a bookseller's daughter. The Jews of the province, as Manea reports, "spoke Romanian as well as German, and enjoyed uninterrupted contact with the Romanian population." In the sugar factory where Manea's father worked, there also worked "Czech, German, and Italian 'foreigners'" in what had seemed an increasingly cosmopolitan community. The deportation order issued in 1941 by the Romanian fascist authorities sent the Jews of Bukovina to the Transnistria concentration camp in the

Ukraine and put an end to the illusions inspired by the long experiment in cosmopolitanism.

Though several elderly members of the family interned with them in the Transnistria camp did not survive the war years, Manea and his parents emerged in 1945 and soon struggled to make a life for themselves in communist Romania. In 1949, Manea became a communist youth leader—the episodes of the memoir devoted to this period in his life are alternately hilarious and heartbreaking—but soon he went through a period of disaffection, eventually became an engineer, published several books, and by 1974, with the help of a psychiatric exemption, became a full-time writer. His eight novels and numerous other works gradually made him a significant literary voice in his country, but he also became a suspicious figure in Ceausescu's anti-Semitic, authoritarian universe, though he was not a defiantly dissident writer nor an openly subversive anticommunist. In 1986, he left the country with his wife and two years later settled in New York City.

Manea's fiction and essays (four books are available in English translation) clearly issue from a man who knows gentleness and affection but is too ironic and suspicious to settle for "healing" or "closure" or to ignore the specific gravity of his own nature. *The Hooligan's Return* begins in 1997 with a visit to a landmark deli in Manhattan, where the writer discusses with his friend Philip Roth his decision to visit Romania after an absence of nine years. Like other such exchanges in a book that moves in surprising and briefly disorienting leaps and bounds from melancholy to whimsy, from the sardonic to the lyrical, the exchange with Roth is fragmentary, suggestive, playful, and inconclusive. But in that opening episode of a long book we see at once the tenor and the abiding strategy of Manea's imagination, which encompasses a great many moods and events and projections. Nothing stands still for long in this narrative: back and forth and away the narrative persistently swings, so that the long journey to Transnistria in 1941 is intertwined with the repatriation journey of 1945 and the later trips to the West and back again to the homeland in 1997. In Manea, the flow of language is by turns murmurous and singleminded, remembrance and reflection, time present and time past so entirely interfused that the one seems invariably the face of the other.

There is not much of the "certified martyr" in Manea. He did, after all, survive the serial ordeals to which he was subjected, and if survival did often seem to him a dubious privilege, he did live long enough to observe the demise of fascist and communist Romania—and also to bury some of the glamorous lies associated with extraterritoriality. Like Kafka, he is "claimed . . . by the dark fogs of Eastern Europe," but he is loath to appropriate the "certifiable" despair of Kafka's "I am allowed no moment of calm, I cannot take anything for granted, everything has to be fought for." Yes, Manea declares, he recognizes himself in Kafka's words, though one must beware of affiliations precisely because they are so tempting; those whose boats are leaky are preternaturally susceptible to resonantly downward-drifting accents.

Manea's resistance to posture and myth takes many forms. More often than not it arrives with an inflection, a voice, the sharp accent of a friend disinclined, in Manea's version, to let the writer get away with anything. Am I a nuisance? Manea wonders. Yes, "quite a nuisance occasionally," Roth concedes. And do I not resemble, as I have long seemed to myself, that familiar character of Augustus the Fool, "the pariah, the loser, the one who always gets kicked in the ass, to the audience's delight"? Sorry, another friend replies, but you are, poor thing, a "respectable" writer in residence, "honored with prizes and an endowed chair. . . . In the East European circus, the clown returning from America is a victor, a star." The friend is tolerant, amused. He laughs at the writer's penchant for self-dramatization and certifiable martyrdom. Try as he may, Manea cannot successfully make himself into the figure for whom he would like to mobilize a dreary, all-purpose compassion.

Manea believes that to be worthy not merely of compassion but of admiration, the exile needs to see himself not as a victim merely but as one who struggled, a man never complacent in defeat but moved always to say no, I will not go gently, I will not speak that lie, I will not settle into the empty rituals of solidarity. To this end, he applies to himself—a modest, tentative, sheepish man—the epithet "hooligan," which has a notable pedigree in twentieth-century Romanian history. Manea tells us that in Mihail Sebastian's book *How I Became a Hooligan*, which appeared in 1935, Sebastian affirmed:

[The] "spiritual autonomy" of Jewish suffering, its "tragic nerve," the dispute between a "tumultuous sensibility" and a "merciless critical spirit," between "intelligence at its coolest and passion at its most unbridled." A hooligan? Did that mean marginal, nonaligned, excluded. . . . He defined himself clearly: "I am not a partisan, I am always a dissident. . . . " What does being a dissident mean? Someone dissenting even from dissidents?

But it was not only the Jew Sebastian who staked a claim to the word "hooligan." The young Mircea Eliade, later famous for his scholarly books on the history of religion and a distinguished professor for many years at the University of Chicago, published an early novel entitled *The Hooligans*. There hooliganism was associated with "rebellion unto death . . . perfectly and evenly aligned regiments within a collective myth." This was a hooliganism rather far removed from the "merciless critical spirit" and "cool autonomy" extolled as indispensable components of hooliganism by Sebastian. In fact, at the time he wrote his novel, Eliade was a spokesman for the fascist Iron Guard, eagerly awaiting, as he wrote in 1938, "a nationalist Romania, frenzied and chauvinistic, armed and vigorous, ruthless and vengeful," and prepared to address "the advance of the . . . Jews [who] have overrun the villages." Such observations seem to Manea "ridiculous and disgusting," and the powerful essay on Eliade that he wrote for *The New Republic* in 1991 won for him in postcommunist Romania epithets ranging from "dwarf of Jerusalem" to "half-man" and "louse."

The word "hooligan" has in our language a somewhat archaic ring, in part because it has often been applied with tender affection to naughty children whose transgressions, however habitual, seem to their parents eminently forgivable. Likewise, when Manea applies the word to himself, he does so with the sense that he is the most improbable of hooligans, a man ordinarily too mild and dreamy to represent a genuine danger to the body politic. To read Manea's stories is often to find oneself in a dreamy domain of Proustian inwardness. To be sure, Manea's fiction also encompasses political satire and farce, and his essays often pursue their targets with unremitting urgency. Still, as one critic has noted, Manea most often prefers "the horror of the indescribable to the description of horror," and "the uncanny atmosphere of unreality," along with the proliferating "coded paradoxes" of his fiction, make him seem anything but a typical polemicist.

Still, there is in Manea's repertoire a considerable gift for authentic hooliganism. He is a compulsive debunker. All through the memoir, he leaves behind him a trail of discarded postures and postulates. Manea clearly fears the contamination of "critical" hooliganism by a species of glib appropriation captured by several leading Eastern European writers. In Milan Kundera's *The Unbearable Lightness of Being*—to cite a notable example—the character Sabina leaves Prague for the West in 1968 and discovers in the catalogue for an exhibition of her paintings "a picture of herself with a drawing of barbed wire superimposed on it. Inside she found a biography that read like the life of a saint or martyr: she had suffered, struggled against . . . injustice, been forced to abandon her bleeding homeland, yet was carrying on the struggle." When Sabina protests to friends that "my enemy is Kitsch, not Communism," she is not understood. Manea would never agree that his enemy in Romania had been "Kitsch, not Communism," but he does surely understand Sabina. His determination not to make himself into a dissident noble rider is drawn from the same loathing of falsehood that inspires Kundera's character. To be a hooligan, that is, an oppositional figure who sees through every mask, appeals to Manea so long as it does not entail the pretense of perfect virtue.

This reluctance in Manea goes beyond the customary acknowledgment that heroes are likely to have clay feet. He is wary not merely of ordinary frailty but also of self-deception. And he loathes puerility, which is the "everyday somnambulism" of the hear-no-evil-see-no-evil fellow travelers of every established order. That puerility is perfectly expressed in the title of Manea's *Compulsory Happiness*, which is set in the "penal colony" of "the big lie"; there, in Ceausescu's Romania, citizens "can continue sucking on their dumb lollipop of hope" and deny to themselves what is obvious about the lives they lead. In his memoir, Paradise is the name Manea gives to the great good "daily" place most well-adjusted ciphers agree to be happy in. The memoir opens with the words: "The bright spring light, like an emanation from Paradise, streams through the large picture window wide as the room itself." By the end of the paragraph, "looking down from his tenth-floor apartment" at the New York City street below, he must remind himself again that "in Paradise . . . one is better off than anywhere else." Later, strolling casually past Verdi Square, he notes that "the placid pigeons of Paradise have come to rest" on the presiding statue of the Italian composer.

Everywhere Manea confronts the trivial, familiar, comforting surfaces of ordinary life that tempt him to agree that things could be worse and that only fools long for a "better" or a "best" that will never materialize. Everywhere he notes the propensity to shallowness and accommodation. Try though he may to be grateful for the air-conditioned Paradise of the United States, he cannot summon "the joy of liberation." Moved occasionally to register with due compassion the plight of ordinary people, all, like himself, unable to be other than they are, he reminds himself that the "oppressed masses" are "the not-so-innocent," and that "elementary polarities"—as between East and West, free and unfree, open and closed—"often prove to be in fact complementary." So Manea speculated in *On Clowns*, and so he would seem still to believe in his latest report from Paradise.

For Manea, what has always seemed problematic is the very concept of normality. Normality suggests, after all, that human beings can live their lives without undue recourse to fantasy and exaggeration, with some reasonable expectation that the world will be more or less regular in its rhythms and unfoldings. This sense of things Manea struggles to achieve, though he does so, for the most part, without hope. In Romania, he reports, almost anyone would likely have been invited to serve the government as an informer. A close friend of Manea had been chosen to inform on the writer, and did so for several years, meeting each week in "safe" private houses to deliver meaningless information to a Securitate policeman, later casually reporting to his friend Norman on these "official visits." Such an arrangement was routine in a country where there was "one fully employed police officer for every fifteen citizens," as Manea wrote in *On Clowns*, "and for every police officer, fifteen 'volunteer' informers." But can such an arrangement be, or seem, normal?

But the question of normality cuts in other directions as well. Early in the memoir, Manea reads on a yellow New York City building façade, "spelled out in iridescent blue," the words: "DEPRESSION IS A FLAW IN CHEMISTRY NOT IN CHARACTER." Like so much that passes through Manea's mind, the words are at once preposterous and cautionary, a curiosity and a portent of larger things. Ever alert to flaws, skeptical about therapies and adjustments, suspicious of formulas designed to make people feel good about themselves, Manea routinely recoils from anything soothing or categorically guilt reducing. Scarred by the "toxins" he has long ingested, he betrays in the memoir his long habit of handling what passes for normality with acidic, ironic distortion. Tempted though he may be to earnestness, solemnity, and uncomplicated fellow feeling, he checks himself and remembers the advice of Witold Gombrowicz, who "used to relish sticking out his tongue at himself in an ever-present mirror."

That Manea has no prospect of establishing a "normal," untroubled relationship with any conceivable idea of normality is clear to us from the first pages of the memoir. Even his happy memories are delivered with a compulsive air of ironic distortion. Bucharest itself, a place where Manea once experienced varieties of carnal adventure and other intensities, is remembered as a "Gomorrah." Ordinary events and emotions are transformed into dramatic counters in an ongoing struggle, so that a "normal" sense of the thing unfolding before us has no chance against a diction replete with "revenge," "redemption," "masters of the night," "the ghetto's eternal fear," "the Christian siren," and "the honey trap of defilement, the taboo, temptation."

The distortion and the irony that are essential aspects of Manea's imagination are sometimes directed at ephemeral things such as love affairs and other times at more terrifying events. "Transnistria did not live up to expectations," he writes, "and could only show a balance sheet of fifty percent dead." The irony in that sentence is best appreciated when the sentence is placed next to a passage on the preceding page of the memoir: "From across the millennia, a tragic destiny has united the Babylonian captivity with the inferno of starvation, disease, and death in Transnistria." So wrote the Christian mayor of Czernowitz, a man named Traian Popovici, who had tried until the very last moment to halt the deportation of Jews. So the irony here, though Manea does not declare it to be one, is that Popovici too "did not live up to expectations," that is, did not behave as a "Christian" official would have been expected to behave in Czernowitz in 1941. Popovici's language, marked as it is by an inflationary rhetoric ("across the millennia," "a tragic destiny," "Babylonian captivity," "inferno of starvation"), is by no means excessive here—it expresses in fact the "normal," that is, the highly charged, fully informed, deeply felt response of a "normal" person to a catastrophe that most "normal" "Christian" people in Czernowitz could not have grasped in anything remotely like a "normal" way.

Assaulted by versions of orchestrated unreality and by monstrous deformations of public rhetoric, Manea often doubts his own capacity to maintain "coherence" and "wholeness." He wants to be free of illusion, to renounce all misleading affiliations, yet he needs a place to stand, however much he mistrusts places and cannot long stand still. Is he a Jew? He is a nonbelieving Jew; he belongs to what Jean-François Lyotard once called a "non-people of survivors" whose "sense of communion" depends upon "an endless recalling of things past." But Manea catches at this definition like a man who trusts nothing, least of all a key to identity so seductive and so empty as to connect the communicant to a "non-people." His Jewishness is a fact, but it does not seem to him an adequate place to stand.

Throughout the memoir, Manea turns to many sources in his search for coherence. His mind "fills with quotations, as if only the rhetorical hysteria of other people's words could release [him] from [him]self" and, we might add, effectively deliver him in the end to himself. Manea is haunted, if not often by "actual" ghosts, then by bits and pieces of monologues, dialogues, passages of half-remembered books, vagrant quips, and aperçus. "Wasn't it Maurice Blanchot who said that?" he wonders, or "I might as well have thought of Prague and of Milena Jesenska, yes, Kafka's Milena," or "'You are not Cioran,' I tell myself." Identity-making for Manea is all about "the verbal collages" that he is forever composing, shaping and unshaping and reshaping as he goes, acutely sensitive to every least exaction of language and mood in each fragment he snatches at, tempted but never completely taken by the ingratiations of sentiment.

There is no single figure about whom Manea can say, as Elias Canetti could say of Karl Kraus, that he was "one of my idols," but neither does the insatiably appropriative Manea allow any one source to drive out the others. Manea's passions are so much in flux, his enthusiasms typically so provisional, that he is never entirely disappointed with those he appropriates. Where Canetti writes of his need "to liberate" himself from his enthusiasms, Manea's collage building is an ongoing progress in which no one influence or voice can long seem attractive without the countervailing force exerted by other, often contradictory, voices.

Canetti identifies in Kraus "his truly Biblical quality: his *horror*," and though Manea is without Kraus's other qualities of "arrogance" and "veneration for his gods," he has, surely, in abundance that "Biblical quality," that capacity for registering horror that few other writers have so powerfully conveyed. In Manea, the horror has often to do with his sense that language lies. What seems truest to him is a language far removed both from the "daily communal language" and from "literary" language. Though his mother was not, in any ordinary sense of the term, an eloquent person, she does seem now and then to Manea to speak truthfully in what he once calls "the language of the ghetto." This is a language "moaning, murmuring, demanding, living, surviving." He hears it in the nighttime rambles of the mother, elderly, diminished, in the hospital for an eye operation, hears it in her "coded laments, incomprehensible requests," in part incomprehensible because spoken in Yiddish, in words "alien" to Manea's wife, who lies beside the old woman in her narrow bed. Night after night she hears "first a murmur, like water, short guttural signals, followed by an agitated, secret confession, an arcane lexicon, wailing and reproaches, lyrical, tender refrains, meant for the ears of initiates only," mixed dialects, "Slavic and Spanish inflections, biblical sonorities, oozing forth like some linguistic alluvial mud, carrying with it all the debris gathered along the way . . . her monologue is punctuated by spasmodic sounds that could be laughter or pain, one cannot tell." Characteristically rich in color and sonority, the passage enacts within the texture of its language the drama of Manea's struggle toward truthfulness and coherence. In her way, the blind mother produces a true utterance, "oozing forth," as Manea writes, and "carrying with it" everything she has "gathered," in which the intermingling of "laughter or pain," the "wailing" and the "lyrical," the "agitated" and "tender" bespeak some indisputable authenticity of feeling that no true writer would fail to envy.

For all of Manea's enormous learning and wit, his political sophistication and ironic cunning, he seems in the memoir never to let the mother's voice move very far out of reach. For the horror quietly conveyed so often in the memoir has much to do with Manea's fear that the figures who have meant most to him are now receding, the places and conditions that made them real to themselves irrecoverable. Neither can Manea reverse the more general process of corruption: the trivialization of suffering and the reduction of experience to a free-for-all in which, as Manea writes, "Everything [is] compatible with everything else." One version of that free-for-all is the process by which the exile efficiently adapts and learns to live comfortably with the loss of the world, the people, and the meanings that alone can furnish the ground of his coherence.

Manea writes as if his rightful place on earth had not yet been discovered, as if his true place were anywhere, but somewhere else. He looks back with longing not to a place but to a sense of place. *This* is what was forever denied him. That is why he understands so well his mother's fondness for the cemetery, beyond anything she felt for the synagogue:

> It was a form of natural, unmediated, but also transcendental, communication, a way of inserting herself into history . . . the past and the present . . . fused. We come out of Egypt every year as they did, without ever leaving it behind altogether, we relive other Egypts again and again, their fate is ours, just as our fate is theirs, forever and ever.

This, Manea says, is "a mystical connection" to the past, and it is not at all to be confused with the simple longing to be back in the familiar rooms and streets of one's place of origin that so afflicts many exiles.

If Manea is a kind of hooligan, it is because he does not trust himself to be what the world wishes him to be: neither an exemplary little prince nor a grateful survivor, neither a principled activist nor a modest citizen. The irony on display in Manea's memoir is so corrosive because it respects no boundaries, is slyly subversive no matter in which direction it is aimed, and holds itself to be almost without exception too little and often too late. Though Manea permits himself more than occasional expressions of vulnerability and affection, though he seems to us at moments companionable and tender, he is always on his guard, alert to the dreaded possibility that he will slip into the posture ridiculed by Brodsky, of the "certified martyr" or the ineffectual "retrospective and retroactive being."

This memoir—a genuinely great book, an entire teeming life seized and made permanent—is the record of a long, as yet unfinished apprenticeship in hooliganism. For he would learn, this Manea, what it is and how it is to be, with all one's heart, what he can only with misgiving claim for himself. Not a hooligan, exactly, but one who might well be taken for one, a hooligan in waiting, perhaps, or a would-be hooligan, attempting to have things more ways than one and in the process satisfying no one, least of all himself, for whom "failure is what legitimizes you," and doubleness.

To which the alternative is . . . what? The prospect that he might in fact achieve what is projected is not easy for such a man to embrace. Manea's apprenticeship is mainly good for making the prospect of a heroic hooliganism seem ever more improbable. The would-be hooligan hopefully calls up one or another of the moments when something he wrote or an interview he gave created a scandal, made him a palpable enemy of the people, only in turn to be mocked by his own wicked intelligence, or by a friend: "There's a tank division general inside you struggling to get out, you know," one friend says, and "your liberals are acclaiming your liberal courage." Elsewhere, another friend in Manea's head smiles at him: "You, a hooligan? That is sheer imposture, borrowed armor." To which the apprentice can only wryly accede. The truth of his own doubleness, of his incurable multiplicity, of the integrity of his bemused, ironic, incorrigible estrangement and self-estrangement, he cannot, must not, will not, contradict.

NORMAN MANEA

8

THE NORMALITY BLUES

PETER SCHNEIDER

I

Is there nothing so grim that it cannot be turned to comedy? Twentieth-century German history would seem to provide a test case. The land of war criminals and skinheads, of festering guilt and revisionist denial, of blood sausage and blood libel, has inspired plenty of farce and satire, but most serious German writers in the twentieth century have opted for the lugubrious or the solemnly admonitory, for the rueful or for an especially vengeful species of black humor. To be sure, Günter Grass long ago demonstrated, with an assurance bordering on megalomania, that a German writer might make anything he likes of the German century, that it would yield as readily to *divertissement* as to tragedy, to every kind of exorbitance as to anguish—but the one thing that has seemed more or less out of reach for German writers is the comedy of ordinary life.

Ordinariness has often seemed problematic for German writers. In Grass, the ordinary is typically associated with kitsch or with "the bourgeois smug," with a comforting dream of "happy hours bestowed by an electric plug," with "carpet slippers" and "Sunday's roast and Friday's kippers." In such a land even murder can be accommodated by ordinary men and women endowed with the capacity to "transform feelings into soup." Typically, in Grass, the man who wears a Nazi pin on his lapel, disinfects a gas chamber, or commits one or another mundane treachery is the victim not of an ideology but of a conformity that is the true face of ordinariness.

Just so, in the radically different work of Heinrich Böll, the sensible or the "realistic" is often given a bad name by a writer alert to the easy self-deceptions of ordinary people whose defining features are modesty and adaptability. In Böll, the character who makes "allowances," who operates from a "sense of duty" or "a calm broad-mindedness," is decidedly not to be trusted. Even ordinary language, ostensibly straightforward speech, is suspect. To put one's thoughts into "some useful order," like the narrator in Böll's story "At the Border," is very likely to dissemble, to evade unwanted thoughts. The very word "useful" is pejorative in Böll, as are words such as "theoretical" or "practical."

The major German writers train us to suppose that an ordinary person is a dangerous person, one who misuses or distorts language without knowing quite what he is doing. But there is an important exception. Peter Schneider is as alert as Heinrich Böll or Günter Grass to the limitations of common sense, but he regards the ordinary with nothing like the animus so pervasive in the others. As a political journalist, Schneider has written about a great many subjects with wit and wry compassion. He has noted that ordinary people are of course susceptible to meanness and brutality, but he has also noted that writers, intellectuals, environmentalists, and professional do-gooders are at least equally susceptible to treachery and self-deception.

East German "citizens" ostensibly committed to the rescue of Vietnamese refugees in the aftermath of the Vietnam war "made no connection," Schneider has observed, between the so-called "heroic struggle of the Vietnamese people" and the actual Vietnamese who lived in their midst. Refugees in the German Democratic Republic found themselves intimidated by ordinary people, who spray-painted graffiti on local walls, insulted their customers in shops, and in general displayed no interest whatever in the lives or the needs of their guests; but not-so-ordinary Germans, including people in very high political and legal positions, have often been guilty of flagrant violations of human rights and a "cynical self-assurance" that makes a mockery of any effort to claim for such people a superior sensitivity. Though Schneider is typically scrupulous about distinctions and knows better than to equate callow insensitivity with outright brutality, he registers with unfailing candor the tendency of just about everybody to fail to meet one's expectations.

Schneider has published three books in the last decade. *The German Comedy* appeared in 1991, a volume of essays and vignettes studying "the paradoxes and absurdities of life in the absence of the legendary [Berlin] Wall," introducing us, as Schneider says, "to the West German family man who counted on the Wall to keep his East Berlin mistress a secret or the East German baker dismayed at the loss of work-breaks now that flour is in steady supply." The tone of the book is at once severe and forgiving, rueful and bemused. Serious issues are engaged with an odd combination of earnestness and comic irony. Ostensibly "independent" German minds are ridiculed or teased with much the same satiric brush that is used to paint Stalinist functionaries and new capitalist entrepreneurs.

Selective memory lapses are the order of virtually every day in virtually every precinct of German life, Schneider reports. "The chiefs of dissent march beneath" the same banner that reads: "Whatever you do, just be sure to save face." Though Schneider is drawn to big questions, to questions of "character" and "freedom" and crime and punishment, he beautifully conveys his sense that people will be people—which is to say, they will be less than we might hope for and yet remain unpredict- able; they are interesting, if only because they thwart every explanatory theory or idea.

Many factors make for comedy in Schneider's Germany. It often seems that even petty or mundane matters assume absurd dimensions in the German context. Consider his observation that in 1990 it was absurd to expect much from "the juridical attempt to overcome the past" in communist East Germany. There, as in post-Hitler Germany, it was almost impossible to find "qualified jurists," and "one can hardly expect those who administered injustice to pass judgment on themselves." It was reasonable, perhaps, to suppose that ordinary goodwill, summoned in circumstances resembling a decent, orderly, democratic system, would sometimes call forth decent instincts even in people tainted by their long complicity with a corrupt and murderous regime, but Schneider argues that it was probably more reasonable to suspect that goodwill would never quite produce—at least not until a great deal of time had elapsed—comprehensive changes in a society inured to "juridical transgressions." "Detective writers," Schneider writes, "have apparently overlooked the only truly perfect crime: the one in which an entire society is complicit."

The comic element here, as pretty much everywhere in Schneider's work, is a reflection of his abiding conviction that moral superiority and "exceptionalism" are difficult to credit when they are underwritten by the idea "that no one else has the right to judge somebody else." In a country in which denial is routine and "sins of omission" have no serious status as sin, indignation will usually seem excessive and disproportionate to the weight accorded even large failures or indecencies by

PETER SCHNEIDER

ordinary people. Comedy seems better suited to people who have grown adept at deflecting criticism.

No doubt many Germans would bristle—they have bristled—at the suggestion that they are specialists in denial or omission. They can cite—they have cited—instance after instance of soul-searching and hand-wringing, and Schneider often reminds us that German debates about guilt and reparation have sometimes generated morally impressive results. But the Germans, suggests Schneider, are specialists, if not in brutality, then at least in varieties of sentimental paranoia. They have a peculiar appetite for what he devastatingly describes as "pleasant high tragedy," so that the fall of the Berlin Wall in 1989 inspired in many of them a sense that they were losing something vital to their sense of life's essential savor.

Other Germans, including the many who worked as spies in the East German Stasi, betray the peculiar blend of idealism and "merciless logic" that Schneider finds at once fascinating and appalling. As he reads the testimony of former Stasi functionaries, he is struck by "the degree of personal dedication and faith" inspired by East German Stalinism, so that those who did the dirty work of informing and spying often "did so with little or no selfish interest." In confessing at last to their misdeeds, in apologizing and asking forgiveness of their victims, ordinary Stasi collaborators typically insisted upon the "honesty, truth, uprightness" that they believed they upheld; and it is not at all surprising that when one collaborator heard from another who could not quite bring herself to do all of the terrible things that her colleagues had done, the first simply replied, "Well, so I'm a better comrade than you!" This, says Schneider, is an example of a peculiar "idealism," according to which someone can feel morally superior by committing herself wholeheartedly "to carrying out an obviously base act."

And what, in the German context, would be the logical outcome of an "idealism" involving routine betrayals of ordinary norms of decency and the consequent renunciation of those betrayals? Schneider detects in the new Germany a fervent cynicism, a principled dismissal of ideals, a general agreement that "whoever believes in anything is an idiot!" Thus the repentant Stasi collaborator vows never to "act in the name of any idea ever again," with a "heroic" disdain that reminds Schneider of avowals uttered by "the average Nazi after the war." Blind idealism leads, in the new Germany, to "no more ideals" and to a conviction that if you keep your eye trained on the practical and material, you can avoid any possible temptations to crime.

II

As a critic and a journalist, Schneider has always sharpened his political reflections with a novelist's instinct for detail and anecdote. But Schneider is also a novelist. *Couplings*, which appeared here in 1996, and now *Eduard's Homecoming*, are lively, attractive, and sobering narratives, extending Schneider's portrait of things German and raising questions about the ability of an essentially comic imagination to deal with ordinary German life. On the evidence of these two novels, it is possible to say that the exigencies of the comic novel have released in Schneider unsuspected strengths. His writing has always been brisk, worldly, instructive, amiable, sharply focused, and irreverent. The fiction adds to these qualities a feeling for character, a gift for paradox and hyperbole, a nose for searching out and skewering every species of political correctness, and a large talent for satire.

Though Schneider is very much a German writer interested in German characters and German situations, he creates figures of genuine if sometimes flawed feeling, and he discovers in them, as in their situations, all that we need in order to feel implicated in their complicated fates. Schneider's fictional characters are not in any ordinary sense ordinary men and women. They risk more, desire more, suffer more, think more. Generally, his male protagonists are intellectuals, creative types, scientists. Their wives, their women, are liberated, eccentric, fiercely independent, exceptionally adept at assuring "the smooth descent and touchdown of [their own] body-ship after its intoxicating [sexual] flight."

Yet these characters do not expend their energies dwelling on how exceptional they are; they do not suppose that they are anything but ordinary human beings afflicted with the standard anxieties and pressures all too familiar to everyone else. And for all of their theories and disquisitions, for all of their passing references to *Don Giovanni* or sado-Marxism or Ernesto Cardenal, they are essentially right about themselves. They are quite as silly and self-absorbed and vulnerable and insufferable as any ordinary person could possibly have a right to be, and in writing about them Schneider is as little inclined to exempt them from

PETER SCHNEIDER

common standards of judgment as to pretend that, owing to their intellectual merits, they are somehow less likely than others to say or to do perfectly idiotic things. In Schneider, ordinary is as ordinary does, and there is pleasure to be had in observing the many ways in which people endowed with obvious advantages delude themselves and manage, almost invariably, to make even their more substantial advantages look ambiguous, dangerous, and perhaps not quite desirable at all.

In *Couplings*, the action revolves around a molecular biologist named Eduard, who keeps a notebook on "the Average Half-Life of Love Relationships" and conspires with his friends and lovers to do something about the "separation virus" that rages through West Berlin. The novel promises to "look at how the generation that came of age and rebelled in the sixties is coping with love and commitment." The politics of the novel comes through intermittently and in several different guises. An anarchist poet named Theo, who lives in East Berlin "behind" the wall, provides many opportunities for playful contrasts between East and West, and complains that socialism in the East is a "petit-bourgeois" affair, while the West is nothing more than a "peep-show society." Klara, one of Eduard's "serious" girlfriends, provokes reflections on the war between the sexes and the politics of gender. Everywhere there is a tendency to think fleetingly about the Nazi past and to consider what the mania for "innocence" and clean hands says about Eduard and his friends.

The plot of the novel is a simple mechanism, and rapidly we come to feel that very little is at stake. Eduard's conflicts have mostly to do with women. How committed is he to Klara? What meaning ought these people to ascribe to the casual infidelities that they commit, or to the comparable infidelities committed by their closest friends? Ought one to deny or resist a constant readiness to fall in love, to feel deeply, if only briefly, for several women at once? Is it reasonable that someone who is regularly falling in and out of love should be disturbed by the thought that his own parents were similarly engaged on several fronts and thereby caused each other pain?

These questions emerge again and again in a novel whose plot mechanisms exist principally to raise them and to offer some semblance of a reflection on their importance. Characters talk and argue and tease one another with little prospect that anything of consequence will ensue. Of course there is always the possibility that a separation will occur, but with separation more or less inevitable in Eduard's world, this hardly seems a major consequence. Even characters who fear heartbreak or re-crimination quickly recover from their disappointments and move on to new, comparably robust affiliations.

Couplings is a comedy not merely in its playfully orchestrated im-probabilities, farcical encounters, and witty observations. It is a comedy in its conviction that, even in a world shadowed by catastrophe and riven by ideological strife, life goes on more or less as it must, and even more or less as it should. People are resilient, however anxious they may seem, however vulnerable to occasional misery or more than occasional doubt. Yes, the novel seems to say, feelings are sometimes hurt—the newspaper reports that a terrorist bomb was exploded in a crowded district, with numerous people injured, or a dear friend has just learned, again, that he has cancer; but we have learned to expect no less. We ask ourselves why this happens and not that, we discuss ideas with one another and weigh the words that we use, we resolve, yet again, not to be taken in by clichés, by stale versions of an outgrown "bourgeois morality." But we know, more or less, who we are, and we know better than to expect from ourselves a perfect consistency. We find ourselves pathetic, needy, laughable. And we smile at our efforts to forget that we are pathetic, needy, laughable—and, most of all, inconsistent.

As we think of Peter Schneider in all of this, controlling the deft thrusts and parries of a novel that is never less than amusing, one can-not but think of him as a serious man for whom the questions raised in *Couplings* are weighty ones. We do not doubt that for him the novel is something considerably more than a light entertainment. Yet it is hard, all the same, to accord to the affairs of this novel the entirely admiring engagement that we accord to the affairs elaborated in philosophical comedies such as Kundera's *The Unbearable Lightness of Being* or Svevo's *Confessions of Zeno*. Those books convey the sense that an essentially comic imagination, alert to every possibility of absurdity, pratfall, and self-delusion, has found itself confronted by matters of life and death, by questions unanswerable though inescapable, by obsessions some-times trivial or ridiculous but nonetheless compelling and, at bottom, critical to an understanding of the spiritual hungers that animate us. There are hungers in *Couplings*, to be sure; but they are not spiritual, not constitutive of anything essential in Schneider's characters. Nor are the vagrant obsessions of his characters a manifestation of some fertile oddity. Even when his characters confront illness and mortality, there is little sense that the prospect of an imminent death is inescapably related

PETER SCHNEIDER

to an abiding concern with the meaning of life. Here there really is a lightness of being.

And yet this failure, if that is what it is, may well express the very heart of Schneider's intention, of his ambition to write a book about things German that did not traffic in the lugubrious ultimacies and the morbid infatuations so prevalent in German writing. Perhaps he wished to engage "relevant" issues without suggesting that they are or need to be matters of life and death. Is it not possible to create, with no sacrifice of interest or credibility, characters with relatively ordinary problems and manageable obsessions, and to place them in circumstances only vaguely and occasionally associated with the more dire circumstances that are called to mind by words such as "German," "Nazi," "Stasi," or "collaborator"?

Schneider does acknowledge that in the German context thoughts will sometimes turn to dark things. An apparently good man such as Eduard will be moved to speculate about traces of anti-Semitism that he may have picked up. His more radical students at the university will insist that he confront the ethical implications of the animal research that he conducts. Still, if Eduard refuses to be defined by these issues and if Schneider does not permit his narrative to be overwhelmed by them, this may indicate that Germans of Schneider's generation are free not to be defined by terms, ideas, and events that they did not choose for themselves.

Looked at this way, *Couplings* is what may be called a normalizing work. It sets in motion a cast of characters alternately earnest and frivolous, and it subjects them to a scrutiny that makes them at every turn all too human. When they wonder who they are, they expend little energy, enough only to suggest to themselves that they can stand still for a minute before rushing headlong at this or that mostly indifferent object. Their processions are never gloomy, their reflections at best provisional. Always they are caught in the act of making up and moving on. Impressed or provoked by truth-claims associated with one or another idea or faction, they are standard bearers only for the right to think a little and feel a little and regret a little. What we like best about them is their naturalness. Though we are not quite ready to go along with the student radical who upbraids Eduard with the words "What happened to your rage, your restlessness, your sensitivity?", we have reason to understand what the young man means, and we accept that a heavy price has been paid for the normality, even the banality, to which these mostly decent Germans have accommodated themselves.

THE NORMALITY BLUES

The comedy in the novel allows for scathing indictment and pointed reflections on power and betrayal, but the dominant accent is light satire and jovial send-up. Guilt is summoned in dream encounters that present transparent caricatures of genuine conflict. Pangs of conscience are calmed or blown away by erotic games. For every complaint of loss there is a compensatory movement forward. Schneider has a gift for the bittersweet and the unquenchable, but he is impatient with loss or grayness, and he is disposed to make light of "existential horror." The new Germany that he evokes in *Couplings* may be a bit of a chaos, affording occasional glimpses of a darkling plain and mostly ignorant ideological armies, but he is not much tempted by the prospect of recompense, and his book expresses an essentially sunny and admirably deflationary outlook.

99

III

The sequel to *Couplings* is also a comic novel, though *Eduard's Home-coming* offers a darker portrait of Germany after the fall of the Berlin Wall. It is an angrier book than its predecessor, though it has its share of farce and its passages of playful verbal extravagance. The action of the novel is propelled by the return of Eduard to the former East Berlin, after years in California with an American wife and three children. He is lured back to Germany by the prospect of a new job and the news that he has inherited an apartment building. But postcommunist Berlin is a chaotic and disappointing place. Edward's property is occupied by violent squatters determined to prevent him from taking it over, and he finds them only slightly more intimidating and enraging than the lawyers, policemen, and journalists he meets. Meanwhile, his wife is reluctant to resettle in Germany, and her reluctance inspires Eduard to think the worst of himself, and to invent ways of winning her back—to himself and to the city.

The novel contains material that will remind readers of Schneider's earlier work. Eduard is clearly the man we remember from *Couplings*, and his friend Theo is again the erratic, brilliant, exasperating anarchist poet, though he now lives in what was West Berlin and is claimed by both the political left and the political right as a "bridge-builder" and "savior." Schneider remains an equal-opportunity satirist, targeting all varieties of political dogmatism, including bridge building,

PETER SCHNEIDER

confessional breast beating, and the more virulent forms of identity politics. But *Eduard's Homecoming* is an autonomous work, in no way dependent on its predecessor, and it marks for Schneider a considerable advance.

Committed still to a normalizing view of German life, and also to an essentially comic and forgiving perspective, Schneider is here more focused on the intransigent *données* of the universe that he studies, and less inclined to swerve away from irresolvable issues or to let a character dismiss them with a clever line or a good joke. Though the novel refers to an "important rule . . . scrupulously adhered to" by some writers, namely, "that any distinction between the important and the trivial was prohibited," *Eduard's Homecoming* is deeply invested in the making of such distinctions. He is by no means a visionary writer, but Schneider intends nothing less than a re-envisioning of the recent German past, a project requiring a reconstruction of attitudes so rooted in his countrymen as to seem almost unalterable.

The dominant attitudes to which Schneider's satirical imagination is drawn come in several shapes and dimensions. At the apartment building that Eduard inherits he encounters squatters whose behavior is explosive, unruly, and not altogether clear in its political orientation. These are familiar countercultural leftists in their rhetoric ("Eat the rich!") and in their "socialist" conviction that "buildings belong to their inhabitants." But these same people, defiant about their "rights" and ready at any moment to resort to violence, also paint swastikas on the walls of their buildings and express contempt for foreigners and racial minorities. Apparently sensitive about "the rights of mothers and the unborn" and angry about media control of public opinion, they display no respect whatever for the truth and are adept at using the media for their own purposes. In the complex of attitudes that they embody, they seem unsavory, despicable, menacing, and not quite forgivable, however impoverished or unfortunate they are. In the end, they are an expression of circumstances for which no group or party can be held exclusively responsible. Those circumstances, as Schneider understands them, are the unification of two decidedly "unequal" Germanys and the ideological maneuvers required of all German citizens who wish to lead more or less untroubled lives.

What Eduard finds after he returns to his homeland is a world in turmoil, though many of the ideological markers on display are strangely familiar to him from the past. It is not simply that East and West are now no longer separated, or that "capitalists" and "entrepreneurs" from the West are now taking over properties in the East or buying up with plentiful Western dollars all of the scarce, inexpensive merchandise available in the East. It is not simply that, with the opening of Stasi files in the newly "liberated" East, everyone can see that the infamous secret police kept security files on fully half the adult population of the German Democratic Republic, and that a large proportion of the population was at least some of the time employed as informers. Nor is the turmoil that Eduard witnesses merely a reflection of the guilt and the uncertainty experienced by affluent Germans who know not how to deal with their more needy brethren from the East. No: the trouble has much to do with uncertainty about "normal" civilized behavior and with doubts about a future that may well be, as the poet Theo says, "the root of all evil."

101

As in earlier books by Schneider and in the postwar novels of other German writers, the concept of normality itself is subjected to particular scrutiny here. Eduard worries over his right to profit from his inheritance if the building left to him by a grandfather was improperly extorted from a Jewish owner in the Nazi era, though there are normative conventions in place to suggest that if he was not himself responsible for extortion and did not contribute to the situation that made it possible, then he owes it to himself and his family to "make the most" of his inheritance without assuming guilt for something beyond his control. Similarly, there are norms and conventions that teach that "freedom of decision didn't exist: human beings were products of their environment and all behaved similarly if subjected to enough pressure." By this standard, as Theo instructs Eduard, Theo's younger brother cannot be condemned for informing on his "subversive" older sibling. After all, "he couldn't compete with me as an enemy of the state; the only role open to him was of custodian and defender of the beliefs I was infringing. His reports on me described the path he might have trodden himself if I hadn't got there first."

Yes, Theo concedes, "you always have a choice between being a bastard and a reasonably decent person," but once you look at the relevant factors, the grounds for a resolute moral condemnation fall away. An enlightened person will avoid "pious fiction" and accept that just about any behavior—including the behavior of "a bastard"—may be normal and in its way acceptable within the framework of an ordinary existence. Eduard is by no means content to go along with Theo on such

PETER SCHNEIDER

matters, and Schneider is surely reluctant to credit any such normalizing perspective—but neither is there in this novel a fully elaborated theoretical alternative to the ideas formulated by Theo and several other characters.

Resistance emerges fitfully, though powerfully, in brief vignettes, isolated sentences, and sharp reversals of a carefully constructed anticipation. Eduard's lovely, volatile, unpredictable wife Jenny, who bristles with feminist indignation when introduced as "Frau Hoffmann," wife of Eduard Hoffmann, and insists that "whether married or divorced, we're all single mothers," also insists in all sincerity, "in answer to [Eduard's] question about my sexual fantasies: I don't have any at present, to be honest, nor do I miss them." And with that, Eduard reflects, all the "superior forces" responsible for the presiding and allegedly enlightened assumptions of the age—the feminists, "the sexual gurus and theorists whose talk shows daily revived the dictatorship of the satisfying sex life"—are put to rout.

The issue is not, of course, whether women have sexual fantasies, or ought to have them, or ought to miss them. The issue is whether or not women are free to feel "alright," satisfied, "normal," when and if they do not have the full panoply of appetites that they are told they must have if they are not to consider themselves victims of patriarchal oppression. The struggle for the definition of "normative" behavior extends to just about every aspect of Schneider's novel. Everything is contested, and the spectacle is more or less comic depending upon the quantity of will expended by people determined to believe that theirs is an "advanced" stance on critical issues.

In the old GDR, for example, "official doctrine stated that there could be absolutely no genetic basis for human aggression; acts of violence were held to be symptoms of a misanthropic capitalist environment." At the same time, "since crimes of all kinds were committed in the GDR but could on no account be attributed to environmental factors [in a society that officially proclaimed itself exempt from the usual charges of abuse, corruption, or injustice], the guardians of pure theory were confronted by a painful choice. They had to define acts of violence as relics of capitalist culture or to take a radically biological view and derive them from human nature," with theoretical and political consequences difficult to assess. Schneider's language, here as elsewhere, gives the game away. He invites us, with Eduard, to regard as potentially ridiculous an "official doctrine" based upon recourse to the idiom of the "misanthropic capitalist environment," while the "guardians of pure theory" are mocked by the very terms used to identify them.

Here as elsewhere in Schneider's novel, the comedy lies in the transparently hopeless efforts of ideologically committed parties to make sense of the world without betraying their principles, which amount to a fixed view of the way things must be. Thus Eduard discovers that he is himself inured to a sense of guilt—deserved, he believes, by anyone who is German, sensitive, more or less comfortable, and positioned to profit in ways not generally shared by others. Is this a fixed ideological disposition? Insofar as it operates in Eduard even when he knows better than to take it altogether seriously, and exercises over him a force that is unwarranted by anything reprehensible that he has done, it is unmistakably a fixed disposition. Ideologically it would seem to stem from the belief that where there is no justice or nothing that looks like formal justice, one is not permitted to enjoy profit or pleasure.

As expected in a German novel, the normative assumptions and the questions raised to challenge them often have to do with the Nazi past. The questions chiefly ask how far normative assumptions may be said to serve or to obstruct the work of memory and the work of thought. Comedy is not easy to come by in this precinct, though Schneider manages some effective riffs and inspired set pieces. Eduard recalls a lecture that he attended in "the summer before the Wall came down," and reflects that the unspeakably dismal GDR regime "was nowhere more doggedly defended than at the Ivy League universities." Though there are no longer "respectable" academic defenders of the Nazi regime, it is clear that ideology will find ways to support the unspeakable and unsupportable—that even the Nazi past will not for long seem definitively buried, for good and all. Not for nothing does Schneider see to it that the entire novel is required to engage issues bearing on "collective conscience," the "little cowardices" and "despicable acts" of "the generation of Germans" loath "to delve into their parents' or grandparents' antecedents because they risked coming across unpleasant details."

Eduard's wife Jenny puts the case for fear and trembling before the past as bluntly and hilariously as anyone could wish—"How did you yourselves turn up in Germany? Like angels who tumbled out of hairless angelic pussies and little pink clouds onto that particular patch of ground? You Germans can't even tell your children who bequeathed them their red hair or talent for music or predisposition to diabetes"—but Eduard and others in this novel never quite put their trepidation behind them. Is it "normal" to persist in such feelings of moral worthlessness, in the suspicion of a taint that one cannot by any action remove, when the deeds inspiring the morbid disposition were performed by others and are a half-century old? Is it the fate of ordinary men and women, people only ordinarily sensitive and neurotic, to persist so?

There are voices in the novel to suggest that perhaps it is time for Germans to move on. Eduard's lawyer Klott warns against "premature self-accusations" and admonishes his client that "this isn't a psychotherapy group where your tears would do you credit." But it is Jenny and another woman who most sharply admonish Eduard and by extension his generation. They are not to "let things take their course," Jenny says, not to allow "a false version of events [to] prevail." A man, such as Eduard, with but "one eighth of his brain responsible for self-preservation . . . still functioning," must not allow himself to be tied to the injustices committed "during the Nazi era." In a society whose intellectuals "vied with each other in pronouncing themselves capable of all manner of misdeeds" and who therefore found themselves committed to a species of "crazy logic," Eduard is susceptible to a "beguiling, infectious apathy."

It would appear that Schneider, like Jenny and Klott, would like to shake his hero out of his vague compliant guilt. But he does not leave the matter there. Though he resists a programmatic rejoinder to the guilt-tripping and hypocrisy of a society long inured to the formulaic moral pedantries of leftist propaganda, he does offer a highly suggestive complication. Obsessed with questions about his possibly ill-gotten inheritance, Eduard travels to Palm Beach to interview a onetime acquaintance of his grandfather. There he learns that, wonder of wonders, Egon Hoffmann was a decent man, even a courageous man, who did his best to shield and to assist his Jewish friends, and paid considerably more for the apartment building than its 1930s market value. The revelation does not change the larger picture, and Schneider makes no claim for a thoroughgoing extenuation. In fact, as Eduard says, his grandfather's story "wouldn't make a suitable apologia for Germans"—indeed, it "magnifies the [actual] guilt of innumerable conformists and accomplices" by showing that "it was possible to sabotage the machinery of persecution and destruction," though few attempted to do so. As for Eduard himself, there remains some doubt as to whether he will prove adequate to the responsibility that has devolved upon him with the discovery of the facts of his grandfather's life. "True," his newly acquired Palm Beach confidante says, "you can't claim credit for the courage and decency your grandfather displayed," though there is a "duty to make the best of it," that is, to bear witness to the existence of "the few Germans" who were not complicit in atrocity. "Any German third-grader," she says, "can spell the names of Hitler, Goebbels, and Eichmann, but he's never heard of the Egons. . . . What sort of examples do you want to imprint on your children's hearts and minds?"

There is a danger, in all this, of a facile sentimentality, a danger to which Schneider's novel never succumbs. In part he owes this success to the patience with which he has Frau Marwitz, the Palm Beach connection, elaborate the financial, legal, political, and personal aspects of the righteous grandfather's stratagems. Not for Schneider, in this book, the ellipses and elisions that he knows well how to employ. The weight and the intricacy of the evidence mobilized on the grandfather's behalf prevent an idle, feel-good mystification. Schneider's object is not to paint an oh-so-poignant picture of a heroic German whose example might redeem the record of a generation. His object is, rather, to suggest how hard it is to retrieve an adequate record of the past, and how complicated are all efforts to construct a valid and marginally satisfactory identity.

The comic strengths of Schneider's novel include its robustly acerbic and sometimes amiable eccentricities, its sharp distaste for cant, and its delicious way of putting in the mouths of intelligent characters sentiments that often quite fail to do them justice. Though he is not at all averse to eruptions of the broad humor that we associate with farce, the humor of *Eduard's Homecoming* is more often structural or epigrammatically pointed. Schneider has a rare gift for situating action and for precisely laying out the relevant political and cultural determinants of an individual's thoughts or actions. Small gestures and single phrases are in this way prepared so that they can seem suddenly hilarious and illuminating without having to be labored or overexplained. Though there is plenty of playfulness and some wit in the dialogue as well as in the descriptive prose, the effect is never ornamental or superficial. With his wise, light touch, Peter Schneider appears to have solved the problem that has long plagued German writers. He has found a way to write the comedy of ordinary German life without denying that to be German has been, will continue to be, and might even deserve to be a special fate.

PETER SCHNEIDER

9

DISCIPLINE AND PUNISH

FLEUR JAEGGY

We have grown tired of decadence, and surely of what passes for decadence today. Coy, artificial, a mystification without mystery or transgressive power, it no longer inspires cults or effusions on the tonic effects of fetish objects. Instead we get only the unsubversive postures of subversion. Objects of art and style that are designed to seem diffident or nasty seem to most of us only quaint, willed, and excessively literary. Works whose models were celebrated for their capacity to enthrall are more apt now to amuse, faint reminders of a time when representations of sex in a freshly dug grave had the power to provoke and to arouse.

Of course, there were always varieties of decadence. The perfumed, lushly tapestried concoctions of turn-of-the-century artists inspired by Huysmans or Wilde are so different in almost every way from the radical fantasies of later decadents such as Bataille as to call into question the very use of "decadence" as an analytical or descriptive category. And yet, in the pages that Huysmans devoted to Baudelaire in *À Rebours*, for example, there is a clear statement of qualities that do in fact continue to dominate what remains of the decadent imagination: the preference for "those districts of the soul where the monstrous vegetations of the sick mind flourish," for "the mind that has reached the October of its sensations," the pervasive sense "of a despotic and freakish fate," of creatures "skilled in self-torment," of "ennui" and "lassitude." Alternative sensibilities are typically derided by decadents of every stripe for their "common sense," their sentimentality, their "moralizing inanities."

For Nietzsche, decadence had more to do with the promotion of an abrasive, comprehensive negativity than with the striking of perverse, violent, or melancholic postures, though he was not averse to striking a few poses himself now and then. The *épatisme* inherent in decadence still had a certain grandeur. It was an element in the struggle against what Nietzsche called "impoverished life," against "conventional morality" as a denial of life. Yet it was not long before critics began to notice what might be called the decadence of decadence. Adorno was alert to the phony appropriation of oppositional stances by twentieth-century artists pandering to a popular appetite for novelty, and Trilling carefully anatomized the process by which decadence—like other advanced forms—became a mode of accredited, and therefore empty and debased, subversion.

This is not to say that decadence has disappeared as a temperament or an aesthetic phenomenon. The category still assists in the differentiation of one sort of work from another. Thus we recognize at once that Russell Banks's *Cloudsplitter*, for all the violence and the perversity of its central figure, is in no sense a decadent work; its author takes no special pleasure in going against the grain of established moral tenets and has little feeling for the excitement thereby generated. Neither would anyone mistake for a decadent sensibility the dark, haunted, even suicidal cast of mind that permeates W. G. Sebald's *The Emigrants*. What James Wood has called the "internal wasting sickness" of Sebald's characters would in the hands of a decadent writer become the occasion for a kind of persistent, studied, ostentatious nihilism; but the quiet music of Sebald's work reflects his deep resistance to every kind of posturing.

This resistance is not apparent—not at first, not always—in the work of the Swiss writer Fleur Jaeggy. The author of four novels (only one of them, *Sweet Days of Discipline*, is available in English) and a new collection of stories entitled *Last Vanities*, Jaeggy is unmistakably fascinated by decadence. She trades, persistently, in the standard moods and devices of the decadent imagination, and she invests in the cult of violence, without claiming for it a moral or psychological purpose. Attracted to the aberrant and the irrational, Jaeggy pursues them sometimes for their own sake and sometimes for the sake of the effect that their expression will produce.

The familiar association between decadence and "sickness"—psychological, sexual, physiological—is ratified in her work, which features madness, murder, and persistent fantasies of revenge and dismemberment. It is characteristic of the sky in a Jaeggy fiction that it calls to mind "an infected sheet," of a child's eyes that they are filled with "menace," of ordinary domestic life that it is haunted by "the stealthy tread of catastrophe." A young girl allows herself to be caressed "like a corpse."

The faces of boarders wear "a mortuary look." Daydreams are suffused with "trophies of poison and sorrow," "the dark green of the gloom," "palpable suffocating bodies."

The danger, of course, is that works drawn to such specifications will seem as trite and mechanical as the more comforting works drawn to what were once commonly called bourgeois specifications. When characters habitually harbor toward one another murderous sentiments and are not much troubled by them, we can hardly feel that we are in the presence of a fresh and demanding view of human relations. When violence is routinely gratuitous or patently inexplicable, it is likely to seem frivolous.

It is not that we do not believe in the reality of such instincts. We are perfectly willing, some of the time, to credit the fact that what happens—in the occasional short story, in the apartment next door—may well be terrible and largely beyond our powers of explanation. In a work of fiction, however, we wish to feel that what we do not understand is nonetheless worth thinking about. We may rightly demand of material that ought by its nature to inspire vertiginous thoughts that it do no less.

One of the stories in *Last Vanities*—there are seven in all—involves a young mother who hates her new daughter, "hated her from the moment she appeared in the world," and cannot make up her mind whether or not to give the child to a wealthy couple still grieving from the loss of their own child. "No Destiny" is narrated in the third person, limited-omniscient perspective, much of it in the implied voice of the young mother. When we read that the garden was "white in winter. Dirty white," and that "in spring it was dirtier still," we are hearing the dominant narrative voice of the story and, at the same time, the peculiar sour voice of Marie Anne, the darkly unpleasant, embittered mother who often gives herself up "to her rage." When Marie Anne visits the home of the wealthy couple and it is described as a "nice house" with a "nice garden," we feel the barely contained resentment expressed in the repetition of the complacent word "nice," and associate it with the perspective of the young woman herself. We are prepared, more or less at once, for a story about the disfiguring effects of envy, destitution, and vengefulness.

Jaeggy mischievously inserts into the story a few stray elements to suggest that she is up to the sort of thing that we find in well-meaning, sensitive fictions alert to the miseries of the poor—but class is not at the root of Marie Anne's hatred of her daughter. No more is poverty the cause of her reflection, when confronted with the dead infant's dolls, that "the little girl hadn't had time to smash in their faces or pull off their legs or maybe an arm." The malignity in the story is patently motiveless. It is directed not at the rich but at everything. It is pervasive and indiscriminate.

Nor is the malignity to be understood as a psychological condition, as a distortion of feeling with more or less determinate social causes. The wealthy couple, only faintly evoked, is almost as susceptible to depravity as Marie Anne and her friend Johanna. Celebrating what they take to be the imminent adoption of a replacement figure for their lost daughter, they "pull to bits" the children's dolls. The husband crouches down and has Marie Anne climb onto his back. The wife takes off her dress, and all of them play, and "happiness bit into them like a burning blade." The mood is artificial, overheated. There is menace in the air, and it comes not from characters who are themselves the source of the disturbance, but from the foul ether that circulates freely through every passage of Jaeggy's brief story.

The decadence that we identify in "No Destiny" is not what in the late nineteenth century used to be known as *mal du siècle*, that mood of pervasive dissatisfaction that insisted that pleasure is finite and desire is insatiable. Neither does the decadence in Jaeggy have much to do with the exaltation of artifice and the deliberate denigration of nature that are so central to the poetry of Baudelaire. Jaeggy has no apparent interest in promoting particular ideas about nature or desire.

There is no place within the terms of this compact for the earnest expression of carefully considered ideas or for the acknowledgment that reality is, for most people, a very different matter. Good taste, in such a fiction, always demands that the dominant perspective seem irrefutable and that the obsessiveness of the central characters seem axiomatic, with no need to justify itself against any other standard of behavior. To explain or to qualify would be to disturb the mood of the fiction, to violate its carefully maintained opacity.

There is something haughty and peremptory in Jaeggy's fiction. For all the pressure of unrelieved anxiety that often permeates her work, its aura of torments undergone or anticipated, we never feel that the writer herself risks a loss of control. The peremptoriness is obvious in Jaeggy's unapologetic, even deliberately crude, plotting. Like other stories in *Last Vanities*, "No Destiny" abruptly terminates the main action and springs forward, within the space of the final paragraph, by at least a decade.

Jaeggy's sovereign willingness to dispense with the niceties of ordinary narrative construction is evident also in a story called "Porzia," where an event that transpired twenty-five years before the main action is made to play a disproportionately large role in the unriddling of the narrative problem; or in "A Wife," where the young daughters of a family are suddenly, without transition of any kind, "sturdy" adolescents "ruled by instincts." No effort is made in these stories to justify the fast-forwards and the recursions. No reason is offered for the refusal to develop material in the indicated directions. Stories end where they end because that is what the writer has decreed.

Jaeggy writes with the confidence of someone for whom the perverse and the vacuous are always absorbing. If they seem to others pointlessly menacing or otherwise distasteful, that is perhaps what confers upon her own breezy mastery an air of brio and an arrogant singularity. She is aware, as she moves with severe aplomb from one unsavory tidbit to another, that she is administering little savaging shocks to our system, but she betrays no hint of discomfort herself. The elderly couple to whom a pathetic bulldog is given in the story "Porzia" is said to have "then"—immediately—"poisoned the dog," but this occasions neither pause nor comment, and it is hard not to smile at such casual references to carnage or cruelty as they routinely succeed one another in this book. No more are we surprised that a small, troubling detail—the old couple's grandson is "bitterly" said to look "like a girl"—should quickly occasion a flurry of kindly conventional remarks, more or less out of nowhere. It is as if the story existed simply to liberate these small shocks and reversals, to play with the harsh thought that anything is possible and move right along.

Even reflection, what would elsewhere pass for thought, is in Jaeggy an ephemeral disturbance in the stir of incident. The young woman who thinks that "when others die we become their masters and mistresses" is rather severely corrected by the narrator: "It has never occurred to her that the opposite might be true, that perhaps our lives are governed by them." But this correction has no force; the narrator might well have said something altogether different, for all the effect that the actual correction has on the development of the story. But Jaeggy is a writer who knows better than to invest in anything so easily contradicted and betrayed as an idea. Everything conceivably solid in her fiction is shot through with intimations of impermanence. The earnest statement, like the monstrous and the freakish, is only a short step removed from the put-on, the playful stab of nauseous whimsy.

FLEUR JAEGGY

Yet Jaeggy's best work is richer and more various than some of her stories would lead us to suspect. In the title story of *Last Vanities*, as in the novel *Sweet Days of Discipline*, we note that she is not invariably limited or defeated by her inordinate attraction to the splenetic or the nihilistic. Where in a number of her stories we get little more than mood and static poignancies without depth, elsewhere we find a real talent for implication, a subtle modulation of sentiment and voice. In these writings, Jaeggy does not shrink from the suggestion that words and actions have weight.

Jaeggy is always recognizably a writer of an almost ascetic intensity, with a gift for the elliptical, the cryptic, the distracted; but these qualities amount to a great deal in a story such as "Last Vanities," where we have not a studied annulment of feeling but a curiously anxious inquisition. To be sure, it begins in the usual way. Reproach is said to "spread out like a foul-smelling fog." The principal characters loom "above these vapors, like evil spirits." The word "dirty" is intoned frequently, and in its vicinity are words such as "soiled" and "smears," "warp" and "sinister." Later we find "rancor" and "revulsion," "the filth of sweetness," the "Death" that is "first and foremost something that contaminates." Here again is Jaeggy's appetite for the feral, the haunted, the mortuary.

Entering such a work, we are prepared to resist what is obviously overwrought—except that in this case resistance does not come easily. For Jaeggy's design here allows for a number of competing emphases. The destructive elements are anything but spurious, and they are in the service of something more than a thrill. "Last Vanities" revolves around an elderly Swiss couple who suddenly, for the first time in a fifty-year marriage, entertain murderous thoughts about each other. Kindly, honest, and shy, these apparently exemplary octogenarians, "ever thankful to God," go through their customary household rituals, hoping to keep themselves safe from harm. Provincial and fastidious, Kurt and Verena Kuster have known all their lives how to banish torpor, grief, and illness. But then the prospect of decline and death insinuates itself at last into their midst, and the *gemütlich* fastness of their retirement nest, the cozy adjacency of other apartments like their own, and the couples next door conducting lives that "were the continuation of their lives" cannot protect them from the great fear.

So successfully does Jaeggy convey the inescapable panic that overtakes the husband that we accept at once his rapid transition from fear to suicide. The stages are brief, the motives more or less transparent.

Afraid that his wife is ill and will soon die, and unable to live with the dark uncertainty of a loss that seems inescapably imminent, he throws himself from the window. His wife has watched him go through the final motions. Afterward, she believes that she "helped her husband to throw himself down from the window." In an imagined courtroom proceeding, she asks how she could "go on living with a man who was upset that she wasn't dead?"

In all of this it is not Kurt who commands our attention; it is Verena. It is she who observes, reflects, wonders. The fragmentary memories and the quotidian mysteries that flit lightly through the narrative are hers. The Kusters' brief honeymoon is, to us, her experience of marriage. ("The first night she felt like an actress, trying to perform what others had done.") The ignorance so central to a resolutely provincial life is her ignorance. ("What did she know of the world, beyond the border?") Even the menace, the carefully deposited reminders of Jaeggy's attraction to the poisonous and the homicidal, are here marks of Verena's drifting and increasingly morbid imagination. It is she who stares at the laundry "turning in the glass" and thinks how "one fine day their bones would be as clean as fresh laundry."

For a person so long closed to all thought of death and decay, Verena comes to morbidity with a curious if entirely believable ease. We believe in that ease of transformation, as in other aspects of "Last Vanities," even if they do not conform to natural law. It is not the burden of Jaeggy's story to offer a theory of old age. Her characters move us not because we are inclined to think "I could be like that," but because they participate in a fully evolved metaphor in which every aspect of the story is implicated. It is a gorgeous metaphor of decline, in which love, fear, despair, flight, antipathy, and regret are intermixed, so that nothing in the story seems in the least extraneous, willed, or unassimilated.

In this tale, the appurtenances of decadence are properly subordinated to other, larger purposes. Here the foul humors are neither generic trappings nor exotic contrivances. The vagrant touches of rot and rancor have their proportionally modest roles to play, and they are inextricably linked with competing accents of affection and contrition, in combinations that do not yield to formula. When, absorbed by the thought that she is responsible for her husband's death, Verena thinks "the murder was her prettiest embroidery ever," we do not hear in this the self-congratulating voice of a writer impressed by her own perversity. Instead, the assorted vapors and smears are rooted in the mind of a profoundly disoriented woman. The bird perched on Verena's windowsill, with "something human about its face, the painted face of women in brothels," is not a static emblem of a corrupt world, but a vivid fraction of a mind also preoccupied by celestial courses, the precarious wave in her own "soft blue hair." The melancholy of "Last Vanities" is humane.

Jaeggy's spare, bleak, haunting novel *Sweet Days of Discipline*, which appeared here in 1993, is a more troubling instance. Set in a postwar Swiss boarding school for girls, it betrays a nostalgia for decadence, for the effects that are still presumed to follow from the relentless plying of the void. A first-person fiction spoken by a young woman remembering her captivity in a school that effectively deprived her of life, Jaeggy's novel has a refined though never precious air. It is in its way quite beautiful.

There is, throughout, the suggestion of madness, or at least fanaticism. Here and there we hear a distinct Nietzschean accent. There is the silence surrounding the name of God, the eloquence beyond good and evil, the gallows laughter. There is also the marked predilection for the lurid, the somewhat exaggerated intensifier: the narrator's girlhood is "senile," the faces of her friends wear "a mortuary look," the looming future is anticipated as "crimes I hadn't yet experienced." The atmosphere is thick with "aromas of servitude." The novel's opening page sets the action in an area where Robert Walser "used to take his many walks when he was in the mental hospital," an area nicely described as "an Arcadia of sickness."

Again, there is no mistaking Jaeggy's delight in plumbing the depths of "graves that nest in our minds." And yet *Sweet Days of Discipline* is a rich and affecting book, animated by a disciplined austerity, its terse beauties falling on the reader like a chaste gray rain. What is diseased and stagnant in its landscape is not set out to shock or to titillate. There is no preening at the edge of the void. The gloom and the sourness, the traces of "fervorless indolence," evoke a condition of spirit that is never self-satisfied.

The key to Jaeggy's achievement is the relationship between the narrator and a student named Frederique, whom she courts with the hopeless idolatry of youthful infatuation. Though other characters move through the novel, Frederique is critical to its extremity, its terse ambivalence. For she is a kind of fanatic, an absolutist whose example makes everything else seem by contrast paltry, childish, ordinary. From her first appearance she is described as "disdainful," "an idol," a person who "had no humanity." Her hands are cold, her writing artificial. Contact with her is invariably "so anatomical that the thought of flesh or sensuality eluded us." She shows neither emotion nor vanity. She is "impregnable," "a nihilist with no passion," "a sickle moon in an oriental sky. While the people sleep she cuts off their heads." In later life she remains for her childhood companion a force, a goad, one who "goes on ahead of me."

This novel is not in its deepest instincts a work of decadence. There is nothing peremptory about it. It keeps its distance from Frederique as from every prospect of consolation. What "goes on ahead" in this book is a kind of hard, gratuitous indifference to the ordinary investments and sentiments of this world. Yet the indifference is never achieved; the hauteur is never completed. For Frederique is admirable *and* repellent: an example of perfection and an example of sickness, aversion, incapacity. Her lassitude and her despotism are at once mesmerizing and pathetic. She is clearly a disturbed young girl, and we are not at all surprised to learn in the end that she spent many years of her adult life in a mental institution. Her acolyte, the narrator, will always lag behind Frederique in her knowledge of the void and in her identification with solitude and death, but when she recalls that as a girl she "envied the world," it is the mark of her difference, her saving distance from Frederique and her alluring nullities.

A novel of decadence would not permit its central character the regret and pathos that we hear in this novel. The narrator tears up "the rare letter from my mother or father" and she associates "exhilaration" and cheerfulness with "selfishness" and "vendetta." But she is no flower of evil. She takes a kind of satisfaction from avoiding Frederique. She tastes, now and then, a voluptuous pleasure in disappointment and pain, but it is not pleasure that she tastes when, at the station in her uniform, she waits for a train that will stop for three minutes before moving on. "There I stood," she reports, "spruced up, to see her pass by, go through the station, then she would be taking the Andrea Doria and sailing across the ocean, my *maman*." To be sure, she "foresaw the pain, the desertion, with an acute sense of joy," but this peculiar joy is associated with something "malicious, there's poison in it." It is pain that is not truly mastered, unwelcome pain, pain that contaminates.

Jaeggy's novel has been described as "a prose poem." Joseph Brodsky saw in it the "engraver's needle depicting roots, twigs, and branches of the tree of madness." But though there is in the novel, as in Jaeggy's successful stories, a continuity of pitch and idiom, there is also an undermusic that works against the grain of the austerities and the abnegations. Jaeggy may seem to take her familiar pleasure in showing us that the "happy" family seated near her youthful narrator—they "generated an air of such happiness . . . displayed an almost stubborn happiness"— will shortly be blasted by the suicide of the youngest daughter; but this authorial pleasure is short-lived, bitter. She notes "the icicles weeping on the branches outside." Whatever the inclination to melancholia and denial, we hear the steady, distant, elusive call of "the good things in life," the "good news" that some of us have been "taught" to resist, to "renounce," to "fear."

Does any of this amount to a philosophy? Jaeggy is a writer, not a philosopher. She is content with the evocation of a tension in which the idyll of the happy housewife is as remote as the fanaticism of renunciation. Of "order and submission," her narrator says at one point—she might also have included revolt and torpor—"you can never know what fruits they will bear. . . . You might become a criminal or, by attrition, a normal conventional person." The result of this uncertainty is not a cultivated indifference or a reckless licentiousness; it is an elegiac longing for something—Jaeggy knows not quite what it is—that she might almost wish to believe in. And there is nothing less decadent than an elegy.

10

PRIMACIES AND POLITICS

NADINE GORDIMER

For quite some time, cutting-edge literary theorists and postmodern writers have proclaimed the impotence of art and their conviction that the novel as an instrument of knowledge has exhausted its resources. What one critic called "the platitude of meaning" and another "the loss of significant external reality" came rapidly to inform and constrain anything that might be said about the work of many sophisticated writers eager to be taken seriously. Those who regarded with relative indifference the manifestos of influential spokesmen for "advanced" art were routinely dismissed as hopelessly out of touch with their own cultural moment. Novelists who betrayed in their work an interest in the world were often thought to have forfeited any claim on readers for whom the novel was an "autonomous" art and primarily an occasion for the flexing of imaginative muscles.

Meanwhile, ever since the first stirrings of the postmodern, a number of writers have resisted the attempt to set against each other the "advanced" and the "traditional," the "autonomous" and the "worldly," the "imaginative" and the "pedestrian." They have sought, moreover, to make a case for "meaning" and "reality," while refusing to concede that either is an inevitable reflection of bourgeois ideology or of a commitment to genteel decorums. Though experimenting freely with literary forms and voices, they have refused to accord special status to the experimental or the arbitrary. The best of these writers have gone about their work with a remarkable determination not to be distracted or forestalled by the academic distinctions and theoretical imbroglios that have made a good deal of "advanced" writing seem vain or puerile. Though committed to telling plausible stories and creating believable characters, they have readily acknowledged the partiality of their vision and the inability of art in general to formulate commanding or fully satisfying truths. Tempted by the breadth and flexibility of novelistic form, its capacity to take on the most demanding of subjects, they have retained—through all of their exertions—a deep, sometimes primary absorption in language itself and a sense that serious fiction can never be more—or less—than a continuous raid on the inarticulate.

Of all of the contemporary fiction writers who are routinely associated with a literature of engagement, Nadine Gordimer has most strenuously challenged the familiar categorical distinctions between the "art novel" and the traditional, "realistic" novel. In no way a didactic or self-consciously programmatic writer, she has used the novel much as others before her have used it, while yet insisting upon its power to test the resources of language and to focus attention on the creative process itself. To think of her as a political novelist is understandable, given the characteristic range of her subjects and the interests she promotes in her essays and speeches. To think of her as a writer for whom reality is a given, and for whom the novel is a set of determinate procedures for encompassing reality, is to miss entirely what she has done. If when we speak of "realism" we refer to the novelist's demonstrated interest in a world beyond the word, then Gordimer may rightly be described as a realist; if by "artist" we refer to the novelist's absorption in her own medium and her ability to involve us in a created universe that looks and feels like a region of the mind, then Gordimer is by every token an art novelist.

Early in her career, Gordimer seemed to some readers a gifted but unapologetically traditional writer. Few supposed that the author of *The Lying Days* in 1953 would go on to write a formally demanding novel like *The Conservationist* in 1974, or that her classic 1970 political novel *A Guest of Honor* would seem like a great nineteenth-century work when set alongside later novels like *Burger's Daughter* or *Something Out There*. Critics have made much of the obvious continuities in Gordimer's fiction, often charting the evolution of her thought as a way of identifying constants in her preoccupations and themes. Rare are the commentaries that dwell on the development in her work of multiple, frequently incompatible narrative perspectives, or her increasing absorption in problems of voice and syntax. One need not undervalue her earlier fiction to recognize that in the full flowering of her art Gordimer has produced a kind of fiction no one quite foresaw. From the first a cunning observer of human affairs, with a fine ear for speech rhythms and an eye for telling, psychologically revealing gestures, Gordimer has more and more become a writer whose very sentences arrest attention, not because they are pretty or rude or willfully eccentric, but because they move in several directions at once, often with great speed. One never loses oneself in the thickets of Gordimer's prose, or forgets that she is writing about the fate of South Africa or the delusions of liberalism, but one feels oneself constantly maneuvered, snared, alternately pleasured, unsteadied, set back on one's feet, briefly released, by a prose that is everywhere an instrument of astonishing self-corrections and exactitudes.

Consider, from her novel *My Son's Story*, a characteristic passage. It describes the movement of many people, black and white, toward a township where they will hear a speech delivered at the grave of recently murdered South African blacks. The language is at once expansive and concrete, the speaker tempted to move beyond observable facts and conditions but ever alert to those conditions as the ground of his massing, tumultuous feelings:

> The blacks were accustomed to closeness. In queues for transport, for work permits, for housing allocation, for all the stamped paper that authorized their lives; loaded into overcrowded trains and buses to take them back and forth across the veld, fitting a family into one room, they cannot keep the outline of space—another, invisible skin—whites project around themselves, distanced from each other in everything but sexual and parental intimacy. But now in the graveyard the people from the combis were dispersed into a single, vast, stirring being with the people of the township. The nun was close against the breast of a man. A black child with his little naked penis waggling under a shirt clung to the leg of a professor. A woman's French perfume and the sweat of a drunk merged as if one breath came from them. And yet it was not alarming for the whites; in fact, an old fear of closeness, of the odours and heat of other flesh, was gone. One ultimate body of bodies was inhaling and exhaling in the single diastole and systole, and above was the freedom of the great open afternoon sky.

The passage has unmistakable objectives. It must remind us in summary of how black people live in South Africa, of their quotidian sufferings and the indignities to which they are routinely subjected. It must remind us that for South African whites, conditions are fundamentally different, but that they pay a price for their privilege. More especially,

NADINE GORDIMER

the passage must introduce the prospect of an almost unimaginable commingling of whites and blacks that would uplift and transform everyone involved. The burden on this single paragraph of incommensurable messages—of misery and hope, separateness and intimacy, fear and release from fear—is so evenly and dexterously handled that we are through the paragraph before we have quite registered the distance it covers. The detail in the front of the paragraph—queues, work permits, crowded living quarters—eases us into the ever-expanding spatial metaphor that dominates the passage, carrying it from a closeness—which is stifling—to a distance—which is a form of deprivation—and across finally to another sort of closeness that is a manifest of freedom. Moving back through the passage, we see clearly what had so taken us in our initial movement through it: the inexorable merging of opposing terms, sentiments, and ways of imagining. The "women's French perfume" and "the sweat of a drunk" constitute an opposition no more stark than that between fleshly "odours and heat" and an absorption in "spatial aura" or "one ultimate body of bodies."

Of course, one may wish to resist the visionary thrust of Gordimer's paragraph, believing that the culminating apotheosis is not fully earned. In that case, one would point to the overly obvious early images or to the predictable quaintness of the oppositions (the black boy's "little naked penis" next to the professorial leg). But it is precisely the accessibility of the imagery, its routine quaintness and unremarkable familiarity, that makes us wonder at all that is made of this material. In this sense, resistance to the visionary thrust of the passage is a premature response, based upon the certain assumption that the writing—or the writer—has designs on us. And indeed, if Gordimer did want us to be swept off our feet by her rhetorical sleight of hand, then we would have some plausible reason to resist her invitation. As it is, we are better advised to let ourselves be moved without yielding utterly to an optimism that has for support only a rare and temporary projection. Precisely the predictability, the easily verifiable accuracy of the fundamental opposition—between black and white experience in South Africa—ought to make it impossible for anyone to believe in the durability of an optimism so expansive and so sudden as to dispel old fears and hatreds in the course of a dozen stirring lines.

The brilliance of Gordimer's paragraph—and it is by no means unusual in her writing—has much to do with its ability to invite capitulation without quite permitting it. This has nothing to do with the slyly trivial games many avowedly postmodern writers play, luring and teasing only to show that nothing is secure, no emotion genuine, no ostensible evidence an adequate warrant for anything. In Gordimer the instinct to lure and invite is the expression of a scrupulous generosity. Inviting our hope, it demands our strenuous effort to imagine a possibility that rejects familiar oppositions. Gordimer's handling of metaphor is not a glib exercise in sleight of hand but a sign of her refusal to abide with the usual terms we use to confront "reality." Her language, with its rhetorical extravagance and clearly literary esprit, is also remarkable for its scruple and weight of address. To be generous here is to think of possibility in an entirely serious and hopeful way, without supposing that what is yet to be done has in fact been done. Is it conceivable that people coming together on a symbolically charged occasion can honestly feel themselves transformed, brought close to one another as never before? Of that much we are surely willing to be persuaded. Are we ready to conclude therefore that a permanent transformation can be so effected? The word "freedom" at the close of Gordimer's paragraph would seem to suggest that we consider that possibility. But it is something else to say that Gordimer's judgment is dominated by her own wishful thinking or controlled by the propulsion of her own rhetoric.

In fact, Gordimer has long worked with similar conflicts and temptations in previous books. In her 1987 novel *A Sport of Nature*, she introduces and remains absorbed by the idea of a "rainbow family," a thoroughly satisfying union at once black and white and able to overcome every reluctance. But the paradigm family in the novel is destroyed, the foundations of its optimism everywhere challenged by incomprehension, provinciality, and cynicism. Even as the novel evokes its exemplary marital couple in their sexual pleasure and their instinctual connectedness, it is regularly given over to the interruptive reflections of narrative voices that cannot participate in the celebration of this special closeness. Nor are these voices made to seem altogether frivolous or dismissible. However cynical or provincial they may seem, they do also convey cautionary perspectives or reasonable doubts that the novel intermittently or ambivalently supports. To what degree, we wonder, is the exemplary connectedness of the rainbow couple a reflection of avidities that have little to do with the ordinary passions or capacities of most other people? Is it not clear that the long-term commitment of this particular white woman named Hillela to her black revolutionary husband Whaila has more to do with sexual temperament than with a capacity for genuine growth? Such questions remain with us as we think about *A Sport of Nature*. No reader of the book will come away certain that Gordimer has tried to represent her central figures as exemplary human beings. Neither will any reader suppose that the language of the novel is inexact or misleading. The language registers ambiguity and paradox because that is in the nature of the characters and situations it wishes to evoke.

This is true also of Gordimer's 1979 novel *Burger's Daughter*. Even there, in a work with clearly admirable central characters, the language assiduously registers alternative impressions and fluctuations. The point of view in the novel is regularly complicated by the introduction of narrative perspectives that correct or subvert the dominant voices and sentiments. No matter how fine and noble the character Lionel Burger is made to seem, one cannot get out of one's head the cynical, insidious whisperings of a character named Conrad, for whom the altruism and commitment of Burger are at once intimidating, awe-inspiring, laughable, and suspect. In the same way, Gordimer's Rosa Burger can be made to resist and sometimes mock the "good people" to whom she has been connected all of her life, and the very language of compassion and humanitarian striving can be made to seem predictable, sanctimonious, and pitifully decent.

My Son's Story clearly operates within similar narrative and linguistic boundaries. The central character is somehow believably admirable and foolish, intelligent and vain, caring and indifferent. The point of view is continually slipping, here totally omniscient, there limited, the tone of the narrative voice now confident and sincere, elsewhere derisive and troubled. The language moves now with perfect assurance and unselfconscious fluency, alternately with deliberate attention to its own privations and audacities. Content to move within a universe of meaning, language here is closely alert to the betrayals of meaning that come from the misuse of language. So characters here reflect not only on what "friendship meant" or on what "comradeship meant," but on the adoption of jargon or other kinds of ritualized expression. So words like "disaffected," "discipline," or "out of character" are anatomized or repudiated at the very moment they are taken up, though with nothing like an academic or pedantic intention. Always with Gordimer there is the alternating movement from openness and fluency to closeness and scruple. The intermittent recoil from language-as-given, language-as-available, language-as-sufficiency, is an expression of a deep moral urgency that is never mere earnestness or solemnity. One is not surprised to find in Gordimer an unapologetic absorption in the language of "obligation," "betrayal," "dignity," and "understanding." But neither is one surprised to find a concern about the way that admirable words and preoccupations may be susceptible to the cheapening we associate with sentimentality, glibness, and pomposity.

Gordimer would probably have little to say about the "loss of significant external reality" much proclaimed by postmodernists. Certainly *My Son's Story* moves with the conviction that what makes life easy for some people and hard for others is about as significant as anything can ever have been. And as to the reality of the conditions to which human beings respond, well, one might anguish over one's ability to do them justice, but surely one would resist the suggestion that reality doesn't exist or that one has no chance of sharing with others what one has felt or observed.

In the following passage, for example, it is obvious that different readers will discern different emphases, but it would be ridiculous to assert that "significant reality" is lacking or that in these words no two readers will see many of the same things:

How black they always were, these women; black blackened by labour in the sun, it's as if nature, which supplied our founding parents with the right degree of pigment to inhabit this continent, also supplies them with the camouflage under which to appear to submit to slavery. If you're mixed you don't have the protection. She strips the green leaves and spills the floss back from the cobs, digging her earth-rimmed nail to spurt milk from a row of nubs, because I ask her for young mealies, and her black face has no recognition for me, my half-blackness and this half-white man's street we live in as one of my father's political acts. She doesn't know I have anything to do with her. So much for his solidarity with the people.

And then I found I didn't have enough money in my pocket to pay her. She smells the same, of the grease smeared on her red-black cheeks and the smoke of wood-fires in her clothes, but mealies have gone up in price since the days in Benoni-son-of sorrow. One of our Afrikaans neighbours had come out to buy, as well, and she intervened to pay for me—Ag now, don't worry, you can give me back later, it's nothing—once you get one of them round to making an exception of you, there's no limit to their neighbourliness. My mother's dignity and beauty make our

NADINE GORDIMER

family an exception, although my father says exceptions change nothing, they merely confirm mob racism. For him, we are in this street to challenge the general.

In unpacking such a passage one sees at once that it trades in many "significant" facts. Inevitably in Gordimer's South Africa a "colored" person like the speaker will regard color as central to every human transaction. To buy a mealie from a street vendor is to note her color. To note her color is to consider the implications of color and to measure one's own relation to those implications. Further, if the speaker is a thoughtful person, he will recognize that the way one deals with color in such a place will determine one's political outlook, and that to think of politics is to consider how honestly and clearly one's positions are held. The words "so much for his solidarity with the people" are "significant" in several respects: (1) they express the speaker's feelings toward his father, (2) they probe the problematic quality of commitments to people with whom one often has only a vague or symbolic relationship, and (3) they suggest that the facts of color within a particular kind of system may be more important than any emotion one may wish to summon. That such considerations are significant—and how can they not be?—there can be no doubt.

There is also no doubt about the ability of such a passage to summon something like reality and to make it seem palpable. Of course, racial sentiment may well be the crucial reality for such a book. But there is also the reality of the mealies and their preparation, to say nothing of the reality of Afrikaaner neighbourliness and the difficulty of getting past long-held assumptions about what is possible for whites or blacks. In the face of the reality offered in such a passage, programmatic objections based upon overfamiliar postmodern prejudices have little to tell us. No reader needs a postmodern critic to tell him that the observations in this passage belong to a particular someone and are not "true" for all in the same degree. But of course as readers of this novel we know the difference between more or less accurate observations and what are clearly unreliable assertions. When the speaker refers uncharitably and even bitterly to his own father in a way that seems gratuitous, we are made suspicious of his assertions. When he speaks rather too knowingly of things he doesn't or couldn't fully know, we are likewise mistrustful. But in the main we do trust this speaker—not in the sense that he has the truth, but because he does consistently offer a plausible version of reality as available not only to him but to others. This would be too obvious to say if it were not routinely overlooked or denied by the "advanced" critics for whom Gordimer's new work will no doubt seem as "naive" in its assumptions about art as her previous novels.

Clearly, Gordimer is naive about nothing, though the incorrigible freshness of her writing and her capacity to take us inside an emotion as if we were exposed to it for the first time often make us feel that she is seeing with young eyes things quite familiar. But of course we understand, even as we are moved by the high emotion or naive wonder of a passage, that it is framed, controlled, and quickened by an artfulness that has many aims in view. This is not always easy to remember, given Gordimer's willingness to use—in a single page devoted to a new love affair—expressions like "the most precious aspect of his new life," "a kind of magic," "a wonderful spell of intimacy," "what secret pleasure," and so on. But again, what might seem in other hands indulgence or pathetic fallacy is in Gordimer chastised and inexorably undercut by other urgencies. Not that Gordimer violently interrupts the reveries of her lovers or subjects them to a predictably lacerating irony just as they peak. She is tolerant, patient, insisting that her narrator—however acidulous his own perspective on the lovers—do his best to give them and their transports their due. We know when we read "If his need of Hannah was terrible—in a magnificent way—then there was no need of anything or anyone else" that "in a magnificent way" is an impression belonging to Hannah's lover, not to the narrator. But such an expression is permitted to fall upon us with a certain force—given its placement near the end of a long ecstatic passage—that almost makes it feel that it comes with the authority or approval of Gordimer herself. In such a passage, the undercutting is accomplished not by way of pointed juxtaposition or acerbic commentary but by the framing of the narrative as a whole, by its persistently reminding us of a world elsewhere—of people and interests not apt to be impressed by any lover's feeling that the bed he shared with his lover was "an everywhere." In some way, the moments of reverie to which the narrative voice commits itself are all the more striking for the sense otherwise communicated of a reality not generally susceptible to such sentiments.

There are other kinds of freshness in Gordimer, passages less wholly given over to the emotion gripping her characters. In some, we are impressed chiefly by the way the voice represents conflict, torn as the speaker is between the desire to get inside an emotion as those experiencing it would wish to see it and the need to get it right, however harshly. So we get "Don't talk, don't talk any more, Hannah said, although she was the one he talked to, she was the one with whom he shared what there was to live for outside self, she was the one friend he ever had. They quickly made love—no, he fucked her; it was all he had left in him to expend." Here the formulation about "what there was to live for outside self" expresses the point of view of the narrator's father, not the narrator himself. This we know certainly by the way the words "She was the one friend he ever had" are made to follow, signaling the father's inability to acknowledge his earlier attachment to his wife and to his present, blinding infatuation. By the time we reach the corrective "no, he fucked her," we see how the narrator has struggled to keep within the perspective and the voice of his character, the father whose behavior has so alienated him from his own son. In "no, he fucked her," the force of recognition is achieved not merely by the sudden use of the word "fucked" but by our renewed sense that an internal conflict has been seething all along.

Elsewhere, the freshness has to do with the bluntness of an impression, the way it is driven home by means of a metaphorical or discursive expansion of the field of vision, only to be returned to the ground emotion underlying the impression. This we see, for example, in the narrator's effort to account for his father's continuing infatuation: "The face of a woman who uses no make-up has unity with her body," he observes, as if with his father's eyes, though with an acuteness that would seem beyond his father:

> Seeing Hannah's fair eyelashes catching the morning sun and the shine of the few little cat's whiskers that were revealed in this innocent early clarity, at the upper corners of her mouth, he was seeing the whole of her; he understood why in the reproduction of paintings he had puzzled over in the days of his self-education, Picasso represented frontally all the features of a woman—head, breasts, eyes, vagina, nose, buttocks, mouth—as if all were always present even to the casual glance. What would he have known without Hannah!

The movement from the at once innocent and sophisticated Picasso reference to the grateful earnestness of those final exclamatory words is really quite remarkable, and captures in miniature much that carries us in Gordimer's novel.

For doctrinaire enthusiasts of postmodernism, the faltering of language and its inherent inadequacy to the task of representation are facts to be ostentatiously or playfully trumpeted by writers confronting the immensity—and absurdity—of their task. Measured by this standard, Gordimer may seem insufficiently intimidated or defiant. She does not wear her inadequacy on her sleeve. Her fictions tell us nothing of the novelist's sleepless nights, and she has little instinct for playful self-derogation. Gordimer's confidence in handling surfaces and textures is no less apparent than her confident mastery of political conflicts and ordinary human interactions. Her language inspires neither irritation nor knowingly ironic laughter. If it is not quite a sufficiency unto itself, it is nonetheless free of the impulse to wallow in the slough of self-defeat or to divert attention to the exhaustible skills of its author. For all of the novel's devices, it never seems mechanical or gratuitously flamboyant. To say of Gordimer's language that it is "responsible" is to say that in wielding it she refuses to congratulate herself for simply letting fly in every which way—as if to do so were in itself a sure token of the liberated imagination.

It may of course be argued that there can be no responsible use of language, no responsible fiction, if reality itself is taken not to exist. In that case, the language would have nothing to be responsible for, or to. William Gass suggests as much when he writes of the inevitable antipathy between art and truth. But *My Son's Story* is responsible in a way that would seem to proclaim the irrelevance of any such assertion. Proposing nothing it is unwilling to examine, the novel may surely be said to be responsible—if not to reality, then to its own premises. If the language of the novel evokes nothing that cannot be made to serve the broad expressive purposes of the work, then again it may be said to be responsible to the project itself, to the potentially liberating effects the novel may exercise upon properly responsive readers. For such a novel, the idea that reality does not exist and that therefore everything is permitted and nothing is of significant consequence can only be an empty metaphysical speculation. For a writer like Gordimer, the "reality" of a novel is not strictly speaking mimetic but creative. It sets the terms of its unfolding and is scrupulously attentive to them as if they were underwritten by objectively verifiable and enforceable conditions. That attentiveness is the source of its seriousness and of its claim upon us.

The movement, speed, and occasional extravagance of Gordimer's prose belong neither to modernism nor to the literary modes that have succeeded it. Such writing is neither breakthrough nor retrogression. Its movement is not alone in the pacing or continuity of events, its speed not simply in the rapid alternation of insights or points of view. Its extravagance is neither excess nor studied disequilibrium. In fact, one thinks of *My Son's Story* as most characteristically Gordimer's in its unpredictable mixing of resources, its use of both formal modes and improvised snatches of this thing or that. Here and there are the ritual exchanges between characters one associates with standard novelistic narrative, but more striking are the fragments of dialogue, the shards of overheard voices, the briefly coloring word or phrase introduced to heighten an abstract reflection. Shifting as the narrative does from one to another such employment, one is aware always of the ceaseless movement of the discourse as a movement in consciousness itself. Speed occurs as much in the withdrawal from a mode that has been briefly taken up as in the resolute shifting into another fully fashioned tone or manner. Like other major writers—one thinks even of so different a novelist as Saul Bellow—Gordimer moves deftly from high to low, from the sophisticated to the demotic, from the refined to the casual. The restlessness of the narrative voice and of the mind it expresses appears in these alternations as also in the frequently interpolated questions that evoke an anxiety more encompassing than the issues named in those questions. "Where is he going?" in Gordimer is an expression of concern focused on a particular character, but it also expresses doubt about our ability to follow the motives and actions even of those we love, and finally about the ability of any narrative to penetrate the lives of those it pursues. The constant movement away from answers to questions even as answers are offered, the reeling in of speculation as the line is paying out, is central to the movement we admire in Gordimer. To suppose that she gives us anything approaching pure mimesis or an utterly unselfconscious omniscience is to miss the way that consciousness formulates and supervises its own trajectory in such a novel.

To resist talking about the content of *My Son's Story*—as I have tried to resist it here—is not to argue that the thematic content is marginal to the novel's purposes. That would be foolish. Gordimer has never written a novel principally about language. She has no interest in making her work a battleground for a war between form and content, language and reality. She would no doubt agree that the novel is a more or less complete system, a reality unto itself, but she would also insist on the inevitable pressure constantly brought to bear on that system by extrinsic factors. Because she has been extraordinarily successful in representing those extrinsic factors, inspiring readers to describe her fiction as "a brilliant reflection of a world that exists" or a depiction of "interrelationships that characterize the citizens of South Africa," her artistry has often been taken for granted. To attempt to correct the balance is of course to risk going the other way, making Gordimer seem the sort of "poet" whose richly textured sentences and finely calibrated modulations of voice alone set her apart from other engaged writers.

In fact, *My Son's Story*, considered solely as a further attempt to study the situation in South Africa, is unquestionably a fresh addition to Gordimer's opus. It describes not only the radicalization and growth of particular people, but also the way that the most intimate relations are affected by political affairs. In this the novel deepens insights developed in previous works by a writer whose struggle with liberalism has been central to everything she has done, and whose concern with the human consequences of political action has been unwavering. But the novelist here shifts emphasis to the erotic and psychological dimensions of the conflict in a way that seems at once natural and surprising. Always in the past a fiercely attentive student of erotic ritual, Gordimer here charts the rise and implications of erotic pleasure with a sustained meticulousness that is new in her work. Similarly, she treats the evolving dynamics of Oedipal conflict with a steady curiosity that enhances our understanding of identity and growth. Nowhere in her recent work does Gordimer go so far in allowing the political to seem if not less important then certainly less interesting than the personal lives of her characters. Having confronted the possibility that politics would consume everything in the conflict coming to a head in the South Africa of 1990, Gordimer has in no way recoiled from the political, but she has recalled us to primacies that underlie our worldly exertions.

Though it is a first-person novel narrated by the son of Sonny, the "coloured" protagonist, *My Son's Story* most often feels as if it belongs not to its narrator but to his father. At times it moves into what feels like an omniscient third-person mode, so that we forget for the moment that there is a particular narrator, however often he reminds us of his presence. Sonny interests us as a study in contrasts. A decent, compassionate, gentle man, his obsessive involvement with a white radical named Hannah detaches him from his wife and family. Enlightened in most of the important ways, he can be numbly insensitive to the needs of other individuals and blind to the contaminating effects of his own behavior. A committed activist and something of a leader in the liberation movement, he can seem terribly naive about politics, and is surprised to find himself increasingly mistrusted by political colleagues who by their lights have good reason to doubt his steely capacities.

The action of the novel turns on Sonny's relations with family and lover and his sometimes satisfying, sometimes confusing and even disillusioning relations with the political movement he serves. Relatively modest attention is paid to the growth of Sonny's wife Aila, whose disaffection from her husband drives her into a political involvement that had not seemed possible for so mild a figure. The white lover Hannah is a fully realized character, though Gordimer avoids close examination of her motives and background, probably because this would go beyond the speculative capacities of her appointed narrator, who must after all determine what we can learn. Though the young man takes us inside his characters, the knowledge he imparts would seem not to violate our sense of his understanding. In any case, the action of the novel is strictly tied to the plausible development of characters whose strengths and limitations are carefully posited, and with due allowance for the unforeseeable and wayward.

In short, though a case might well be made for *My Son's Story* as a novel about politics, it is principally a novel of consciousness, and is most distinctive in its willingness to entertain ideas without succumbing to them. The fact that all of the characters in the novel are in one way or another involved with politics and ideas misleads us if we take that fact to determine the tenor and purpose of the book. Though, as we have argued, the book is not a postmodern, self-canceling artifact, it consistently commands attention as a deliberately invented, intricately patterned work. Anything but compulsive about calling into question its resources and prerogatives, it nonetheless draws us to issues—the limits of representation, the deployment of point of view, the allowable range of metaphorical expansion—that more typically absorb us in rather different novelistic precincts. That Gordimer can sustain a bristling and deeply feeling interrogation of what seems to be reality while remaining alert to problems inherent in her medium is cause for further study—and for celebration.

11

THINKING ABOUT EVIL

KAFKA, NAIPAUL, COETZEE

A few years ago, in the pages of the *New York Review of Books*, the poet Charles Simic—born a Serb but long an American citizen—conceded that "it's hard to find anything good to say about Serbs these days. Burning villages, killing women and children, chasing hundreds of thousands of blameless people out of their homes hardens the heart of anyone watching. To set neighbor against neighbor is not only evil; it's also stupid."

The burden of Simic's brief essay is not to declare that we know or should know evil when we see it, or that the spectacle of remorseless evil tends to harden every heart. Simic argues, rather, that "many perfectly normal and good people are to be found" among those somehow involved in or supporting evil in Bosnia and in Kosovo. "Do they also deserve," he asks, "to be demonized and punished for being trapped with lunatics?"

The turn in this kind of argument has by now become quite familiar in Western intellectual circles. Sophisticated people, after all, are supposed to know better than to "demonize" whole peoples, and there are always those, in Serbia and elsewhere, to remind us that not everyone was willing to go along with the atrocities committed in their name. Even Simic, who "knew [as he says] what our people were capable of" well before the "blood bath" began, is appalled that Western intellectuals should believe in the "collective complicity of ordinary Serbs," even if ordinary Serbs—a great many of them—were complicit in atrocities. To speak of evil, so Simic would seem to argue, is legitimate. To suggest that ordinary people are sometimes capable of monstrous deeds is likewise acceptable. But to suppose that "ordinary" Serbs not only went along with the evil committed in their name but were actually invested in and may therefore in some way be held responsible for the crimes of

Milosevic is to demonize them and to embrace the patently absurd "idea of collective guilt." Those who participate in the folly of demonization, Simic argues, generally do so the better to sleep "the sleep of the just," and to avoid guilt when they rouse themselves to take retributive action against the evildoers—for example, by bombing their cities. But, so Simic contends, no justice can come from such self-serving behavior.

It is easy, to be sure, to be scornful of demonization, to say, fine, of course, there were and are wonderful Serbian men and women who did everything in their power to obstruct the ethnic cleansing policies of their government; to say, sure, there are, obviously, Palestinians who deplore the terrorist atrocities directed against Israeli civilians, and Israelis who deplore the brutal mistreatment of Palestinians that is an endemic feature of Israeli occupation in the West Bank and other territories within the greater Israel. But the argument against demonization often confuses—not complicates, but confuses—the case against evil.

Consider for the moment Simic's argument in its movement from "I knew what our people were capable of" to the complaint that somehow, thanks to a good deal of faulty "reasoning, Milosevic's dream has come true: Serbia is now a nation of ten million war criminals." At bottom, Simic's complaint is underwritten by his sense that it was principally "the ruling elite" who were to blame for "mass murder and ethnic cleansing." He does not make his case in these terms, but the logic of his argument would seem to be clear on this count at least. Evil deeds executed and abetted by countless people in conflicts inspired by ethnic hatred have principally to do—so Simic would contend—with the orders handed down by "the ruling elite." Thus, "perfectly normal" people are presumed to be more or less "normal" and more or less "good," and if they do terrible things, that is the consequence of their having been "trapped with lunatics." We need not debate here the historical and philosophical issues raised by writers like Hannah Arendt (in *Eichmann in Jerusalem*) or by Daniel Goldhagen (in *Hitler's Willing Executioners*) to say that Simic's understanding of evil is entirely problematic. It may well be that in a great many places, ordinary people are not merely complicit in but enthusiastic about the evils committed in their name. To cry "demonization" every time this fact is invoked is to cut off potentially meaningful discussion. In a recent essay in *The New Republic*, the philosopher Amartya Sen complains that Western intellectuals are "artificially magnifying the voice of religious authority" in the Islamic world when they might instead dwell upon "our [common] right to choose how we see ourselves (with what emphases and what priorities)." Like Simic, Sen deplores the Western tendency, as he sees it, to demonize people by imputing to them features that belong, presumably, principally to their leaders and to rather modest numbers of fanatics. By supposing that religious fanaticism is pervasive in Islamic countries, Sen argues, we come to believe that Islam is "an essentially belligerent culture" and that therefore a so-called clash of civilizations is "inescapable." We would do well, he urges, to think of Islamic peoples the way we think of most ordinary people in the West: not as people inspired to do evil deeds by a venomous antipathy to modernity, secularism, and liberal values, but as people, like ourselves, with an inalienable right "to choose how [they] see [them]selves."

The problem is that Western intellectuals do not in the main arti-   ¹³³
ficially magnify the power of religious authority in the Islamic world. Neither do they delude themselves when they observe that the exercise of the right "to choose how [they] see [them]selves" is at present pro-scribed in many sectors of the Islamic world. Evil is routinely commit-ted by people who believe that they are authorized by their religious leaders to blow up school buses, massacre civilians, and brutally mistreat those among their own coreligionists who challenge the reigning ortho-doxies. Islam is by no means a monolithic, "inescapably" adversarial system, but it is worth noting that at present a great many people in the Islamic world are determined to outlaw and severely punish dissent, no matter how modest, and to prosecute a conflict with the West. They believe fervently in the coming clash of civilizations. Sen and others who deplore "demonization" and the imputation to others of evil motives seem to imagine that the standard Western belief in "plural identities" is shared by people who by no means define themselves in that way. Such people, in fact, often behave as if the diverse features of their iden-tity—as spouses, say, or as parents of children in whom they have an obligation to instill a respect for their own lives at least—were entirely negligible when set beside their primary responsibility to create a culture of martyrs.

All the same, many in the West declare themselves unwilling to de-fine as evil even the massacre of innocent civilians. "Liberation struggle," some call it. Resistance. A war of national independence. The "circum-stances" are said, often, to differentiate what is evil from what is more or less legitimate, understandable, and necessary, however "unfortunate." The standard political discourse familiar to most Western intellectuals

KAFKA, NAIPAUL, COETZEE

will occasionally contain references to evil, but rarely nowadays is the term used without real or implied quotation marks. The Nazi era, in this sense, has provided an exemplary instance of real evil in contrast with which most ostensible subsequent instances must seem at least somewhat problematic. If, in Yugoslavia, it can be demonstrated that atrocities were committed not merely by the Serbs but by their opponents, then many will conclude that neither side was or did evil, that the crimes were, all of them, "relative," not to be subsumed under some categorical or metaphysical epithet. And if it can be demonstrated that the Israeli regime of Ariel Sharon in so-called self-defense tolerated or incited the wanton killing of Palestinian civilians, might it not be said that Palestinian "retribution," no matter how widespread and vicious and indiscriminate, thereby ceased to be evil, as it had once seemed, and instead became "merely" deplorable? Human, all too human? So many in the West have said; so they will continue, no doubt, to say.

A good many Western intellectuals, chiefly in the government bureaucracies or in Washington think tanks, often resort to another rhetoric intended to sanitize the killing of civilians as unavoidable "collateral damage" in a righteous war on terrorism or an equally righteous crusade for "democracy." These intellectuals, and the right-wing journalists who make the case for them, routinely use technocratic or providential language to justify actions that are in fact evil and would have seemed so even in these circles, before they decided that malevolent intentions always belong to others, and that the liberal unwillingness to use power for self-interest is itself a mark of unforgivable faintheartedness.

Even in the pages of journals once associated with a liberal reluctance to use preemptive force or to countenance the blunt assertion of an arrogant American power, the word "evil" is routinely applied to others without the slightest suggestion that anything "we" do may be morally grotesque. More than one editor at *The New Republic* argued that even a war whose long-term outcome is unknowable and that may well make things in the world worse than they were before the war began ought still to be described as a just war, however ugly or hellish. Never mind that the war—I am speaking here about the war in Iraq—will cause enormous suffering, or that the grand moral aims invoked by those in charge are impossible to take seriously when coming from people whose cavalier disdain for the good opinion of mankind makes them the last people one would associate with moral vision. Intellectuals who see no possible evil in a military adventure undertaken by such leadership and additionally see no evil in an essentially unprovoked attack on a nation whose internal divisions and traditions make it an altogether unpromising target for imposed, belligerent, Western-style "reform" have little hope of instructing others on the subject of evil.

To be fair, not many have succeeded in sorting out these matters, and few are the philosophers, historians, or journalists who have had enduringly useful things to say on the subject of evil. Even our so-called creative writers do rather badly on the subject when they speak, as it were, in their own voice, especially when their purposes are essentially polemical. The effort to differentiate one thing from another gives way, most often, to the sense that it is essential chiefly to deplore what is deplorable and to avoid casting blame on people when it is "systems of domination" and "ideology" and "fanaticism" that are "responsible" for brutality and hatred. Even writers like Simic, who know evil when they see it, are most often reduced to discussing circumstance and system in a way that makes evil itself seem somehow the wrong word and the not-finally-legitimate idea for grasping what human beings do to one another. Even brutal deeds committed by individuals come to seem, in the several frameworks erected to understand them, the product of "impersonal" forces best analyzed with the instruments typically deployed by social scientists trained to anatomize bureaucracy, stratification, and the "rationalization of terror."

Franz Kafka knew a great deal about bureaucracy, rationalization, and the domain of impersonal forces. Even in fictions apparently preoccupied with the most intimate of relationships, Kafka was fully alert to the control exercised by arrangements and assumptions that seem to have been set in place by forces and systems somehow outside of or just beyond the experience of the ordinary people affected by them. Did Kafka operate from a sense of radical evil in the world? Clearly he understood that it was possible for human beings to do evil, and that the most disparate conditions might well permit or encourage evil deeds. The death or absence or silence of God was in Kafka's view a signal factor in the emergence of modernity, but the modern did not promise, by any means, to eliminate evil, however much the new perpetrators or architects of evil might learn to rationalize their activities in previously unimaginable ways.

The most penetrating of Kafka's works on the subject of evil is the long story entitled "In the Penal Colony." There, evil is associated with a "traditional" order once dominated by an "old" or "former" commandant, but it is also associated with the regime of a "new," ostensibly more modern and enlightened commandant. Throughout the story, Kafka demands that we ask which of the two dispensations we prefer, which is more apt to deal with the problem of evil in an acceptable way. He also demands that we consider the possibility that the existence of evil is not, in fact, the most important of the issues we confront, for if evil is everywhere a feature of the lives human beings construct for themselves, then it may be that other features of our lives will seem to us more susceptible to change and therefore more compelling.

In Kafka's story, the evil endemic in the traditional order is embodied by the "remarkable apparatus" that figures so prominently in this work. It is an elaborate harrowing device, an instrument of edification and torture. Those who violate the laws of the society—or who are presumed to violate the laws—are summarily subjected to the cruelties inflicted by the apparatus: the "criminal" is placed on a bed of needles that slowly pierce his body, inscribing on it the significance of the law he has violated or ignored. In this way, the "criminal" is made to "absorb" the law, to take it in, to feel it as a constitutive feature of his very being, even as he is finished off by the apparatus, so that enlightenment and termination are achieved more or less at the same moment. The accused have no means of defending themselves against the charges leveled against them; they are victims of a system in which absolute justice is never to be questioned. Equally reprehensible, no attention is paid to degrees of seriousness, to the relative weight of crimes committed, so that violators appear to be punished severely simply on the grounds that they have broken the law and thereby challenged the sacred system of justice upon which the society depends. At the center of the story Kafka places an explorer, who is appalled by such features of the traditional system in the penal colony and whose responses will surely seem plausible to Kafka's readers.

The evil apparent in the operation of the apparatus is also a function of the sheer pain it is designed to inflict. Efforts on the part of its adherents to rationalize the suffering inflicted on criminals, though ostensibly sincere, are by no means intended to be persuasive. Rather, the enlightenment said to follow from the administered punishment is specious and ridiculous, and accounts of the transfiguring bliss discernible on the faces of those who have been tortured and simultaneously "enlightened" about the meaning of justice are apt to provoke in Kafka's readers paroxysms of disbelief and anxious laughter. The horrors outlined in Kafka's story are at once horrible and, in their rationalized context, satirical. If there is evil in the world and it sometimes takes the form of flagrant violations of the law that do great harm to others, Kafka would seem to suggest that there is evil too in the operations of the law, in its indiscriminate employment of harsh punishment and in its inhumane failure to consider individual people with the tact and dignity they deserve. The solemn administration of justice by legally sanctioned officers of the law is often so far from achieving its avowed objectives as to be ludicrous in its pretensions and its palpable violations of ordinary standards of decency.

But there is evil, too, Kafka suggests, in modern efforts to improve upon traditional systems and procedures. At the time of the explorer's visit, the colony has been taken over by a "new" commandant, and an extraordinarily conscientious "officer" now administers the apparatus. Though the colony is still nominally committed to a system of justice and to the principle of enlightenment, it has become ostensibly more humane than it had been under the auspices of the old commandant. The condemned man is visited, before succumbing to his punishment, by "ladies" in pink, charitable people who commiserate with him and stuff his mouth with sweets. These creatures of sentiment, compassionate sisters of charity, can do nothing to save the object of their mercy from his appointed end, and their transparent ineffectuality is part of the point Kafka wishes to make about the improving sentiments. It is not that the ladies with their tender mercies are in any obvious sense instruments of evil. The evil they do is by no means incidental to their empty charity, but it will seem evil only when the effects of their charity are fully understood.

Those effects are best grasped in the account given of the prisoner's suffering when at last he is subjected to his punishment. Stuffed with sweets, overfed, as it were, the prisoner is nauseated by the gag placed in his mouth and vomits uncontrollably as the apparatus goes through its intended motions. Sick and miserable and unable to "appreciate" the slow "edification" administered by the harrowing mechanism, the prisoner misses entirely the intended effect of the punishment. His experience is worse than it would have been had he not been stuffed with sweets and subjected to the cloying attentions of the ladies in pink. So much, Kafka suggests, for mere fellow feeling.

In much the same way, though with nothing like the broad, playful strokes he lavishes on the ladies, Kafka anatomizes the other features of the new regime. The apparatus itself is in terrible shape, its several parts regularly breaking down while nothing is done to repair or replace them. The condemned man vomits at once on the gag set between his teeth because it is sodden with the saliva of previous victims. When the officer himself climbs onto the apparatus to demonstrate to the explorer, in one desperate final effort, that the system works as it is supposed to work, there is no gradual imprinting on his body of the "truth" he wishes to learn. Instead, the needles of the harrow brutally puncture his body, and he is fatally impaled before any semblance of enlightenment can occur.

The evil here does not reside in any group's or person's intent but is a function or condition of a culture's willing what cannot be willed and insisting upon it in obvious denial of the available reality. The culture wills that civilized people find a way to have things both ways: to have, on the one hand, law, punishment, obedience, and strictness of conscience; and, on the other hand, reluctance, civilized misgiving, and compassion. Kafka's story is designed to express the fundamental irreconcilability of the joined efforts to uphold some orthodox conviction of truth and at the same time yield to the sentimentalities enjoined by the imperative of Christian charity. Though by no means a sentimentalist, nor, in fact, a believer in modernist pieties associated with liberalism or skepticism, Kafka fully accepted that traditional notions of truth, justice, punishment, obedience, and the absolute were bound at last to seem insupportable and ridiculous. The refusal or inability to abandon them, on the grounds that life without those notions would be intolerable, is neither great nor edifying, and, in fact, the failure to accept that the game is up and to close down the apparatus ends, in Kafka's story, with a scene that is altogether grotesque. Permitted to function when it is clearly breaking down, and with virtually no adherents remaining to sustain and repair it, the apparatus becomes arbitrary, brutal, and absurd.

Kafka does not offer us an attractive "experimental" version of a liberalism that might plausibly address evil in an effectual way. The apparatus makes a mockery of the whole reformist project, which typically aims to teach the criminal a lesson that he might then go on to apply when he resumes his ordinary life. One reason Kafka's story is so horrifying is that "enlightened" methods of reeducation or reform are shackled to the "traditional" aims of inflicting pain and achieving retribution. If there is any semblance of liberalism in Kafka's story, it is at best a parody.

What all of this can say about the existence in the world of evil is simply that it was a good deal easier to speak of evil when perfect obedience was not merely a requirement but a civilized expectation, and when every violation was a breach of the human contract deserving not to be "understood" but to be punished. If we say of the arbitrary and gratuitous—and of the denial of reality that is self-deception—that they likewise constitute a species of evil, we do not mean that they constitute violations of the same order as overtly vicious or flagrantly transgressive behaviors. Rather, we say that the arbitrary and gratuitous are evil or may be regarded as such when they inflict on human beings a suffering that in no way strengthens the spiritual purposes or the political stability of the community in whose name the suffering is authorized. Likewise, the denial of reality is to be regarded as evil when it allows self-satisfied people to conduct their business with no suspicion that what is customary might and ought to be otherwise. Theodor Adorno noted that denial, an "intellectual defect," may well become an "immoral defect," a reflection of a "prevailing baseness to which thought and language accommodate" themselves when those faculties facilitate the denial of reality.

Kafka intended to establish within the framework of his fiction an adequate counterweight to this sort of evil, and there is promise of a certain kind in the figure of Kafka's initially intrepid explorer. He recoils, as he must, from the spectacle of wanton cruelty he observes in the penal colony, and recoils more especially from the representation of the violence as a species of justice. He is an outsider, and his detachment is an expression not merely of his alien status but of his official perspective as an observer, whose purpose is to examine without drawing conclusions to which he is not really entitled. He has sympathies, but Kafka sees to it that for the most part he contains them. Though the reader is perhaps moved to expect from the thoughtful explorer some sort of intervention on behalf of the ostensibly civilized values he apparently holds, Kafka insists that the explorer betray no will to escape his limitations as an exemplar of more or less lucid, disinterested observation and reflection. The evil observed by such a character is likely to seem to him at once appalling and interesting, and typically he will know better than to undertake an intervention in which he is too well bred to persist. If such a figure seems to us terribly disappointing—his analytic habits in the end no match for the reality he observes—his failure will surely seem to us perfectly familiar, a failure nicely illuminated by Karl Kraus when he wrote that "the most dangerous kind of stupidity is a keen understanding." The confrontation with evil produces in the explorer an understanding not at all commensurate with the magnitude of the

KAFKA, NAIPAUL, COETZEE

unfolding spectacle before him, and his inability to take arms against evil, to lift a proverbial finger, must have seemed to Kafka a sufficient indication of the "stupidity" that is satisfied, with whatever tremors of misgiving, with its own principled disinterestedness. In the end, the explorer's ignominious escape from the penal colony and his refusal to carry with him any reminder of the intractable dilemma he found there indicate Kafka's verdict on the man. He is, without question, not at all equal to the varieties of evil associated with the remarkable apparatus.

The confrontation with evil is central to the literature of the last century. Novels by Koestler and Grass, Solzhenitsyn and Semprun, Kundera and Manea, among others, have taught us how to think about evil in the context of war and totalitarian violence. Such novels, though they are to some degree invested in the problems of society and politics, are by no means sociological works. Though they aim—some of them at least—to embrace all aspects of the individual and collective experience of the people they examine, they are hardly systematic, and they tend to be more interested in ultimate or metaphysical questions than in settling political scores or mounting dissident postures. Grass's confrontation with evil in the *Danzig Trilogy* is concretely situated in mid-twentieth-century Germany, and is unthinkable outside the familiar parameters of recent German history. But Grass's fiction is neither positivist nor polemical, and his interest is largely in corruptions of language and spirit, the understanding of which is essential to an understanding of the evils to which human beings are susceptible.

Not surprisingly, the representation of evil will often seem particularly compelling when the scale of incident is small, the injury meted out apparently modest, the suffering almost tolerable to witness, and the prospects for effectual response more or less concrete. At the beginning and end of his book *In a Free State,* V. S. Naipaul sets brief vignettes that read like both fiction and memoir. In each one an observer, perhaps Naipaul himself, witnesses a form of cruelty or abuse that may well seem to some readers too trivial to stimulate reflections on evil. But Naipaul's book, which also contains a novella and two long stories, is clearly concerned with evil, which comes in many different forms. For Naipaul, the "trivial" incidents presented in his prologue and epilogue constitute varieties of evil, and therefore require a response commensurate with their importance.

In the prologue, set on a "dingy little Greek steamer," a diverse array of travelers—Greek, Austrian, Egyptian, Yugoslav, Lebanese—look on as a "tramp," possibly English, possibly some sort of literary man, but "grimy," elderly, and with "a tremulous worn face and wet blue eyes," is persistently threatened and tormented by two Lebanese passengers. Not much happens in the story, which steadily reminds us of the tramp's fragility, his "stained trouser-legs," his "distress," his inability to connect with anyone, his odd habit of looking, apparently, for "company" or "attention" while wanting really "not to be noticed." Clearly pathetic and distasteful, yet also in his way mildly fascinating, he inspires in Naipaul's narrator much the same distaste he inspires in others: "I feared to be involved with him," the narrator writes.

But soon we see that a certain mood has been gathering among the passengers, and we read that "it was to be like a tiger-hunt where bait is laid out and the hunter and spectators watch from the security of a platform." The tormenting of the tramp is to be conducted according to "the rules of [a] game" and to be pursued even if—especially if—the tramp himself refuses to "play." The game itself amounts to rather little, in such circumstances the usual sort of thing, perhaps, wherein people bored and angry and tired turn on someone defenseless, shout at him abusive epithets, snatch his rucksack, pretend to hit him, administer a less than lethal kick or two, fling him by his filthy scarf to the deck, reduce him to spluttering and humiliation and fear, drive him away into hiding, and strike renewed fear in him when at last he reappears to take a meal. Trivial, no doubt, familiar, so that in the end, with the passengers queuing for departure and "the passion" for the game definitely "over," the tramp and his trials will seem of no further interest at all, surely not to his tormentors.

But Naipaul set the modest vignette at the front of his masterful book because it seemed to him to announce something momentous that he wished, throughout the book, to examine in a number of settings and aspects. The problem of evil is central to the vignette as to everything in this work, and is particularly compelling in its very brief playing out precisely because what may be called "the absent cause" of the pointless suffering inflicted on the tramp is the passivity of those who merely observe. There is evil, genuine evil, in that passivity, Naipaul suggests. To be sure, the Lebanese men who do the actual tormenting are the actual, responsible agents in the usual sense of "agency" most of us understand. But their behavior, as described, is merely brutal in a limited, desultory way, their absorption in what is done clearly passionate, but for that very reason difficult to know how to think about, beyond the easy conclusion that such behavior is unfortunate, deplorable, a demonstration of the elementary fact that ordinary people sometimes or often allow themselves to become furious and passionate about things that have nothing whatever to do with the true sources of their own discontent.

The passivity of the onlookers, however, is more disturbing, even though it is not so immediately distressing as the short-term physical assault on the tramp. For, not passionate about the tramp, not caught up in an overmastering frenzy of persecutory zeal, not feeling the tramp's very presence among them as an insufferable humiliation, an offense against their very dignity, the others might have been expected to respond to the assault with some conviction that it was a thing not to be done. Why was it a thing not to be done? Not merely because it was cruel and needless, surely, or because it was pitched at a man defenseless and miserable. No, the assault was a thing not to be done and not to be borne because it was so obviously an assault upon the very idea that there are in this world things not to be done and not to be tolerated.

The force of Naipaul's vignette has much to do with its not confronting us with an extreme situation and thus not allowing us as readers the excuses or absolutions routinely invoked when "innocent" people fail to behave as they should. Often in discussions of extreme situations one hears it said that it is impossible to pass judgment upon those who merely look on passively when terrible things are done. How can you know, it is asked, what you would have done had you been present in terrible times and had to risk your life in order to intervene, to lift a finger against the brutality visited upon other human beings? Who can know what will seem tolerable to ordinary people, to us, when enormous courage is required to intervene or protest?

But such questions are not asked in Naipaul's prologue, a first-person narrative whose narrator would seem to be the author himself. And it does seem to the reader that here it would surely take very little for an ordinary person, for the narrator himself, to intervene, or at least to protest, however mildly, the cruelty of the assault. Obviously, Naipaul has no fear of demonizing anyone, no reluctance to make characters, us, himself, look weak, vicious, complicit in atrocities. He is no kind of sentimental humanist. In fact, in the prologue, he permits everyone to seem perfectly awful, disgraceful, unappealing. We may infer on the basis of what we are shown that the best of Naipaul's characters are morally blank, indifferent ciphers, with nothing whatever to recommend them as human beings. And if the narrator himself feared to be "involved" with the tramp—Naipaul's word is deliberately imprecise—that must be the consequence of his visceral aversion not only to the tramp but to the other degraded beings who together make up the human fraternity on the God-forsaken Greek steamer. He has nothing to fear from the tramp, nothing but contagion of the sort one may well absorb by considering oneself a member of a degraded, rather worthless mass of people from whom even minimally decent behavior may rarely be expected.

Evil is by no means too strong a word to use in connection with Naipaul's prologue. One feels it circulating stealthily in the foul ether that permeates the little narrative. It is a corrosive presence, something that defiles everything it touches, reveals the tainted interior of every ₁₄₃ single person who belongs, truly belongs, to the compact, diverse, yet morally undifferentiated fraternity. The name of the evil is never given, but it is no less obvious for all that: when what is not to be done is done, and even those who have little to lose were they to protest are silent or passively complicit: there, Naipaul suggests, is evil.

The issue is made rather more explicit, the question of "involvement" more forcefully brought to the fore, in the epilogue. Where in the prologue the steamer was headed for Egypt, here the narrator travels there by air. At a guest house he and other "sunglassed tourists" are served coffee by a "brisk middle-aged Egyptian in Arab dress," while all around them "the hummocked sand was alive with little desert children." He notes that, though "the desert was clean, the air was clean," the "children were very dirty," that is, unsavory, perhaps even repellent. There is no tendency here to be moved by the exoticism or comeliness of the filthy desert waifs. Concern for what may be done to them can have little to do with them as particular attractive beings or even as notably vulnerable people in need of "humanitarian" protection.

And so it is that when the Egyptian waiter with a "camel-whip at his waist" devises a part for himself in what is clearly "an Egyptian game with Egyptian rules," the narrator's interest may not be said to be a function of his attraction to or concern for the desert children. On that score Naipaul is entirely unambiguous. And what is the game he observes? Not permitted to enter the grounds of the guest house, the children come as near as they dare to the tourists, who entice them with pieces of food, half-sandwiches and apples, thrown onto the sand so that the children will fetch them and receive for their venturesomeness the frantic, excited whip-blows of the Egyptian waiter. "It was hardly a disturbance," the narrator notes. The tourists were "cool," one of them amused enough to stand up and point his camera to record the game, while others "paid no attention." Again, a small thing, no doubt, and to speak of the whip-blows as a species of evil when the blows do not deter the children from scrabbling forward again and again would perhaps seem excessive. For if this small "game" is evil, and evil in spite of its apparently having no effect on the dignity of the children who are its willing victims, then what words must one use for deeds of an entirely different magnitude?

And yet, the narrator tells us, "I saw that my hand was trembling," so that he is moved, compelled, to act, though he makes no "decision" to do so, and is aware of "lucidity, and anxiety . . . only when I was almost on the man with the camel-whip." The unraveling, the termination of the "game" is then effected at once, the narrator "shouting" as he takes the whip away, throws it on the sand, and threatens to "report" the incident to "Cairo," whatever that may mean.

Nothing in the mood or posture of Naipaul's narrator suggests that he has the slightest appetite for theatrics or for aggressive intervention of any kind. From the moment he acts, he observes that his behavior seems to the others present extravagant and peculiar, puzzling to the children, perhaps a bit embarrassing, and surely unnecessary to most of the tourists looking on. The narrator feels exposed, "futile," a figure utterly without interest to the several witnesses who might, one supposes, have been moved in some way by his gesture. But indifference and boredom are all he has inspired. Worse, as he prepares to be driven away, he notes that the children will soon be back to resume the game, "raking the sand" for what will be thrown out.

As often in Naipaul, the communicated sense is that things are as they are because they can be no other. One would have to be "innocent," as he says, to believe that the world will substantially change in response to gestures passionate or lucid, well-intentioned or malevolent. Yet the narrator's hand "trembled" when he observed the grotesque little game enacted before him, and he found himself shouting, creating the sort of spectacle he clearly loathed, and for no good reason, given his certain knowledge that nothing whatever would change as the result of his intervention. Presumably, his hand trembled because he felt that something critical was at stake, that some deep violation would occur beyond the violation already there before him, were he not to bestir himself to intervene—however futile his brief gesture. If there is in the man's whipping of the children not evil exactly, there would be, so Naipaul seems to feel, evil precisely in a comfortable, bland toleration of the thing, as if it were of no importance whatever, as if nothing could mean anything in the face of one's settled impression that human beings are never more than an indifferent lot, casually cruel, casually amused, casually bored, casually able to regard others as things responsive to their will, and just as able to abjure responsibility for having done what is anyhow commonplace. The "futile" intervention thus becomes a sort of protest against the passivity, detachment, reasonableness, and fear of exposure or ridicule or futility that together constitute, though on a very modest scale, a form of evil familiar to everyone.

Naipaul operates from no orthodox sense of a unitary truth that may be said to confer meaning upon things. But the futile gesture or protest he enacts in the epilogue is not a gratuitous or arbitrary action. Neither does it proceed from a denial of reality or a self-deception. He knows that there is meaning in his gesture—knows perhaps without quite being able to formulate what he knows—and though his gesture will in the long run make nothing happen, it affirms something essential. He makes no untenable claim for his gesture, and refuses to blind himself to the loathsome spectacle he observes. But he surely sees that his is not an arbitrary gesture without significant meaning. The failure to effect a change in the routine ways of the world need not entail a moral failure. The simple refusal to yield utterly to the usual evils, to the laws or ways of the world—what are sometimes referred to as the facts of life—is enough to confer upon a person some significant moral stature.

Of all contemporary writers, J. M. Coetzee has had the most striking and sustaining things to tell us about evil and the struggle to achieve moral dignity. Though his fictions are often built around figures caught up in self-loathing and resigned to irrelevance, he contrives persistently to test his characters, to demand that they make serious choices or register fundamentally their failure to choose. Evil in Coetzee's universe is not only the thing that is done, but the thing that tempts or provokes. It is in many ways the primal condition, the given, the means by which we come to know or to think about what we are.

The encounter with evil is perhaps most pointed in the novel *Waiting for the Barbarians*. A magistrate long resident in a modest frontier settlement finds himself joined by a security official, an army colonel named

Joll, who has been sent to assist the magistrate in the interrogation and handling of suspects. Though there is little crime in the settlement, Joll and his superiors have reason to believe that a rebellion is under way, that "barbarians" are preparing to overrun the settlement and other regions of the unnamed country. At no point in the novel are those suspicions definitively confirmed by events, but the consistently brutal mistreatment of prisoners remains from beginning to end a central fact of the novel, and the testing indispensable to Coetzee's purpose requires that the magistrate respond to that brutality.

Coetzee makes nothing easy, which is an aspect of his commitment to the truth of things as he understands them. He knows evil, and knows how to show us what it is, but he knows too that there are evils not so readily identifiable and all too easy to confuse with something else. To torture a person on the suspicion that in time he may reveal something one wishes to learn—so Coetzee insists—is indisputably evil. To treat a person as one would a beast, or worse, is evil. There are, in other words, categorical judgments that most human beings are presumably not reluctant to affirm, and Coetzee shares in the assumptions underwriting those judgments. This we infer as readers of his books, and so we infer that he regards as evil other varieties of behavior less amenable to categorical stricture.

From the moment Joll appears, on the first page of Coetzee's novel, we see that the magistrate wonders at him: wonders first at his dark glasses, then at his cool resolution and his easy way of talking about torture. When he questions Joll and learns that he harbors no misgivings whatever about the "set procedures" he is prepared to go through, the magistrate is briefly appalled and troubled, though he holds back and recalls quickly who he is. "On the other hand," he reflects, "who am I to assert my distance from him? I drink with him, I eat with him . . . I afford him every assistance." Though he rapidly acknowledges that his "easy years are coming to an end," when he "could sleep with a tranquil heart," content to do his duty, "serving out my days on this lazy frontier waiting to retire," he hopes still to muddle along without troubling himself very much about things he can do little to alter. He finds it difficult to be "more than correct" in his bearing toward Joll, yet he is determined upon extending the elementary courtesies so far as he can manage them. A modest man, he wishes not to see what he sees and think what he thinks, yet, looking at Joll, he is moved to "wonder how he felt the very first time":

Did he, invited as an apprentice to twist the pincers or turn the screw or whatever it is they do, shudder even a little to know that at that instant he was trespassing into the forbidden? I find myself wondering too whether he has a private ritual of purification, carried out behind closed doors, to enable him to return and break bread with other men . . . or has the bureau created new men who can pass without disquiet between the unclean and the clean?

These are essential questions that Coetzee's magistrate raises early in the novel, and it is the burden of the narrative that follows to be worthy of them. In some ways, Coetzee's willingness to employ the language of "trespass" and the "forbidden," "the unclean and the clean," is one of the more bracing aspects of a work committed to the examination of evil. But equally bracing is his refusal to allow the magistrate employing that language to take comfort in the assumption of distance or difference. Though he is in unmistakable ways different, by no means a torturer, his subsequent intimate relations with an injured "barbarian woman" call to mind the zone of the torturer in their implicitly coercive though never brutal dimension. More, as the novel proceeds, early and late, and especially in his relations with the woman, the magistrate reflects that "the distance between myself and her torturers . . . is negligible." He had seemed to himself a modest man, small in ambition and intensity, a man responsible only as a servant is responsible for carrying out orders. But he is made to realize, for example, that "I should never have allowed the gates of the town to be opened to people who assert that there are higher considerations than those of decency." A man not given to oratory or sententiousness and characteristically resistant to the higher sentiments, he feels "contagion" in the air he breathes as one who has allowed evil to have occurred on his watch.

His consolation, his justification, had always been the law. To act within the confines of the law had seemed to him, as to most others, acceptable, and where the law itself had seemed deficient or unjust, that was felt to be an acceptable defect, given the protection offered most human beings by the law most of the time. He had at times felt, he recalls, that the law was more than occasionally unjust, and had itself caused—as in Joll's brutal abuse of his prisoners—unspeakable suffering. But he had known how to deal with that. "When some men suffer unjustly," he had said to himself, "it is the fate of those who witness their suffering to suffer the shame of it." Willing to bear witness to the shame of a shared injustice and to the shame of a vaguely shared responsibility, he had been able to go on with his life, "until," as he says, " one day events overtook me."

There is a great deal to reflect upon in Coetzee's novel that bears on the subject of evil, but in some way the most compelling feature is the impression it conveys that bearing witness may not be—cannot be—enough. Shame is a constitutive component of a human response to witnessing what is not to be done, the shame, presumably, or humiliation or horror that Naipaul's protagonist registers however briefly in the epilogue to his book, when he rises to intervene in spite of knowing that it will not matter. But the gesture there is more than the experience of shame and more than the bearing witness that is done when a writer points and says *look* and *see* and *absorb* and *recoil*. The shame there, in Naipaul, is enacted, as it is enacted in a more protracted way in Coetzee's novel.

Naipaul, we recall, had described the intervention in his epilogue as futile, quite as the explorer in Kafka's story might well have regarded his own intervention had he done more than bear witness to the brutality he observed. Likewise, there is obvious futility in the exertions of Coetzee's magistrate who, for all the suffering he brings upon himself, ends up with nothing to show for his pains at novel's end. And yet neither the sense of futility nor the shadow of impending suffering can effectively cancel the gesture of the magistrate, who is moved to respond to evil simply because he cannot do otherwise. He takes no stand and has no position to defend, or at least no position beyond the sense that there are things in the world not to be tolerated, not even when one has no hope of altering a thing.

Coetzee's magistrate has no army at his command and no following in the settlement. He has no experience of revolt or protest, no record of dignified resistance to anything. Intervention, in his case, can only assume the form of assertion, the verbal equivalent of removing the whip from the hand of a man who will immediately take it back and resume his work after dealing summarily with the intrusive fool. When the magistrate throws caution to the wind and says things that can only enrage the other servants of empire who have taken control of the settlement, he undertakes a gesture whose futility is at once palpable and irrelevant. He says that, of course, the empire's expropriation of barbarian lands is disgraceful, as are the "acts of wanton cruelty." But he is especially moved to describe what is "disheartening" and a more widespread species of evil. "It is," he says, the "contempt for the barbarians . . . contempt . . . founded on nothing more substantial than differences in table manners, variations in the structure of the eyelid." How, he wonders, "do you eradicate contempt," and would it not be refreshing for "these barbarians" to "rise up and teach us a lesson so that we would learn to respect them?"

These are mostly idle reflections, particularly as regards the notion that a meaningful lesson will be learned when the subject peoples rise up. But the magistrate surely knows that this is an idle thought, and does not suppose that any such eventuality is likely. The point in Coetzee's handling of this material is that the magistrate is moved to identify with the other, and to utter sentiments that are bound to make him seem dangerous and unstable to the guardians of empire. Though he knows himself to be weak and anything but reliable, though he is skeptical about the "distance" between himself and Joll, he knows too that in his heart he wishes not to become the thing he loathes and fears. What becomes important to him, as to Coetzee, is that in some fundamental way he not be "contaminated." It may seem to him, as to us, that by refusing to join in the commission of atrocity he will save himself from contamination. It may seem, moreover, that by recording what he observes, truthfully bearing witness not only to what has been done by Joll but by himself in his own unsavory transactions with a subject population, he will preserve something.

But he understands, gradually, that this will not be what is needed, that he will need to risk exposure to ridicule, to the charge of futility, to isolation and suffering, if he is to avoid contamination. The evil, so obvious when it is incarnated as the torture of innocents, is compelling also in its less dramatic forms. "I was the lie that empire tells itself when times are easy," the magistrate says, the lie, in other words, that evil consists only or principally in the wanton infliction of suffering, and not in the failure to assume responsibility for the fate of those with whom one lives or among whom one suddenly finds oneself.

Coetzee understands that people are largely created or influenced by the circumstances in which they live. The magistrate is as much a product of empire as is Joll. But there is, just the same, will and agency and self-consciousness in Coetzee's more reflective characters, and Coetzee does not permit them to take refuge in the delusion that they are "trapped" by their leaders, controlled utterly by the ideology of the dominant political system, or merely ordinary and not to be held responsible for things they can do little to change.

KAFKA, NAIPAUL, COETZEE

In this sense, Coetzee, like Naipaul, provides in his work an essential corrective to the standard discourse on evil that has become customary in Western intellectual circles. Perhaps "collective guilt," as Charles Simic would have it, is ultimately an insupportable idea. Perhaps there is in arguments that tend to "demonize" whole peoples a spurious political motive. But there is—so Naipaul and Coetzee suggest—an evil that is not simply "deeds that must be punished," as Auden wrote, but something closer to "our dishonest mood of denial." We know, as these writers insist, what is expected of us, though often we deny what we know. There is evil in that denial, in the usually comforting assumption that if nothing effectual can be done to bring a permanent halt to evil deeds, we have no binding responsibility to do anything at all. Evil, in Coetzee especially, is to be understood as the failure to regard ourselves as fully responsible beings. "Psychology," Coetzee says in his book *Doubling the Point*, "is no excuse," and neither is circumstance. What we have, what we know, is "one man, one soul." If we cannot acknowledge that much at least, then we have no hope of thinking about evil beyond identifying its most obvious, brutal, or lurid features, which are always apt to seem so remote and exotic that the thing itself will seem not to have anything much to do with us.

12

PATHOS AND RESIGNATION

PAT BARKER

There is little inclination to elegy or nostalgia in the work of Pat Barker. *Regeneration*, *The Eye in the Door*, and *The Ghost Road*, her trilogy of novels set during World War I, recover sentiments and issues that were once compelling and still seem in her hands remarkably interesting, though often out of reach. The Europe of Barker's imagination is a real place worth remembering, but decidedly dead and gone. She evokes the world shattered forever by the Great War in prose notable for its disinfatuation, while the war itself seems to us, as we read, a conflict no one could conceivably wish to reenact or celebrate. There were, to be sure, heroes who fought in that war, and others who exhibited a variety of strengths both primitive and ethical. But Barker devotes little attention to sublimities. She looks at everything with an eye unclouded by romantic longing. She is a writer for whom seeing things as they are, or were, is more important than creating myths about the past or about staunchness of spirit or honor or obligation.

Of course the commentary inspired by Barker's trilogy makes much of its "antiwar" status. Routinely it is said to be "so much more than . . . excellent historical" fiction, work that functions also as "a cautionary tale about the price of cultural conformity." And indeed it is possible to see why Barker should be read in this way, though she is not, clearly, a writer of "cautionary" tales or a novelist primarily interested in ideas or positions. No one can read the final book in her trilogy (*The Ghost Road*) and not be appalled by the senseless waste of human life it anatomizes. And yet we feel as we read that Barker is more interested in actual people and encounters than in their potentially exemplary function. Just so, no one who reads the second novel in the trilogy (*The Eye in the Door*) can fail to see that Barker herself is disappointed in the conventional limitations exhibited even by people who seem in many respects impressively intelligent. But there are no sustained sermons or lamentations in the novel, no parables or allegories. Typically, Barker grows rapidly impatient with argument. To be sure, there is a good deal of reflection, especially in the first volume of the trilogy (*Regeneration*), on justification and choice and the "*fundamental* questions." Characters often admire the "rational" qualities: precision, restraint, honesty. But the intermittent debates that punctuate *Regeneration* are not permitted to add up. An air of unease circulates steadily in Barker's fiction, and even her most thoughtful characters achieve what passes for resolution only by willfully banishing the doubts and scruples that are so much a part of them when they are most fully themselves.

152   Of course, it is the business of war and of those who wage war to make people other than what they are. That conclusion is hard to avoid as we read Barker's trilogy. Characters accustomed to agonizing over difficult moral issues are urged in wartime—by colleagues, officers, journalists, and therapists—to get over their misgivings and commit to the job of killing at hand. In *Regeneration*, Dr. Rivers must find ways to convince combat soldiers disabled by hysterical paralysis, terrifying nightmares, tremors, stammerings, memory lapses, deafness, and blindness that their "unconscious protest" against the war they have been fighting must be overcome, their sentiments denied, their scruple quietly consigned to irrelevance. The poet Siegfried Sassoon, a key figure in the novel, becomes a candidate for treatment because he has drafted a document of conscientious objection while serving in the army. That he has served heroically is not in doubt. Neither does anyone doubt that his protest is sincere, his explanations "impressive," his disdain for ordinary "complacent," "unimaginative" civilians as pronounced as any war recruiter could wish. But under the circumstances of war he must be counseled not to be the complex person he is, not to insist upon making others uncomfortable. "You seem," Dr. Rivers tells his patient, "to have a very powerful *anti*-war neurosis," and however much the doctor may agree with Sassoon's view of the war, it is his "duty" to send his patient back into combat. The war determines entirely what must be done, as it identifies what "values" are and are not to be credited. Barker's novel demonstrates not only that in war human beings must often be urged not to be what they most deeply are, but that even the best and the brightest are entirely complicit in this radical subversion of authenticity.

"Are you," a soldier asks Sassoon late in *The Eye in the Door*, "the same Sassoon?" The question as intended is innocent—the man asking it wishes simply to ascertain the identity of his companion—but it helps to lay bare one issue at the heart of Barker's trilogy. As Dr. Rivers notes, Sassoon's protest "was derived from a striving for consistency, for singleness of being in a man whose internal divisions had been dangerously deepened by the war." The striving in itself may be admirable, Rivers suggests, but it entails in the circumstances of war a demand that may well be impossible to meet. After all, for a soldier to achieve "singleness of being" will require that he banish misgivings about the purpose and conduct of the war in which he has enlisted. Should his misgivings be reasonable, he will need, in the interests of "singleness," to disavow reasonableness and to give himself over to a form of unreason that dare not acknowledge what it is.

153

The immense challenge Barker sets herself in her war trilogy is to set reason against unreason, and authenticity against inauthenticity, in such a way as to unsettle our grasp of these terms. Often in these novels, principles would seem to be at issue and to underlie the actions of characters. But Barker insists—or allows her novels insistently to suggest—that principles are merely principles, as singleness is but one paltry idea, and that really we ought not to allow ourselves to be governed exclusively by ideas or by reasonableness. For one thing, we can never successfully govern ourselves exclusively as we think we ought, and reason itself, as we so well know, is often a defective instrument for reaching conclusions.

More important, Barker forces her readers to ask, again and again, how most of us can decently carry on without capitulating entirely to disillusionment and cynicism. For it is one thing to concede that we are divided, and that we are sometimes required—by circumstance, by obligation—to pretend that we are not divided or to behave as if we were not. But it is another thing entirely to feel, in the face of these concessions, that everything we do is a matter of pretence. One feature of Barker's trilogy that may well seem unfathomable to us is the absence of cynicism in characters who have good reason to believe that nothing they do has much connection with the ostensive reasons assigned to their actions.

Of course, without a considerable exertion of the historical imagination it is difficult for many of us to fathom the elementary sense of obligation that seems so real to many of Barker's characters. Likewise, we can only wonder at their belief—can it be, truly, a belief?—that the loss of their one and only life is not too high a price to pay for the satisfaction of having answered a call. We understand much more readily what Lieutenant Prior means when in a letter to Dr. Rivers from the front he writes "in my present situation the only sane thing to do is to run away," and we are—some of us—apt to be disappointed in him when he says "and I will not do it." To be sure, as he acknowledges, he has thereby "passed" the "test" administered to him by "fate," but it may also be that he has failed the more important test, that is, to make himself do "the only sane thing to do."

In *Regeneration*, Sassoon and the poet Wilfred Owen meet and begin at once to discuss their impressions of the war. "Sometimes when you're alone," Owen says:

154

> In the trenches, I mean, at night, you get the sense of something *ancient*. As if the trenches had always been there. You know one trench we held, it had skulls in the side. You looked back along and . . . Like mushrooms. And do you know, it was actually *easier* to believe they were men from Marlboro's army than to think they'd been alive two years ago. It's as if all other wars had somehow . . . distilled themselves into this war, and that makes it something you . . . almost can't challenge. It's like a very deep voice saying, *Run along, little man. Be thankful if you survive.*

There is in this passage an accent I do not like, and I must suppose—perhaps it is wishful thinking—that a great many of Barker's readers will like it no better. To be sure, we can understand that a sensitive young man will be moved as Owen is moved by "the sense of something *ancient*" in the trench experience. But do we fathom, really, what follows from this, that we must therefore feel small and insignificant and unworthy to protest this sense of accumulated history? For that is what Owen seems to me to suggest. The present war is to be understood, after all, as a distillation of all the other wars that have been and, presumably, all the later wars that will follow, as surely as the nights follow the days. To set oneself against the present war would be, in this sense, to set oneself against history, necessity, and reality.

Barker does not allow herself to challenge Owen's sense of the thing, or not, at least, where challenge would be chiefly felt, at the point of Owen's eloquent recitation. In fact, she responds by permitting Sassoon to affirm Owen's sense of the matter. "I had a similar experience," Sassoon says, referring to "the flares going up" one night "against the skyline. . . . What you see every night. Only I seemed to be seeing it from the future. A hundred years from now they'll still be plowing up skulls. And I seemed to be in that time and looking back. I think I saw our ghosts."

This is the long view with a vengeance, the present conflict viewed "from the future," a ghostly thing, distilled, as it were, the one war now indistinguishable from "all other wars," protest or misgiving therefore as hopeless as a tiny fist clenched against the night. The "angel of history" sees things in this way, as Walter Benjamin describes it: "His face is turned towards the past. Where we perceive a chain of events, he sees one single catastrophe which keeps piling wreckage and hurls it in front of his feet." From this perspective, Benjamin suggests, it is difficult if not impossible even to imagine making "whole what has been smashed." It is not the business of Barker's trilogy to assert with finality any such perspective, as if she were staking out a position. But it does often appear that for Barker, politics can be at best a gesturing without any significant prospect of hope, not conceivably a stay against confusion so much as the further addition to "the pile of debris" the angel observes "before him," which "grows" inexorably "skyward."

Of course, the trilogy contains a great many observations and instances, and it is perhaps misleading to reduce Barker's understanding of war and society to a single outlook. In *Regeneration*, to be sure, the intermittent emphasis upon Sassoon's trial of conscience is promising for a work that aims at least in part to engage political issues. If we feel, nonetheless, that much of what we take in is hard to fathom, that is because the sense of obligation on display is sometimes unreachably high, while the recourse to "reality" or "reasonableness" is often unimaginative and disappointing. Ordinarily when people, soldiers or civilians, behave badly or well, we have little trouble understanding them, so long as we take them to have acted out of ignorance or custom or fear or ordinary sentiment. Far more difficult to understand is behavior that seems the result of an inability to think at all, to imagine alternatives, to resist an order or contradict a platitude. Barker does not indict her characters for their limitations, and does not find reprehensible what her readers are apt to find puzzling. We accept that as readers we are outside the moment Barker evokes and would surely find less puzzling the assumptions and reflexes she describes if we participated in the worldview shared by her characters. But this readerly generosity (or incapacity) does not make us wonder any less why

Barker should see what she observes as if she too were not outside the observed moment.

Like other works that study war, Barker's trilogy would seem to accept that there can be no coherent moral system by means of which to judge the behavior of people in wartime. In fact, Barker would seem also to accept, as Thomas Nagel has written, that in war there can be "no course free of guilt and responsibility for evil." But it is not a philosophical case the trilogy constructs, and Barker's renunciation of a critical outsider's perspective reflects both an aesthetic scruple and a troubling moral detachment. The war trilogy is decidedly not antiwar fiction, and in fact uses "history" to avoid a lively engagement with the very issues it raises.

To be sure, Barker is troubled by what she observes, but she is also all too eager to affirm the sophisticated insider's view of the war spectacle. "It's odd, isn't it?" Prior says at the end of *The Eye in the Door*. "In spite of everything—I mean in spite of Not Believing in the War and Not Having Faith in Our Generals and all that, it still seems the only *clean* place to be." This Barker permits to pass for "depth of understanding" because she so scrupulously refuses to stand outside the perspective shared by her own characters, most of whom are permitted to exist for us as decent men, at their worst men of "two natures," subject to the "primitive duality" familiarly associated with Jekyll and Hyde. More than once in her trilogy, Barker has characters think of Stevenson's story "as a shorthand for internal divisions." Such divisions make men think of themselves as susceptible to competing impulses. Though they may judge themselves as they judge others, and even resort occasionally to terms like "cowardice" and "honor," they demand of themselves chiefly consistency or transparency, and they tend to take seriously the idea of doing one's duty, even when they are not certain what that entails. Knowing as they do that men are capable of many different things, not all of them compatible with the standard raised by their "better" selves, they accept what would otherwise seem unacceptable, and Barker is not moved to correct them.

The point is made in many ways, none more suggestive than in the "fucking marvelous story" told in passing to Lieutenant Billy Prior in *The Eye in the Door*. The story has to do with "a man who found a [poisonous] snake half-dead and nursed it back to life," only to be bitten by it. "And with his last gasp," the man asked, "but why? I saved you, I fed you, I nursed you, why did you bite me?" To which the snake responds, "But you knew I was a snake."

Does Barker, then, suggest that it is in the nature of men to betray and disappoint one another, even as they inevitably betray their own sentiments and scruples? Is it sufficient for her decent men to say, in one way or another, what the snake says: "But you knew," or "you should have known," or "how can any of us be expected to be more or other than we are?"

Dr. William Rivers is surely what passes for a decent fellow in Barker's trilogy. A "thorough-going rationalist," he is also the person most needed and admired by the various soldier-sufferers to whom we are introduced. Sassoon regards him as a "substitute father," and even those who resist him and insult him acknowledge that they "might do a lot worse." Though he does genuinely care for those who are in therapy with him, the most precious gift he wishes to give them is not his concern but the example of his perfect therapeutic scruple. This scruple he associates with lessons learned in the course of earlier voyages he had made as a young man to the Solomon Islands. From the responses of islanders to his own views on a variety of subjects he learns that others can be as uncomprehending of his assumptions as he of theirs. "And I suddenly saw," Rivers reports, with a kind of schoolboy freshness, as if he had continued to think it a momentous discovery, "that their reactions to my society were neither more nor less valid than mine to theirs." Of course, Rivers goes on, white men naturally and unselfconsciously assume that they are "the measure of all things," so that evidence to the contrary will inevitably seem striking. "And suddenly," Rivers goes on, "I saw not only that we weren't a measure of all things, but that *there was no measure*." Extraordinary, the glide in what may appear to be an argument but is in fact a sort of a confession. The good Dr. Rivers moves from the observation that people see things in different ways to the "understanding" that "reactions" of one sort "were"—presumably *can be*—"neither more nor less valid" than any others. Not only are "we" not "the measure of all things," but we are required to accept that there is *"no measure"* at all.

As a novelist, Barker is preternaturally aware that in fiction, views are merely views, and that they are best understood as coming from a particular person. Rivers is not for her a mouthpiece. When he speaks we are moved to think of him—*his* needs, *his* stance, *his* obligation to *this* patient and *this* task. When we consider his views we recall—we must recall—that Prior once accused him of being a "strip of empathetic wallpaper," and that, at another point, he persuaded him to conclude that he had "put your mind's eye *out*," caused himself not to think certain thoughts or feel certain unwanted feelings. Rivers's susceptibility to the conclusion that there is *no measure* or that one view can be no more "valid" than another is best understood as a reflection of the kind of man he is. We may embrace or reject his conclusions, but we will do so without supposing that there is a reliable "measure" available to underwrite our response. Barker is too shrewd to force this way of thinking on us, but as a novelist she does nothing to help us resist it. She is not a dialectical writer, not interested in setting competing ideas against one another to see which is the stronger or to discover how much, in the end, they complement or resemble one another. Rivers is compelling and attractive because he is lively, humane, and tolerant, but he is not a dialectician. He knows where he wishes to go and where he hopes to take others. The stance is not at all disinterested, however much he takes himself to be a scientist. If he is far too sophisticated to operate from inflexible beliefs, he does believe in the therapeutic imperative, and he allows himself to serve the interests of established power because he associates responsibility—rather too conveniently—with doing one's job. To read the trilogy as if its intention were to ratify Rivers's perspective is to perhaps read it as Barker wishes, but it is also to feel that we are insufficiently supplied with a substantial counterweight.

Of course, it may well be said, Prior is a very different sort of central character, and he dominates much of the action in the trilogy. Early and late and to varying degrees he struggles with Rivers and regards therapy itself with a thoroughgoing hostility. More important, where Rivers is typically kindly and tolerant, Prior can be brutal and disdainful. Where Rivers seems not to have any sexual life at all, Prior constantly needs sex and finds it wherever he can. Walking past a bombed site, Prior notes "some affinity with places where the established order has been violently assailed," and he acknowledges that in sexual relations, as elsewhere, he is "capable of real sadism" and likely to attract persons who "needed to be hurt."

In fact, Barker devotes considerable attention to Prior's sexual activity, and her narrative is most literal when she is describing the stirring of cocks, the clasping of buttocks, the stroking of bellies, and all of the greasings, tongue flickings, and sucking-offs that make for what one of Prior's partners, Charles Manning, refers to as "a good fucking." Only slightly less literal are the descriptions of Pryor's relations with Sarah, whose "yellow skin" and "ginger hair" are "some effect of the chemicals she worked with" in a factory. Barker is as adept at capturing the permutations of sexual avidity as she is at noticing how, even in the throes of sexual transport, characters will often be moved to think of parents and role models and unwanted assumptions. This is no less true of Prior than of others, though it is more like him to hang over Sarah as she works him over and watch "the stretched mouth, the slit eyes, the head thrown back until it seemed her spine must crack," only to think of "other faces" and to reflect that "the dying looked like that." Barker sharply registers the waywardness of Prior's imagination, though she also seems rather too fond of such radical juxtapositions. Similarly, she is too proud of her own illusionless handling of sex, her ability to treat it largely as an affair of the body, her knowledge of the relevant grossly physical particulars. In this, Barker may be said to share with Prior an aversion to mere sentiment, a compulsion to call things by their rightful names, and a tendency to be offended when anything like a swerve into delusion is detected.

At the same time, Barker is very much with Prior at those moments when he seems rather more sympathetic than we had thought possible. In *The Ghost Road*, some of which is given over to Prior's journal entries, Prior thinks of a man he "bayoneted." "What worries me," he writes, "is that he was middle-aged. Odd really—it's supposed to be golden youth you mourn for. But he was so obviously somebody who should have been at home, watching his kids grow up . . . and yes you *could* see all of this in his face—with some people you can. Some people do look exactly what they are. *Fuck it*."

Obviously this is, at its core, an utterly conventional reflection, familiar to us from a great many sources, not least the war poems of Thomas Hardy ("The Man He Killed"). But it is not, for Prior, at all typical or conventional, and Barker would seem also to credit the reflection for its resistance to the cliché about "golden youth you mourn for." Surely nothing is set into the narrative to undercut the authenticity of Prior's reflection, and if his reflection is in its way easy—the reflection after all costs Prior very little, and clearly doesn't worry him much at all—Prior effectively banishes any further exertion along these lines with the words "*fuck it*." Do some people "look exactly what they are"? It may be, it may not be, but either way, with a little regret or a lot of regret, people, all of us, do what we do, *fuck it*, and there is nothing anyone can introduce to alter that very comprehensive fact. So Barker would seem to suggest, with a steadiness of purpose that is admirable.

PAT BARKER

Less admirable is Barker's proceeding, as she does, by juxtaposing two such different central characters as Rivers and Prior without following out the differences so as to discover something she herself did not already know. At bottom, Rivers and Prior are very much on the same page and do not represent fundamentally divergent perspectives. Unlike Rivers, Prior is not a pleasant man. His way to self-control and maturity apparently entails a good deal more internal conflict than is readily observable in Rivers. But in the end, as Prior himself observes, the affinities are more important than the differences. In Rivers, he says, "the power to heal, if you like, springs directly from some sort of wound or deformity in him." Like Prior, Rivers "has a lot of strengths, but he isn't working from strength . . . in fact, for me," Prior goes on, "it's the best thing about him."

160

This sense of the thing is not in itself objectionable. Prior may well be right about the affinities, and if he is not, his observation has at least the virtue of suggesting what he needs to tell himself in order to make Rivers "acceptable." Having fought Rivers from the first, and having resented his "inexorable" efforts to break through Prior's stubborn resistance to therapeutic intervention, Prior has come a long way to the acknowledgment that Rivers does indeed have "the power to heal." But in the novel, these men are intended to function as largely antagonistic figures, their palpable differences as people suggestive of other differences, and the decision to bring out their affinities and thereby to erase or subordinate other potential differences is significant.

How significant we may begin to grasp when we observe that Prior, near the end of the trilogy's final volume, is made to recall the opportunity he had passed up five months earlier to get out of the war and take a desk job at the Ministry of Munitions: "Well, here I am, in what passes for a dug-out," he writes in a late journal entry. "And I look around me at all these faces and all I can think is: What an utter bloody fool I would have been not to come back." We cannot imagine Rivers crouched in that dugout saying any such thing, but of course we do know that he had hoped for just such a development in Prior, that is, for just such a robust affirmation of the rightness of the commitment, whatever the awfulness of the ostensive "cause." If Rivers had at some point, as Prior observed, put his "mind's eye *out*" so as not to see with his full capacities what was going on around him, so Prior here would seem also to have come around to the robust virtue of a merely partial vision stoutly held.

If we say that Barker does not use the conflict between Prior and Rivers to discover anything she did not already know, that would suggest that she holds too firmly to the view of things underwritten by Rivers, with his "terminal stiff upper lip," as he once calls it. In a way, the very structure of the trilogy, with Rivers and his several grateful soldier-patients at the center, almost requires that, if Barker were to follow out an alternative vision, she would need to take on Rivers. But she likes Rivers too much for that, admires too entirely his intelligence and scruple and his own struggle to deal with or at least compensate for the wound he carries. Apparently Barker felt that in making Rivers fully believable, which is to say conflicted, thoughtful, vulnerable, occasionally irritating, she would loosen our attachment to him and allow us to think against the grain of his sentiments.

161

But in fact, by bringing Prior and the others around to Rivers, Barker leaves us with his perspective as the sole dominant possibility in the novel. It does not help matters that so much of the final book of the trilogy is devoted to Rivers returning in memory to his early experience living with a South Pacific tribe. This aspect of the book might have been used to furnish an alternate sense of things, but neither Rivers nor Barker will permit that to develop. The headhunting of the tribe is delicately presented, so that for all of the differences Rivers notes as between the sense of the sacred in the one culture and his own sense of what constitutes the "highest value in the world," the sense of shared values steadily and deliberately emerges.

Prior, moreover, in another journal entry, is permitted to reflect on Rivers as follows: "Sometimes I used to think he was back with his fucking head-hunters—he really does love them, his whole face lights up when he talks about them—and that gives him a slightly odd perspective on 'the present conflict' as they say." Exactly right. The added dimension confers only a "slightly odd" turn to what is, after all, Rivers's characteristic perspective. To say that a South Pacific "culture of death" illuminates the nature of one's own very different culture is not in fact to discover anything very remarkable or challenging at all. Who would not have thought, by the end of the Great War, that those who continued to find it exhilarating, compelling, and necessary would thereby have committed themselves to something like a culture of death? And what, in any case, would the words mean to anyone practiced in translating that commitment into terms like loyalty, duty, or carrying on? To invest in a formula like "culture of death" is precisely not to intend an antiwar perspective, especially when the formula is drawn from an analogy with another culture that is rightly accorded an honorable status deriving from its highly developed sense of the sacred.

Of course, Sassoon might have been permitted to assume a more central position in the novel and thereby to have furnished yet another perspective. But Barker gives up on him rather early in the trilogy, and brings him back only occasionally and without much effort to make him seem freshly appealing. When Rivers, late in *Regeneration*, reflects that "poor Siegfried's rebellion hadn't counted for much," he speaks, apparently, for Barker, who doesn't allow herself to see any essential promise in a mere rebellion of conscience that has little prospect of altering the course of things. Rivers does concede, in his characteristically fairminded way, that Siegfried's rebellion "had been a completely honest action and such actions are seeds carried on the wind," but since "nobody can tell where, or in what circumstances, they will bear fruit," one might as well stop at that concession and leave things where they are. Sassoon himself, hundreds of pages later, near the end of *The Eye in the Door*, describes his own "pathetic little formula for getting [himself] back" into battle as "bloody stupid," adopting "a mincing effeminate tone" when he says in impeccable, contemptuous self-parody: "I'm not going back to kill people. I'm only going back to look after some men." So much self-deception, so much waste: so Sassoon tells himself as he comes steadily around to Rivers's understanding of what is necessary, which is to do as one must do without unduly "thinking about" the conflicts and contradictions. When Sassoon says to Rivers that "it's no good encouraging people to know themselves and . . . face up to their emotions, because out there they're better off not having any," he is uttering an entirely realistic observation and in effect sealing the novelistic fate of Barker's trilogy.

That fate might also have been different had Barker devoted greater attention to the other antiwar figures she barely develops. They are most prominently featured in *The Eye in the Door*, where one of them, a woman named Beattie, is extolled as "one of those who felt every death" and another named Mac is admired—but also "hated"—for "refusing to fight" and "trying to bring the munitions factories to a halt." Barker draws these figures with characteristic vividness, but makes no effort whatsoever to get inside them or to account for their conviction. That they have conviction is clear; no one disputes their honesty or willingness to suffer for their pacifism. But it is also clear that Barker does not wish to take seriously their pacifism or to think through the political consequences of a principled opposition to this one war in particular. It seems to Barker sufficient that Beattie should refer, once, to the "millions of young lives" Lloyd George of Britain and other government officials have "chucked away." Others may wish—so Barker seems to feel—to pursue the matter of antiwar sentiment, but for her it is at most a sideshow demanding little more than minor acknowledgment.

In fact, Barker is interested principally not in these figures and their convictions but in their effect upon Prior. He had grown up among these people now in prison or being hunted down, and his present involvement with them—he is assigned to gather information from them and in effect to betray them—allows him to think about violation, betrayal, and bad faith: allows him, in other words, to be sensitive to such issues without attempting to change his life or seriously confront what would be required of him if he were to follow through on his occasional qualms of conscience. No, Prior assures himself: though he doesn't "like himself very much," and probably shouldn't, "he was not violating anything that mattered." No one, apparently, or very rarely, violates "anything that mattered," reality being chiefly what matters, and knowing what is and is not "honest." Though again, honesty itself would seem at best a dubious prospect for people who know better than to inquire too closely into their own misgivings about their conduct.

The novelistic fate of Barker's trilogy may have chiefly to do with her sense of the work as historical fiction. Barker is moved, obviously, by the variety of the human spectacle, but feels that, at bottom, human beings are more like one another than they are different, and that both history and psychology enforce this sense of things. Psychology, in effect, tells us that we are, all of us, susceptible to primal fears and urges, and that no revision of social forms or ideas can openly prevail against nature. History, on the other hand, but in no less comprehensive terms, demonstrates the ineluctability of the suffering and struggle to which, as human beings, we are bound. In Barker's hands, historical fiction is a means of showing not simply what happened but what had to happen. Barker is drawn more strongly to intractability than to variousness, and if her narrative seems sometimes open to contradiction and conflict, she seems always to know that, in the end, nothing can be done to alter the essential direction of human affairs. Those who suppose that conscience or will or garden-variety reasonableness can be effectual in turning men away from their characteristic pursuits or conflicts—from war, say, or

163

following orders they know to be wrong—may be bold or honest or brave, but they will not understand what it is to live in history and to be subject to laws which, if they are not quite iron laws, are nonetheless durable and not to be undone.

Typically, historical fiction implicitly invokes the authority of fact to support its conclusions, if not each of the narrative turns the novel takes on the way to those conclusions. Barker concludes each of her three volumes with an "author's note" that explains how "fact and fiction are . . . interwoven," though only close study of the many sources she cites would ensure full mastery of that interweaving. Of course, we do not need to know how much the portrait of Prior owes to existing psychiatric case histories any more than we need to know exactly how many of Rivers's reflections are actually drawn from the published papers of the "original" Dr. Rivers. Barker has given us works of fiction that gather and unfold and shift direction and sustain or release momentum in the customary ways of novels, so that there is never a sense that we are reading documents or otherwise authoritative testimony. At the same time, at least in part because the opening novel in the trilogy begins with Sassoon's "Soldier's Declaration" (signed and dated July 1917), we proceed with the understanding that the trilogy is based upon a historical record.

What, precisely, is the authority thereby associated with the entire work? It is not, we are to suppose, a work entirely free to go where it wishes. It cannot make Sassoon a better poet than he was, or Rivers a therapist who willfully abandoned his patients, or the Great War itself a struggle impossible for reasonable people to oppose or question. Its authority has to do with our sense that the novelist operates with constraints she has chosen to honor but that make her necessarily more alert to "reality" than other novelists need be, and therefore somehow more responsible to "the truth." To be sure, there is the true "truth" that exists "out there" beyond the pages of Barker's novel, and the other "truth," which emerges from the narrative Barker constructs. We understand, as we must, that those "truths" are not the same, and that in any case no one can grasp with finality what purports to be "truth," whether actual or constructed. And yet we do accord to books ostensibly beholden to the "facts" as they exist "out there" a special status, demanding of such works that they appear at least to avoid gross distortions of generally accepted "facts" and honor at least the basic outlines of historical reality. To concede that these are conventional demands based upon a conventional view of "history," "reality," and "truth" is not to say that we can readily dispense with the assumptions informing those demands. When Barker announces, in ever so many ways, that she is dealing in the main with "real" people, quoting their "actual" poems and detailing their "actual lives" in the context of an "actual" war, she is determining to a considerable degree how her trilogy is to be read. The authority of the work has everything to do with how consistently Barker then upholds the bargain she has made—refusing to willfully or blithely distort or simplify what we take to be the essential "facts" from which she is working.

We also demand of such a writer that she not succumb too entirely to what James Wood has called "the superstition of fact." This "superstition" Wood discerns in writers who are "obsessed with questions of accuracy and inaccuracy," who display an "informational zealousness," and "do not believe deeply enough in the fictional to abandon the actual world." To think about Barker in this way, armed with these cautions, is to see at once that she is by no means "obsessed with questions of accuracy" or inclined to an "informational zealousness." Barker has so entirely mastered the terrain she covers that she betrays no trace of obsessiveness, awkward zealousness, or eccentricity. What is presented seems, for better or worse, *there*, which is to say, irrevocably what it is and what it had or has to be. Barker writes out of what appear to her readers to be solid verities. She does not, so far as we can tell, make things up in the ways of a modernist imagination bent upon putting its own magisterial stamp on its own evolving, unstable narrative. Barker is a writer who appears to know what is what, for whom the several centers of the conflict she surveys decidedly hold. Ghostly presences now and then invoked in the trilogy are defined by their decidedly "unreal" status, by their being set against the world that is, in the several respects that matter, an actual world. Barker does not write like a modernist who wishes to be a law unto herself. The law to which she is responsive seems to her and to her faithful readers to be somehow *out there*, however loath we may be to give it a single, simple name.

But then, of course, we want to ask whether, in Wood's terms, Barker believes "deeply enough in the fictional to abandon the actual world." From what we have observed, it would seem that she does not. Certainly she does not in the sense Wood intends in his essay on W. G. Sebald, where he observes that in novels like *The Emigrants* "facts seem never to have belonged to the actual world" and that "the real world gains a harsher, stronger life within a fiction because it receives a concentrated patterning which actual life does not exert." The authority we have referred to in Barker derives from the very different sense that the apparent "facts" we observe in the fiction seem "to have belonged to the actual world." And if there is in Barker's telling a harsh strength in seeing things as they were, that effect has much to do with her refusal to permit "a concentrated patterning" to take pride of place in our experience of the material. Barker's facts do not seem to us to become "newly real" or at all seem "rivalrous to" the facts of the so-called real world. Wood's reading of Sebald does not allow us to think of Barker in comparable terms. Neither does this novelist give us the "self-reflection" and "dreamlike reticence" Wood rightly admires in Sebald. But the absence of these virtues does not fatally compromise our admiration for the kind of historical fiction Barker writes.

No, it is not because Barker proceeds without the sovereign high-modernist disdain for the merely real or given that we challenge or at least question her reliance upon "history." It is not that she is paralyzed by trivial facts or limited by a desire to provide an "accurate" account of what happened in the Great War. The problem, the limitation, if I may so put it, is rather that she does not give herself permission to step outside of the perspectives generated by the characters within her own fiction. For she has scrupulously depicted these characters as such characters would conceivably have been, subject as they were to the conditions and thought-currents dominant in their own day. Moreover, Barker has determined that conflicts she has set in motion will be for the most part contained, if not fully resolved, so that the conflicts cannot continue to resonate for us beyond the pages of the fiction. We are not haunted by the facts or conflicts of Barker's novel because she has mastered and consigned them so efficiently to the "history" to which they belong. Had she made her "history" more capacious, had she imagined her characters more variously, or accorded to her more wayward characters—the incorrigibles, the pacifists, the conscientious objectors—a greater weight of concentrated attention, she might have achieved in the trilogy something larger, fuller, deeper than the clarifying disclosure of the way things were and had to be.

The novels built around the materials Barker assembled for this trilogy require a more venturesome political imagination than Barker was able to summon. For the political imagination would have required of her that she consider with greater seriousness the hopelessness of men in wartime who feel that they are engaged in something unspeakable while also wishing somehow to engage in a protest or resistance they know to be futile. We should be more inclined to believe in the obdurate reality of established power as Barker evokes it if she had found a way to capture the passion of those whose vision is not defined entirely by their own historical moment. History is not, after all, reducible to absolutes like "the inexorable logic of history" or to simple choices as between reality and conscience. But history in Barker's trilogy too often reduces to that sort of inflexible opposition, where reality is always bound to seem more compelling because it is so clearly more "true" to the facts. Barker proceeds in the trilogy according to a self-confirming hypothesis about history in general and about war in particular. Had she attempted as well to show us the gradual unfolding of an oppositional perspective on the war, we would perhaps be more inclined to accept that pathos and resignation were for most men the only "reasonable" possibilities.

167

13

STIFLINGS

LÁSZLÓ KRASZNAHORKAI

There is no single, standard Eastern European novel. Neither is there an archetypal Czech or Polish or Hungarian novel against which ostensibly deviant forms may be assessed. The best books by Eastern European writers are spectacularly diverse, and the works that have appeared in the years following the fall of communism have been especially varied. Though it is tempting to believe that one or two aspects of particularly gripping masterpieces—a fondness for the grotesque or the apocalyptic, an obsession with political tyranny—may serve as defining features of Eastern European writing generally, one need only think of the "exceptions" to conclude that they far outnumber the "standard" works.

For most American readers, Eastern European fiction has typically been associated with Czech or Polish writing, but in the last decade several Hungarian novelists have attracted enthusiastic attention. Among them are Peter Nadas, Tamas Aczel, Peter Esterhazy, and George Konrad, the last of whom first made his reputation here in the 1970s and remains a prodigious and resourceful writer. Now the first English-language publication of an acclaimed work by László Krasznahorkai permits us once again to consider, if only very briefly, whether the term "Hungarian novel" means anything more than "a work of fiction produced by a Hungarian writer." Like some but by no means all of the novels coming from Hungary in recent years, *The Melancholy of Resistance* is intermittently retrospective, apocalyptic, and prophetic. It is concerned, at least in part, with the subordination of individual desire to the aims of a more or less official cultural and political apparatus, much as we would expect of a work produced in a nation just emerging from a long period of Communist domination. As in novels by Nadas and Aczel, the prose in Krasznahorkai's book is frequently labyrinthine, the sentences rolling on at great length. As in the novels of Esterhazy, there is in Krasznahorkai what John Banville has called a "stoic doctrine, a kind of *amor fati.*" As in the otherwise utterly different work of Konrad, the communicated sense of reality is oppressive, and the task of reversing injustice and cruelty is what Leszek Kolakowski has called "comically . . . [and] obscenely unaccomplishable."

And yet, to set Krasznahorkai's novel alongside the books of those others is to see at once how hopeless it is to read this unfamiliar work as a typical product of the Hungarian imagination or as a reflection of peculiarly Eastern European circumstances. Originally published in 1989, the novel little resembles any particular work by its author's more eminent contemporaries. It offers nothing of the tumultuous history of Hungarian communism and none of the dispassionate, highly evocative documentary realism that distinguished the early work of Konrad. It is no wonder that W. G. Sebald, among others, sought to understand Krasznahorkai's work by assimilating it to a visionary tradition that is by no means strictly Eastern European.

Sebald proclaimed that *The Melancholy of Resistance* "is a book about a world into which the Leviathan has returned," though the book is decidedly not about the Leviathan, nor even about the effect of the Leviathan upon the world. The Leviathan in Krasznahorkai's novel is a dead whale, a thing, a carcass stuffed and exhibited in a traveling circus. It has, so far as we can tell, no satanic powers, surely no edifying properties, and no capacity to inspire in those who pay money to look at it any trace of spiritual or nihilistic reflection. If Melville's whale calls to mind ultimacies and abysses, signs and wonders, godhead and malignity, Krasznahorkai's whale inspires in the one character potentially equipped to take it in only a "happy stupor," while others—"who continued trudging compliantly around the whale in the stinking gloom"— not only showed no signs of being similarly affected but gave the decided impression that the highly visible object of the advertisement was of limited interest. Though Sebald suggested that Krasznahorkai's novel is a visionary work and that the return of Leviathan is here a soul-making—or soul-shattering—occasion, the intimations of apocalypse that are liberally deposited throughout *The Melancholy of Resistance* are so relentlessly anatomized and caricatured that in the end they seem no more than the eruptions of feverish, childish fantasies, and the novel itself, however reluctantly, a realistic work whose primary ambition is disillusionment rather than soul-making.

To be sure, Krasznahorkai toys with his reader, suggesting now and again that he is interested in the incomprehensible. Characters obsess about omens, "terrifying rumors," and "mysterious" disasters. Ordinary folk speak of a "last judgment" and speculate upon "some vast murderous fury." When the circus arrives in the nondescript village where the action of the novel is set, we have reason to suspect that the featured attraction will prove to embody something fabulous, that ultimately a reckoning will emerge that is commensurate with the intensities of the handwringing expended on the creature's behalf. The insignificant little woman who early in the novel fantasizes about "the sort of creature who 'knew neither God nor man'" is but one in a chorus of excitable townspeople. The idiom of Krasznahorkai's novel is by turns apocalyptic, penitential, and overheated, as if very large and urgent matters were continuously at hand and the fate of the soul itself hung in the balance.

That the whale itself portends in this novel nothing so large is quickly apparent, despite the several noises contrived to suggest otherwise. Those who obsess about the "unfathomable and inconceivable" and the "ever-spreading, all-consuming," are in fact so fearful and obsessive that it is impossible for any reader to view the world as they do. By the time the whale puts in its initial appearance, we are armored against the credulousness of the susceptible multitudes, and neither the "dead eyes" of the creature nor its "vast unmoving tongue" can cause us to invest in it a metaphysical aspect.

In spite of its Proustian sentences and its surrealist feints, Krasznahorkai's novel is in fact a rather elementary tale. A circus arrives in a small Hungarian town and precipitates a frenzy of mob violence. We soon see that the circus is more a pretext than a subject, though the action, such as it is, formally revolves around the mob and the citizens who incite, control, or otherwise respond to the rampaging chaos in the streets. Intrigues are mounted, personal conflicts are dramatized, political implications are bluntly spelled out. Everything seems small, provincial, the stakes significant only by the standards of a place too unimportant to create a stir in the world. Though destruction is wreaked upon the town and lives are lost, we are concerned principally with a few characters who are endowed with characteristic virtues and vices. These figures engage us in varying degrees, though they are static figures, their features writ large, and the action of the novel is designed to permit their features to stand clear and to boldly signify. Though Krasznahorkai bathes everything in a thick wash of darkness and dread, his intentions are all too obvious.

LÁSZLÓ KRASZNAHORKAI

From the first, Krasznahorkai casts all of his characters as fundamentally unreliable witnesses. "To tell the truth," the narrator says, indicating that if we stick with him we shall certainly know what is what. But as for those the narrator refers to as "them," well, the more one registers the rumors and the omens "referred to by a growing number of people," the more one notes all that "people simply assumed," and the more one accepts that "they" are not ever to be trusted. In fact, in this novel, not only are the things that "they" say set between quotation marks, but quotation marks are employed throughout to set off hundreds of phrases, which are thereby singled out—very much in passing—to indicate the stock expressions without which ordinary consciousness would be bereft. When a woman is described as going to " 'her well-earned sleep,' " we are invited to feel superior to the person who resorts to this consoling expression. A man "intoxicated with 'the smell of success' " is a man in thrall to a modest cliché and thus one of "them," where "they" are those who think with the assistance of readymade tags and phrases. We are given to understand that the characters in the novel would resort to such terms if their inchoate sentiments were formulated in words.

Throughout the novel, in fact, extraordinary attention is paid to language itself. One character reflects that in his world "every sober word and thought confusingly lost its meaning" and "statements employing tropes such as 'as' and 'as if' had lost their cutting edge." Though virtually everyone in the novel is to one degree or another subjected to satire—and we are relentlessly detached even from the one or two likable figures—we are never permitted entirely to remove ourselves from "them." We remain, and we know that we remain, subject to the toils of language. This Krasznahorkai will not allow us to forget.

This is not to suggest that *The Melancholy of Resistance* is a book about language. In many ways it is a book about "them," where "they" are the human, all-too-human beings who are, with whatever exceptions, mostly out there, not merely in small Hungarian villages. If Sebald is right about "the universality" of Krasznahorkai's vision, then "they" are a veritable gallery of everymen and everywomen, and the particulars, including the Hungarian place names, serve simply to establish a credible locale for actions that might erupt anywhere. The attention paid to language is, in this sense, an attention that might well be paid to any language susceptible to cliché and deception. "They" are ridiculous, pathetic, frightening, delusional, and self-important not because they think and speak in a Hungarian idiom that betrays their inadequacy, but because they are, like human beings everywhere, inadequate. Their inadequacy is a fact of their lives. The evidence for it is everywhere. Oddly, much that underlies the disposition and the behavior of characters in this novel is simply presented as "the facts" of the case. People are credulous because they are credulous. Others are rapacious or passive because they cannot but be what they are. The word "because" is itself obviously misleading here, suggesting that reason and logic might plausibly be summoned to order and clarify things. But for all its tendency to argue with itself and to allow its primary characters to doubt their own conclusions, the novel tends more or less inexorably to assert that "everything out there actually was 'one damned thing piled on another.' "

The cold, fatalistic logic inherent in such a view is that "chaos really [is] the natural condition of the world" and that "even the words 'chaos' and 'outcome' are entirely redundant, there being nothing one can posit as their antitheses." In such a world, human beings can do nothing but reflect the situations that define them completely. They are creatures born to chaos and confusion, and chance alone would seem to determine how they behave at any given time. One temperament may be mild, another ferocious, and though there is no use in suggesting that they are one and the same, in the end it is probably safe to assume that the forces at work in any instance will remain largely obscure. Those who struggle to make sense of the ordinary chaos will be disappointed. They will come to regard themselves as foolish.

In Krasznahorkai's book, the ordinary chaos is principally embodied in those who are ordinary. These include the bland and the not so bland, the passive and the ambitious, men and women, public figures and private citizens. All are regarded, with virtually no exception, as fundamentally distasteful. The fearful petit-bourgeois Mrs. Plauf fusses over her idiotic knickknacks and fumes about the "foul desires" of every stranger she meets, every one of them in her view "coarse," "degenerate," disgracefully "unshaven." So revolting is this primly disapproving exemplar of the ostensibly decent and orderly that we all but accede to the instinct of Mrs. Eszter, who on a visit to Mrs. Plauf is overcome by "the ever more intense temptation to crush one of those little knickknacks in her enormous palm, to snap it as one would the neck of a chicken." It is not that the visitor herself is in any way appealing. Krasznahorkai leaves little doubt that she is shallow, cruel, and ponderously self-important, but we cannot but share with her a disdain for "the cosy comfiness, the stolid air of inactivity, the treacly prettiness of this 'filthy little viper's nest'" that is the habitation of Mrs. Plauf, whose "wispy tulle curtains" and "lace doilies" and—"behind the glass of the showcase"—"straggling sentimental novels with their hot, sticky, airless contents" are made, like their possessor, to inspire nausea and contempt.

But if the " 'idle pleasures and feeble desires'" of Krasznahorkai's little people invariably inspire a mild disgust, so too do the strivings of the more aggressive and worldly figures in the novel. These are people whose primary motive is power, who in the pursuit of their goals will stop at nothing. The most notorious of these figures is Mrs. Eszter, who may well call to mind Flaubert's Homais. Like Flaubert's despicably "disinterested" pharmacist, she is, in her view, an Enlightenment figure as resistant to "romantic literary nonsense" as to ordinary fellow feeling. Few characters in recent fiction are at once so repulsive and so vividly drawn as this behemoth, so apparently committed to "civic improvement" and " 'the elevating passion of communal action'" while holding in contempt the idealists and the long-suffering, the innocent and the genuinely communitarian. Though most of Krasznahorkai's characters are weak, stupid, or easily swayed by demagogy, Mrs. Eszter is distinguished chiefly by her cunning, the intensity of her determination, her brutish self-sufficiency, and her willingness to use others to forward her ambitions.

A landscape largely dominated by insipidity, brutishness, and insensibility will soon seem artificial, a system rather than an insight, and this is a risk that Krasznahorkai courts. Frequently we feel that an idea—chaos, the war of all against all, the futility of good intentions—has taken hold of the writer's imagination and made of it a willing accomplice in the promotion of this idea. The problem is that none of these ideas is in itself as complex or as interesting as Krasznahorkai apparently assumes. Like other currently fashionable ideas—all of human life as a struggle for power, for example—"chaos" announces that anything is possible and also that no other view of things is conceivable. If everything is reduced to "chaos" or "power" or "disorder," then anything resembling an exception must seem merely eccentric, irrelevant, a delusion of the irredeemably credulous or underdeveloped. Krasznahorkai's novel has the airless feel of a work with a settled view of things. Its brilliant translator George Szirtes rightly describes it as "a slow lava flow of narrative, a vast, black river of type," but the narrative, with all its fits and starts, is constrained to flow in one direction only. The author makes no allowance for the possibility that he may be mistaken. For him, everything inevitably confirms what is already known.

In this sense, the idea of "resistance" can itself be no more than a conditioned, mostly pathetic fiction in this novel, stirring only insofar as it suggests that desolation may take several forms, some of them more edifying than others. The so-called resistance to which the book's title refers is, in fact, never mounted. It has no active component, though it is vaguely discernible in an activity of mind that never threatens to issue in anything effectual. The resistant minds belong to two characters, one an apparent halfwit or dreamer named János Valuska, the other Gyorgi Eszter, once the director of the local music academy and the husband of the behemoth Mrs. Eszter, more recently an illusionless eccentric who has withdrawn from the world and remained for some years in his bed. Though both of these characters circulate in the village—Mr. Eszter for the first time in years—and both have opportunities to interact with others, neither offers any prospect of significant resistance to the chaos that they encounter or to the forces responsible for fomenting and or- chestrating the chaos. Krasznahorkai invests his exceptional characters with qualities that endear them to us, but his attraction to them is sen- timental. He does not require of them that they be equal to their better notions or their more generous instincts. As with the other, very differ- ent characters in this novel, all that is required of these two exceptions is that they confirm the general condition to which all must submit.

Clearly, "the melancholy of resistance," as an expression at once poi- gnant and stirring, may owe its poignancy to the fact that those who resist do not have the strength or the resources to accomplish their noble purpose. The expression would then refer to the activity of people who know better than to expect success but persist in spite of the odds ar- rayed against them. Such resisters would presumably believe that in time their efforts might be seen to stand for something important, and that eventually conditions might somehow improve. That is often what we find in political novels, where principled revolt frequently takes shape with no prospect of imminent success, but with every sense that the willingness to resist or revolt will itself prove indispensable in the future, when conditions may somehow call forth a more effective, more com- prehensive, better organized, and less eccentric resistance.

The resisters in Krasznahorkai's novel are not at all principled or de- liberate in their disaffection. The youthful Valuska, for all his "angelic" disposition, is depicted as "trapped . . . in a bubble," moving about "'blindly and tirelessly . . . with the incurable beauty of his personal cosmos' in his soul." Hungry for approval and affection, he allows himself to be the genial butt of jokes and ridicule, and passes through life with "no sense of proportion" and "a sad incomprehension." Though he is dimly troubled by what he sees, he generally sees very little, and is exemplary only in the sense that he vaguely longs for a goodness and beauty others seem not to miss. When he is caught up in the mob hysteria that sweeps the village, he is unable to pull himself away, and though he commits no evil deed, wracked as he is with terror, he is in every way frozen, useless, pathetic: "he wished to defend the person being beaten," Krasznahorkai writes, "and . . . to be the person administering the beating." Aware, briefly, that he has spent his life in a "forest of illusions," he can do nothing but register the degree to which the "carnival of hatred" erupting around him is not what he had ever previously had in mind, though its claim upon him is impossible to deny.

Whatever one is inclined to make of Valuska, it is clear that in some respects he stands apart from "them" and yet represents no viable principle of resistance to evil or disorder. Innocence in this book is not a sufficient standard or ambition. It may well be that the writer intended to make of Valuska someone more promising, but saw no way to embody that promise in the figure he conceived. More likely, he simultaneously wished and did not wish to embody in the world of his novel some more effectual power of resistance. In the end Valuska serves, like everything else in the novel, to say that no meaningful resistance is possible, not here.

What might, in some other novel, suggest some stoic moral authority, in this work never rises above a bleak absolutism of negation whose specific content is avoidance rather than encounter. No more than Valuska is Eszter an authentically resisting figure. He lives more or less exclusively in his head, and his several improvised notions come to us with no moral urgency, no sense that he must change his life to be equal to them. Like all of the ideas summoned in Krasznahorkai's novel, Eszter's ideas are entertained without real seriousness, and we feel that they can be dropped or renounced as abruptly as they are taken up.

In short, Krasznahorkai's heart is neither in resistance nor in melancholy. His *aliénés* are odd, disconnected, and plausibly imagined, but incidental to the primary energies of the novel. These energies are satirical, though the targets of the satire yield all too readily to derision. The petit-bourgeois figures in the novel are predictably small, selfish, silly, smug. The mob behaves as mobs will, blindly, violently, badly. Corruption is located as it so often is in the most powerful and trusted members of the community. The police chief is a boor and a barbarian with gamy sexual appetites, a man who mistreats his children and drinks himself into a stupor to avoid responsibility for the riots that engulf the town. Everywhere the portents portend the predictable, and even the inexorable surges of Krasznahorkai's manic, intensely patterned prose can only move the narrative where the author has determined it will go.

There are, to be sure, extraordinary lusters in the writing. Much of the time, we allow ourselves to be delighted by turns of phrase and idiom that lend provisional excitement to a forward momentum whose destination is never in doubt. There is no reticence, no austerity in this writer's repertoire, but never do we long for less or imagine that in opting for abundance or superfluity he has abandoned meaning. If anything, there is too much meaning, too much insistence upon omen and harbinger and metaphor. Krasznahorkai's powers of verbal invention are prodigious, but the verbal energy is too often lavished upon a bleak dogmatism, too often harnessed to irreversible patterns of orchestrated chaos or decline.

At the center of the novel is a transparently specious campaign for "moral rearmament" engineered by the unspeakably cynical and manipulative Mrs. Ezster, but there is nothing remotely credible in this campaign, no effort to imagine what a legitimate "moral rearmament"—if such were possible—might entail. Neither is there, as in Robert Musil's handling of the "Collateral Campaign" in *The Man Without Qualities*, an effort to get inside the misguided idealism of any thoughtful participant or to describe the conflicts of purpose and vision that divide supporters. In Krasznahorkai, "missionary endeavor" is automatically known to be laughable, whatever its object, and those who can be moved by words like "vigilance," "common sense," and "solidarity" are of course those most apt to be moved by bad poetry and sappy appeals to "hearth and home." Caricature is piled upon caricature in the setting up of a satire whose purpose is mainly to certify that idiots are idiots, that the spoils inevitably belong to the cunning and the brutal, whose one obvious virtue is their inexhaustible contempt for sentimentality.

And so we wonder, at last and again, whether there may be in this novel something more. Is there, perhaps, a specifically Hungarian or Eastern European dimension to this novel that might lift it beyond the status of a pessimistic virtuosity? Is the novel a belated satire on the several species of moral rearmament so often promoted by tyrannical regimes in the name of socialism or people's democracies? Perhaps Krasznahorkai anticipated, with the revulsion everywhere inscribed in his narrative, that the successor regimes about to replace the moribund communist governments in the Soviet bloc would be every bit as corrupt and vicious as their citizens had some reason to expect. But such speculation is wasted here, where the particulars are generic, the forms of idiocy, corruption, and betrayal are "universal," the revealed patterns of inculcation and subordination are typical, and every outcome is ordained. Whatever the national or regional origins of the worldview that rules this novel, the schematic and overdetermined playing out of the various conflicts is such as to make that worldview seem inconsequential.

14

THE DICTATOR'S DICTATION
AUGUSTO ROA BASTOS

For more than a decade, the Paraguayan novelist Augusto Roa Bastos has been regarded in Latin America as a major writer. In the years since the publication of his masterpiece *Yo el Supremo* (*I the Supreme*) in 1974, hundreds of articles examining the novel have appeared, and an authoritative critical edition was published in Madrid in 1983. When Carlos Fuentes recently declared the book "one of the milestones of the Latin American novel," he was merely confirming what had long been taken for granted south of our border. Now that a superb English translation of this dauntingly complex work is at last available, readers in this country will be in a position to see for themselves why Latin American critics have been moved to invoke the names of Joyce and Musil, Cervantes and Rabelais to describe the breadth and ambition of *I the Supreme*.

A great many Latin American novels have been haunted by the idea of the dictator, and several of the most famous actually revolve around a dictator figure. One thinks immediately of Gabriel García Márquez's *Autumn of the Patriarch*, or of Alejo Carpentier's *Reasons of State*, or of an earlier novel like Miguel Angel Asturias's *El Señor Presidente*. Often, the dictator in these novels is a composite portrait modeled on various originals, with the consequence that the character is larger than life, so awesome in the range of his brutalities that he is less a person than he is a force of nature. Other writers work from a single model, with results that vary from one case to another. Roa has written about an actual dictator, a singular historical figure, but he has nonetheless attributed to him extraordinary powers—and though he has resisted the mystifications associated with novels in which the dictator is a force of nature and therefore unaccountable to any mundane human law, he has made his human-all-too-human character an impressively ubiquitous figure about whose virtues and defects we are often in doubt. As we study the world dominated by this dictator, we may feel that there is no one else to whom blame might reasonably be assigned, but at the same time, we are loath to apply the categorical judgments to which representations of tyranny usually tempt us. To compare Roa's dictator with other despots in Latin American fiction is to feel that Roa's is distinguished not only by the quantity of detail lavished on him, but by his remarkable capacity to seem at one moment a person and at another an embodiment of contradictory elements not usually identified with a single person, let alone a powerful tyrant.

To speak of Roa's dictator as having been drawn from a model is in some sense to misrepresent him, for the character is never really permitted to stand free of the original. In important ways we are dealing here with a historical novel, a work incorporating actual, named personages who have a documented existence outside the pages of the fiction. Roa's dictator is not "based on" the nineteenth-century Paraguayan despot José Gaspar Rodriguez Francia who in 1816 brought his country to independence; in many ways he is, palpably and persuasively, Francia himself. Though much that he is made to say has obviously been invented by Roa, it is difficult to think of the dictator in this novel as an invented character subject to the writer's imperial whim. So consistently does the novel make use of documents well known to students of nineteenth-century Latin American politics, and so frequently are the words used to describe the dictator taken verbatim from nineteenth-century accounts of people who knew Francia, that even the most unlikely statements made by the character inspire us to feel that they might indeed have come from Francia himself. A novel containing numerous footnotes and quotations, as this one does, inevitably encourages us to believe that we are dealing with facts, or at least with plausible hypotheses and extrapolations.

Francia is hardly a household name in the English-speaking world today, but he was much discussed in the mid-nineteenth century. Thomas Carlyle's long essay "Dr. Francia" was written in 1843, in response to several books about the leader who ruled Paraguay from 1816 to 1840, and it seems fair to say that Roa has been deeply influenced by Carlyle's account. By 1843, Carlyle was in the phase of his career that produced "On Heroes, Hero-Worship, and the Heroic in History" and the superb work of social criticism *Past and Present*. He treats Francia as a man with the stuff of heroes in him, a figure impressive and forbidding, alternately foolish and inspired, credulous and cunning.

But Carlyle knows that in important respects Francia eludes judgment, as he eludes any sort of clear definition. Everywhere the figure is surrounded by "a murk of distracted shadows and rumors." Under such conditions, says Carlyle, "who would pretend . . . to decipher the real portraiture of Dr. Francia and his life?" Those who wrote about him during the years of his reign had their reasons for treating him as they did, but out of their accounts Carlyle could draw "mere intricate inanity," "clouds of confused bluster and jargon," "not facts, but broken shadows of facts," and, not surprisingly, "a running shriek of constitutional denunciation."

Carlyle's tentative encomiums to Francia would seem the predictable expressions of an overheated hero worshiper if they were not confirmed by many other assessments. No more than Carlyle is Roa prepared to overlook the "reign of terror" instituted by Francia in the name of law and order, but neither does Roa overlook the beneficent results of that reign, evident when one compares Paraguayan civil society in those years with conditions in countries like Brazil and Argentina. No doubt, as Fuentes says, Paraguay under Francia was "a sick utopia," a peaceful place not unlike a graveyard. But—so Carlyle reminds us—Francia was "driven by necessity itself" to what "was properly a reign of rigor" in a society that had neither popular institutions nor a class of citizens equipped to take effective control. In adapting to his novelistic purposes so many features of Carlyle's equivocal portrait, Roa has built a figure who is richly various, whose strengths of character and intelligence are inseparable from his sense of isolation and his impatience with the decorums of parliamentary and representative democracy.

Having in effect invited us to measure his character against alternative portraits of the dictator, Roa cannot be surprised when readers conclude that there is little new information to be found in *I the Supreme*. Nor is there much improvement on Carlyle's view of Francia as originally a noble fellow, a republican at heart, who led his country to independence only to end by "stealing the constitutional palladiums from their parliament-houses." None of the many thousands of words uttered by Francia in Roa's novel substantially revises or makes untenable that complex impression. And the standard twentieth-century accounts of Francia's place in Paraguayan history are similarly reinforced in the novel. The dictator's decision to seal off the borders of his country to

AUGUSTO ROA BASTOS

avoid contamination or incursion by its powerful neighbors, for example, is presented in the standard way, as an awful but probably necessary strategy to preserve independence. Roa allows for sharp expressions of disappointment in Francia, who clearly betrayed his own republican and populist ideals, but Roa is at one with other commentators who typically recall the perpetual wars that kept other countries in turmoil precisely because no leaders arose to prevent the church and other corrupt interest groups from tearing to pieces what there was of a civil fabric.

With no obvious desire to revise conventional accounts of Francia's reign, Roa must have wished to accomplish something other than a scrupulously balanced historical portrait or a piece of political analysis. Fuentes's prediction that students of the decolonization process "will find much to reflect on in *I The Supreme*" suggests that there are fresh political insights in the novel. There are not. Roa's most audacious idea is the notion that Francia survived his own death in 1840. By having Francia anticipate at various points in the novel events that took place many years later, even going so far as to refer explicitly to a conflict with Bolivia in the 1930s, Roa in effect shows that Francia is implicated in every phase of postindependence Paraguayan history. But one has only to consult straightforward accounts of the country since 1816 to note that Francia is routinely accorded great attention. If the shadow he casts in the novel is disproportionately large, that is more a consequence of the fact that the work is a mostly first-person narrative told by Francia himself than a sign that Roa reads the history of his country in a new way.

To get at the real object of Roa's ambition it is perhaps necessary to consider the novel's peculiar organization. Principally, *I the Supreme* is a record of exchanges between the Supreme and his private secretary or amanuensis Policarpo Patiño. However, Patiño speaks so infrequently that the "exchange" is in effect an interminable monologue that contains the interpolated utterances of an entirely marginal figure who exists mainly as a narrative device. In fact, the dictator may be said to "contain" Patiño just as he contains the many other figures whose complaints, encouragements, and solicitations he permits them to express as occasional voices trapped within his peremptory monologue.

Roa has no interest in the sort of psychological insight that would conclude from all of this simply that Francia was self-absorbed. The self-absorption here is a given, a device that underwrites or rationalizes narrative procedures. These procedures include the Supreme's recourse to a double persona, a *yo* and an *el*, in terms of which an interior debate is intermittently mounted. Exactly how the one persona is to be distinguished from the other cannot be definitively established, but it seems clear that the *el* is the more permanent incarnation of the Supreme, that aspect of him that exists in the world and in the minds of others and is destined to have a posterity. The *yo* has more to do with the self for itself, though the notion of a private identity for a Supreme is not always persuasive.

But a description of the novel as a more or less continuous monologue, though accurate as far as it goes, is inadequate. For besides the disruptions and internal debates, there are also distinctly separate discourses within the book, distinctive styles of expression, each with its own designation. There are sections marked "in the private notebook," which ostensibly contain material written by the Supreme entirely for himself. There are sections marked "Perpetual Circular," which are dictated by the Supreme to Patiño and are intended as orders and advice to state officials. Other sections are in the nature of citations or notes, some integrated within the main narrative (though typographically differentiated from it), others printed at the foot of the page and often containing lengthy excerpts from other books. There are also what might be called special discourses: the more or less extended testimony of another character, the transcript of an official document, and so on. These usually play an important role in the text, conveying necessary information or providing a background against which we can measure the reliability of subsequent remarks coming directly from the Supreme.

It is not always clear to the reader when one particular discourse has come to an end and another has begun. On occasion, what seems to be part of the "Perpetual Circular" sounds more like the intimate ruminations we associate with the private notebook. Elsewhere, the exchanges between the Supreme and Patiño carry over from one discourse to another, so that the separation into distinct discourses seems no more than a self-canceling, transparent artifice enforcing the utter fictionality and arbitrariness of the whole enterprise. Ostensibly put together by a "compiler"—who, in a final note, reveals that it was "culled" or "coaxed" "from some twenty thousand dossiers" and all manner of other documents—the novel is best described as a polyphonic narrative whose perspective is only superficially controlled by a presiding presence.

But what is it exactly that this novel of many voices has to say? What is the nature of the society over which the Supreme ruled, and what has Roa's view of that society to tell us about politics and power? The relation established in *I the Supreme* between the dictator and his people is an all

AUGUSTO ROA BASTOS

too conventional one: the people assume the status of inert objects and the dictator assumes the dimensions of a protean figure. No matter that the dictator now and again refers to his people as "proud, dignified citizens." What is familiar is the easy contempt for ordinary decorums routinely displayed by the dictator in mundane transactions with constituents. But if we are led to ask whether the citizens of newly independent Paraguay deserved better, Roa's novel provides no answer: it allows us to believe what we like about the nature of ordinary people and about the institutions best suited to representing their interests. Roa keeps his eye trained on a single situation, but we never feel that we know much about early Paraguayan society and how it worked; generalizations about politics and power from *I the Supreme* inevitably go beyond anything Roa is willing to provide.

Is it fair to say, then, that politics in *I the Supreme* is merely a background for Roa's portrait of an eccentric dictator with an extraordinary gift for words? Readers will obviously differ on what may be made of the political material. At a number of points, the Supreme refers to atrocities he is said to have committed, defending himself in various ways. He refers to trials, to the undoubted existence of traitors, to the fact that some of those accused of crimes against the state were not found guilty. He also defends himself by resorting to numbers. How many political executions actually took place in the years of his reign? Patiño says that sixty-eight conspirators were put to death in 1820, and the Supreme himself sets the figure for his entire reign at "less than a hundred."

It is hard to judge the accuracy of these claims, but it does seem clear that Francia never embarked on a course of systematic extermination. Do the numbers matter? Can they serve any kind of political judgment? Though they cannot tell us that Francia's was a humane stewardship or that he cultivated in his constituents a respect for what would now be called human rights, they clearly say something about his reign and his character. Still, we must believe that in the real world of politics numbers do matter, that an isolated instance of official misconduct acquires special significance when it may rightly be seen as part of a larger pattern of systematic oppression or terror. The recent memoir of Armando Valladares recounting his experiences in Castro's prisons is important as a political document because it tells us a great deal about the fate of tens of thousands in Cuba for twenty-five years. Francia's human-rights record seems at least to have been better than Castro's; on the other hand, in a more primitive society like Francia's Paraguay, there may have been less need to organize repression and systematize terror.

Finally, the politics of this novel cannot be evaluated in isolation from Roa's conception of language. Like other contemporary writers, Roa uses multiple personae and alternate voices in order to avoid any suggestion that truth is to be identified with a single character or a simple idea. His prose is saturated with the idiom, rhetoric, and wordplay of other writers and other languages. When the Supreme speaks we hear now Baudelaire or Montaigne, now Blake or Shakespeare or Rabelais. Allusions proliferate, the sources not always clear or important, but the fact of intertextual borrowing unmistakable. Now and then exotic Paraguayan terms or Guarani (Indian) words (translated in a special appendix) are freely intermingled with sophisticated literary phrases or bits and pieces of a Rousseauist philosophical vocabulary. Explicit references to and borrowings from Greek and Latin texts support an ongoing sense of language as anachronistic, capacious, and vigorously opportunistic.

We do not infer from this that for Roa all cultures are vexed by the same dilemmas and all languages are more or less interchangeable in their expression of basic ideas and sentiments. We conclude, rather, that language in *I the Supreme* is an instrument for expressing difference and discontinuity, for demonstrating the radical incompatibility of various cultural norms and literary conventions. The novel brings together a wide range of flagrantly contradictory idioms and assembles them in a way that is often disorienting and deliberately provocative. It does this persistently because it wishes to subvert the procedures by which facts and otherwise familiar impressions are routinely processed and accommodated. And this project constitutes the novel's essential politics.

The Supreme himself goes so far as to deny the importance of words, and asserts that his investment in writing is intrinsically ridiculous. "When all is said and done," he laments, "what is prodigious, fearful, unknown in the human being has never been put into words or books, and never will be." To write is inevitably to falsify. "When I dictate to you," Francia tells Patiño, "the words have a meaning; when you write them another. So that we speak two different languages." But ultimately the novel lives most fully in its language, and it implicitly struggles against the negations insisted upon by Francia himself.

If the Supreme is obsessed with his failure to communicate his own authentic cry, and concludes that we understand nothing, we feel nonetheless that a great deal comes through. If to Francia it is "all the better" that no one understands, since then he can feel free to say and write anything he pleases, it is clear to us that he is served by language as much as he is betrayed by it. When Francia declares "I don't write history. I make it," he announces a distinction that persuades no one, least of all Francia himself. For it is precisely the written record that he wants desperately to affect, in order to defend his motives and thoughts from "those rodents" whose "error consists in gnawing holes in documented truth."

To make history is for Francia, whatever he says to the contrary, a matter of "adjusting, stressing, enriching its meaning and truth." Roa's novel affirms the significance of the project even as, in its ambivalent manner, it exposes and undercuts the dictator himself. If the only enduring monument to Francia is an edifice of language known as *I the Supreme*, it is fair to say that his words or the words he inspired are at the heart of that edifice. Francia and Patiño may "disappear in what is read/written" like the rest of us, but always there remains the possibility that language, more properly literature, will accomplish a purpose that warrants the hope and the labor invested in it.

No reader will feel upon first acquaintance with *I the Supreme* that he has adequately come to grips with the novel, or that he can say how well its eccentric, introspective intensities are balanced by a feeling for the surfaces and conflicts of ordinary life. Edmund Wilson wrote many years ago that even when Joyce and Proust turned their sights upon social or moral life, one felt they were giving us an "exercise . . . of the pure intelligence playing luminously all about but not driven by the motor power of any hope and not directed by any creative imagination for the possibilities of human life." It is tempting to think of Roa in these terms. Some have found him a different sort of writer, even going so far as to read his book as a political novel, as an attack upon General Alfredo Stroessner, Paraguay's notorious dictator.

But though Roa's universe is ventilated by strong winds blowing through the sometimes close and tangled thickets of Francia's mind, it is largely what Wilson calls "the shuttered house" of the imagination that we chiefly feel we inhabit. For all the interest we take in the texture of the prose and the virtuosity of the various narrative devices, we are not always certain that the insight achieved is commensurate with the fantastic energy expended on its behalf. Nor are we certain that there is sufficient dramatic development in a work that has more than its share of verbal energy and schematic brilliance. There is no doubting the extraordinary magnitude of Roa's enterprise, but the precise nature of his achievement will be debated for many years to come.

MANY TYPES OF AMBIGUITY

INGEBORG BACHMANN

There is mischief in formulation. Write something striking and decisive and you are bound to open up as many questions as you sought to resolve. When a character in a story by Ingeborg Bachmann declares that "well said is half lied," he is uttering a "truth" and bearing witness to the inherent slipperiness of formulation, especially when it is terse and provocative.

Bachmann was a relentless formulator. She was drawn to language as if it held the key to every human hope. "No new world without a new language," one of her characters intones. It is like Bachmann and her characters to say all sorts of things with conviction, without knowing quite what they entail. Bachmann was not committed, or not exactly, to irrationality, but she mistrusted elementary reasonableness and took refuge in formulation, presumably in the hope that it would carry her past ambivalence and confusion. Although she suggested that the truth was unsayable, she nevertheless said, again and again, what she took to be the truth. "This inhuman fixing," she called the impulse to unimpeachable assertion, "this insanity which flows from people and is frozen into expression." If she was one of the great writers of the last century, she was, all the same, deliriously dissatisfied with her medium, and her characters likewise often insist that words "are only words" and merely allude to the fact that "something exists."

Ingeborg Bachmann was born in Klagenfurt, Austria in 1926, and died in Rome in 1973, in a mysterious fire that some have suggested was in fact a suicide. She won early fame as a poet but devoted the last fifteen years of her life to fiction, which initially seemed to many readers a disappointing species of "women's fiction"; later, however, her stories and her novel *Malina* made her one of the most celebrated writers in Europe. Although her works are available in excellent English translations and a number of films have been made from her fiction, she has never had much of a following in the United States, and it is fair to say that even in American feminist circles she is rarely invoked as an exemplary figure. The publication of a slender new book of Bachmann's "Letters" to a fictional addressee, written when she was eighteen, encourages us to ask why an indisputably major writer should have remained so little known here.

It may well be that Bachmann's failure to attract an enthusiastic readership in the United States has had mainly to do with her unreliability. Although inclined to decisive pronouncements, she seems always ready to disown what she says. Her most famous utterance, which can be found with variations in a number of different works, has it that "fascism is the first thing in the relationship between a man and a woman." This idea also is cited in books and essays devoted to Bachmann's work. Again and again, critics take Bachmann to have been concerned, above all else, with the violence done to women by men, their "exploitation at the hands of men," as Damian Searls puts it in the introduction to *Letters to Felician*. Nothing, it seems, could be more definite than the sentiment inspiring Bachmann's resounding formulation.

And yet there is, at the center of that formulation, a metaphor. To say that "fascism is the first thing in the relationship between a man and a woman" is not, or not quite, to say that gender relations *are the same as* relations between, say, Nazis and Jews. Metaphor, to be sure, is always suggestive, but it operates best when it is not taken to be coercive. We yield to the logic of Bachmann's metaphor about fascism without believing that if we are to read her sympathetically, we must accept that men are fascists and women their victims.

There are readers, however, who will want to believe precisely that, and who will therefore be disappointed when a writer like Bachmann makes it difficult for them to uphold such a simple, terrifying view of men and women. Such readers might find more satisfaction in the work of another Austrian woman writer, Elfriede Jelinek, who was awarded the Nobel Prize in 2004 and to whom, therefore, much greater attention has lately been paid. Jelinek is best known in the United States for her 1983 novel *The Piano Teacher*, which was recently made into a feature film, and she is rightly described by the Nobel Prize committee as "a dauntless polemicist" with an instinct for "burning issues." One might also note that she has an instinct for what Ruth Franklin in *The*

New Republic calls "incomprehensible pseudo-philosophical musings," "banal . . . propaganda," "pornographic imagery," and a succession of crude "gender stereotypes" to which she unremittingly subscribes. Whereas Bachmann was fiercely and fruitfully conflicted about everything, Jelinek is in doubt about nothing. Whereas Bachmann evokes the bitter, the desperate, and the indescribable in a language tense and unstable, Jelinek has an appetite for slogans, simplifications, and rant. If in Bachmann one is always alert to how much is withheld, unsaid, in Jelinek one feels that nothing is left out and that there is nothing this writer will not say for effect and attention.

Bachmann is invested in a delicately patient examination of consciousness, and never confuses the moral life with the striking of ideological postures. Although she sometimes wrote with the baffled anger of a woman with grievances to express, she was never a mere collector of grievances, and her descents into hysteria were oddly balanced by a miraculous and deeply serious lucidity. Attracted as she was to fashionable ideas about the unbridgeable gap between feeling and reason, she was inveterately skeptical about categorical distinctions, and could be playful even in the face of the standard platitudes she entertained.

In a long essay on "The Feminist Reception of Ingeborg Bachmann," Sara Lennox reports that German feminists have long fought among themselves about the meaning of Bachmann's work and its relation to the "theoretical assumptions" informing views of women as "victims of the dominant [patriarchal] order." Did Bachmann urge women to "keep their distance from men"? Did she believe that the culture in which her women lived—the culture of the European middle classes—"was determined to destroy them"? Many feminist critics read Bachmann as if she intended to promote such views. Others argued that "Bachmann's feminism is always full of unresolved paradoxes" and that only "wishful thinking" could account for the attempt to make Bachmann "conform to our ideas about . . . the proper form of feminist (or other) theory and practice." Some even went so far as to challenge the equation of "patriarchy with other structural forms of oppression" (like fascism), maintaining that Bachmann was far too intelligent to believe what some of her more ideologically inclined readers attributed to her.

It will not do, with a writer like Bachmann, to defend her by suggesting that she is not really interested in ideas, or that gender relations in general do not matter to her. She is not a writer who writes just about herself. For all the formal chaos she sometimes allows, she does not let her narratives wander where they will or drift in and out of relevant involvement with what seem to be her principal concerns. Her characters are never permitted to be entirely free of the ideas that define their importance to her. Even where the surface of the prose is given over to the mercurial fever dreams of one or another character, the current of thought is directed by the author's obsessive engagement with recurrent issues or problems. It may not always be easy for us to hang on to the thread that binds one thought to another, but we are never in any doubt about the general direction of the thought process. The center in Bachmann—the sense that certain things are indisputably essential—tends always to hold, however blurred or splintered the many radiating perceptions or sensations.

In fact, the new translation of Bachmann's *Letters* demonstrates how her work grows out of a relatively small number of basic concerns. *Letters to Felician* is by no means "Bachmann's first mature work," as Damion Searls willfully contends. The *Letters* are the affecting outpourings of an adolescent writer who, in 1945, was apparently experiencing love for the first time and somehow managing not to connect her state of mind with the war that had just come to an end. To regard these items as "mature," one would have to pretend that they were not mawkish or sophomoric, not the effusions of a young person who fancies herself to be "enchanted" and "pure." We can locate in this work signs of the darkness and internal contradiction that mark Bachmann's mature fiction, but here they are merely signs, fragmentary foreshadowings, nervous eruptions without context or discernible purpose. When we read in these letters that "two people are in me, neither understands the other," we can say only that this comes from a divided, gifted, and possibly disturbed young woman. We do not know what more to think of her because she offers us no situation in which to place her, no "before" or developmental sequence that would make her more than the symptoms she displays.

What is more striking about these letters, though, is the pattern they exhibit. The author or persona is alternately submissive—often to the point of self-extinction—and assertive. The beloved is for her "everything," her "only altar," the one she is forever "ready to serve." She, on the other hand, is "ordinary and small," prepared to "lose all dignity" in the service of her "Lord." She is also fearful, open and vulnerable before "a mouth trying to drink from me." Exalted by the sacrifice she is prepared to make, she is yet "in the kingdom of bitterest joys," alert to the fact that the consummation she seeks will leave her "by the wayside somewhere," never truly satisfied. The one who is devoutly urged to "come and cast your will over me" is unfortunately going to leave her with "nothing" she can call her own. Her assertions of "unbelievable happiness" are balanced by feelings of "inconsolable depression." Although she is "unworthy," she vaguely refers to "everything that's missing," and she can almost bring herself to imagine that she has coming to her more than she has. She may be, as she says, "incapable of thinking anything rational," but she will not altogether accept that impoverishment.

To read only these letters by Bachmann is to wallow with her in a pathetic species of confused desire and self-contempt. Nothing here is worked out, nothing gets Bachmann beyond what reads like adolescent mania or neurosis. Those who wish to read the letters as windows "into the human condition" or as blueprints for a theory of women's bondage to men are of course free to do as they like, but then they also ought to ask themselves why the persona here should be regarded as exemplary or typical when she is so often hysterical or delusional and given to exaggerated effusions of balked hero worship.

So much that we find in Bachmann's mature writing is absent from the *Letters to Felician* that it is futile to cite but a single missing element. In *Letters* we have the combination of unsatisfiable desire and willed, hysterical identification with or worship of a powerful other. But as Bachmann's work ripened, the longing was more and more represented as impossible, exaggerated, and ludicrous, the objects of worship made to seem unworthy, the self-immolation depicted as strangely sick and fascinating. The standard Bachmann persona, early so defenseless and small, came later to seem intermittently fierce and brilliant, if always fatally complicit in her sorry fate. If in the *Letters* the "two people" locked together were unable to understand each other, in the mature fiction the victim and her "other" are often in fruitful communication. In Bachmann's novella "Three Paths To The Lake," Elisabeth Matrei finds her life "poisoned" by her lover Trotta, and is consumed by "that undercurrent of contempt [toward other people] which had always been characteristic of Trotta." But she finds as well that once he is out of her life, "Trotta's voice" can be important to her, can become the foundation for "her own voice," strengthening her, separating her from the weak voices of others less determined than she to confront the "real things" in life. For every token of subjection in the mature Bachmann there is some countervailing urgency, however little the instinct to self-assertion can sustain itself.

Another way to say this is that there is a fundamental tension in Bachmann's mature work, a vitality that is, if never completely effectual, at least desperate and often savage. She says no to the forces within her that press her to disappear. Walled in by apparently insurmountable forces, she imagines escape and retribution even as she suffers her condition, strangled by fear and ambivalence. The despair of Bachmann's characters is often robust. If they are prisoners, lifers, they are yet not altogether maimed or impotent. Their thrashings about and eruptions of fitful protest or indignation are unmistakable signs of life. They will suffer and accept, but they will continue to ask why, and they will not go gently.

There are exceptions to this pattern in Bachmann's fiction, characters who are treated as objects of satire, figures who are merely pathetic, for whom it is impossible to feel genuine compassion because they are entirely symbols of a condition they can do nothing but reflect. Such characters exist to prove something, and so do not exist for us as if they were fully human beings. That Bachmann was after more than this—more than an indisputable demonstration of the terrible lives to which women are irrevocably consigned—is clear in the great majority of her stories and in her central masterpiece, the novel *Malina*. Tempted as Bachmann was to banish from her thoughts variety, surprise, and optimism, she resisted total capitulation even as she yielded a part of herself to the terrible, reductive impulse. "Dead," thinks Charlotte in the story "A Step Towards Gomorrah." "Dead was the man Franz and dead the man Milan, dead a Luis, dead all seven whom she had felt breathing over her . . . those who had sought her lips and been drawn into her body." That reduction of all men to one man, of all life to no life, of otherness to irrelevance or extinction, is a powerful force in all of Bachmann's work, an expression of a savage recoil from the encompassing sense of subordination. But the work lives in the alternation from the one instinct to the other, in the refusal of Bachmann's imagination to settle for a complacent victimization.

Mary Gordon gets it exactly right when in a review of Bachmann's stories she observes that "the relations of men and women call up at once Bachmann's profoundest dualizing pessimism and her most visionary hopes." Just so, Bachmann moves from pessimism to hope when she thinks about the capacities of women. At one moment her character

Charlotte wants to teach her disciple to speak "slowly, exactly, and not permit any clouding by the common language," but almost in the same breath she scorns the available "language of women," which is, she observes, good for nothing but "a jumble of judgments and opinions."

However various and contradictory Bachmann's fictions, they do, all of them, enact the struggle of characters—not always women—to get free of something: an oppressive partner, a feeling of indifference, a homesickness, a dependence. Often they are disgusted by their own capacity to dissemble, to be dutiful, to pretend to pay attention though they are wholly self-absorbed. In "Word For Word," one of Bachmann's greatest stories, Nadja reflects that she herself "talked about *everything* with the same superficiality." A gifted and successful simultaneous translator, "she lived," Bachmann writes, "without a single thought of her own, immersed in the sentences of others," and although the story allows her moments of wild, sometimes punishing humor, she is never sure what she wants. Signs, small random tokens distributed across the narrative, may be taken for affirmative wonders, but Nadja typically indulges in wishful thinking and indiscriminate criticism. Her repudiation of everything around her is "hopeful" only in the sense that Nadja will not settle for what she is. We understand that the real issue is not her immersion in "the sentences of others." If she is ever to get free, in fact, she will need—so Bachmann suggests—to acknowledge her own complicity in the circumstances that control her.

Bachmann's insistence upon the necessary struggle to get free did not cause her to write as if she had a fixed agenda. Nothing in her work is consolidated, nothing stands still. Unable to live an ordinary life, Bachmann's characters are always burning with rage or impatience or grief. "Bachmann's vision," as Mary Gordon has written, "is structured by a series of mutually annihilating pairs: thought and action, life and truth, female and male." Like her characters, Bachmann has little use for comfortable accommodation, though she imagines she wants nothing more. No sooner does she opt for "truth" than she allows herself to prefer instead "life," pleasure, happiness. If men or patriarchy would seem to signify oppression, then in due course such terms must also be shown to signify more, even perhaps some promise of liberation. The "pairs" in Bachmann are "mutually annihilating" because she thrives on opposition and antagonism, sees things not simply as they are but as they might be. No principle or person exists in Bachmann without its complementary or oppositional other. And because Bachmann sees and

INGEBORG BACHMANN

thinks in this way, she is never susceptible to the simple charity that allows things merely to be. Turmoil is an essential ingredient of her medium, and although she is powerfully drawn to defeat, she never quite allows herself to assume the posture of the principled victim.

Bachmann's greatest work is *Malina*, though this fact is sometimes obscured by scholars who are more excited by the unfinished novels she left behind. These—*The Book of Franza* and *Requiem for Fanny Goldmann*—contain traces of an ideological agenda Bachmann would likely have submerged and obscured had she lived to complete them. The translator of these fragments, Peter Filkins, writes in his admirable introduction of his efforts to "rearrange" passages so as to produce "readable" texts, but he concedes that we cannot know what the "final shape" of the novels would have been. Would Bachmann, Filkins asks, "have scrapped everything and found entirely different solutions"? "We simply cannot know," he writes.

But we do know that Bachmann published *Malina* and completed it at the time she was working on the unfinished books intended for inclusion in a cycle of novels entitled "Ways of Dying." These novels, says Filkins, "would chronicle the multitudinous ways in which individuals, particularly women, are 'murdered' by a society that Bachmann felt erased and silenced them." But such accounts of Bachmann's intentions are at once plausible and misleading: plausible because Bachmann sponsored such accounts in interviews and speeches, and misleading because the fiction itself by no means supports such a summary. To be sure, many passages in *Malina* suggest that "murder" is very much on the mind of the female narrator, and that what she finds "unbearable" includes the efforts of her "father" to pull out her tongue and the tendency of her lover Ivan to clap a hand over her mouth when she is about to say something drastic or depressing. But the "father" in *Malina* is a fabulously bizarre and protean figure whose activities and guises are often contradictory, and Ivan is typically mild, beneficent, and without any inclination to coercive violence. Were the narrator herself reliable, that is to say, a credible witness, we should of course credit what she tells us as if it were simply the truth. But she herself often does not know the difference between what she fantasizes and what she remembers, and the brilliance of *Malina* has much to do with its combination of attributes, its existing at once as meditation, parable, dream-vision, fairy tale, and prophecy. If the novel as a form typically assumes a more or less rational relationship between the individual and her world, *Malina* challenges that requirement, forcing its readers to ask not only what things mean but why meaning in Bachmann must always be problematic.

Walter Benjamin once wrote of Kafka that "to do justice" to him and his work "one must never lose sight of one thing: it is the purity and beauty of a failure." Benjamin may have used "failure" in the conventional sense of the word, but "Benjamin's diagnosis"—so the novelist Zadie Smith reminds us—points to a more radical "failure": "The peculiar beauty of Kafka," Smith writes, "lies in the very impossibility of his project, which was . . . to express concretely . . . those things in life that fall outside of the concretely explicable or expressible." Bachmann, we may rightly say, is in this sense a Kafkan writer, one for whom the novel is itself typically a medium too committed to society and "the real" to busy itself with the inexpressible. Bachmann's work, approached in this way, cannot be expected to make statements, cast blame, even scores, or correct abuses. Bachmann is not committed to a rational program or a critique of any existing order, even though her work serves at least in part as a demonstration of the terrible effect that the established order can have on a deeply intelligent and deeply feeling person. Of course, *Malina* forces us to think about what people do to one another and what they do to defend themselves against madness or the fear of extinction. But no one who reads *Malina*—really reads it—can suppose that it provides answers to the questions Bachmann raises or adequate political responses to "fascism" and the vicissitudes of ordinary gender relations.

At the heart of *Malina* we find a trio of figures. The female narrator, a distinguished Austrian writer, more than a little mad, is in love with Ivan, the divorced father of two young children, though she lives with Malina, a minor writer and functionary upon whom the woman extravagantly relies. Throughout a fragmentary narrative that contains letters, interviews, fairy tales, and dreams, the woman gravitates from the one male figure to the other, now dreaming of "happiness" with the fatherly Ivan, elsewhere attached to the "omniscient" Malina, who seems to know her better than she knows herself. Is the woman "victimized" by these men? Do they represent the standard torsions of male "power" and patriarchal privilege? Everywhere in the novel are signs that may be taken for the effects of male power. Ivan wants her to write only happy books, and briefly, dutifully, she tries to satisfy him. Once she fears that Malina will catch her "kneeling in front of the telephone . . . prostrate

. . . like a Moslem on his rug," hoping against hope that Ivan will call her. When at another point Ivan casually lifts his hand, she flinches as if he were about to strike her, and as he pins her arms back, apparently to stop her from some fit of hysteria, he asks, "Who's done this to you, who's put such nonsense into your head," thereby invalidating her, denying that she has in fact anything to fear.

In addition, the novel often refers to war, rape, and murder. "Most men usually make women unhappy," the woman says. When you get right down to it, she reflects, "every man really is sick," and if things are worse in Vienna than elsewhere, that is because it "is made for universal prostitution" and "all the ramifications of the male disease" are readily played out there.

196

But the woman who furnishes these observations is clearly disturbed. What is more, she consistently resists or undercuts her own "insights." If she did not, the novel would read like a psychotic rant. To be sure, writers like Toni Morrison have used "madness" to identify the pernicious effects of racism and sexism on women, and there are other writers for whom "madness" functions—however improbably—as an affirmation of female selfhood. But Bachmann does not portray madness in this way, and in *Malina* it is represented as disabling, terrifying, and totally unproductive. When Bachmann's narrator says "no normal man with normal drives has the obvious idea that a normal woman would like to be quite normally raped," she does not affirm her character's selfhood or cheer her on. In fact, the narrator's sweeping and irrational generalizations are routinely made to seem symptomatic of her illness, if also unnerving by virtue of the partial truths they express.

But the key to understanding the narrator's pronouncements on "men" lies in Bachmann's treatment of the character Malina. When the woman imagines that her father had ordered her bookshelves "to be torn down," she tears "the French books from his hand, since Malina had given them to me," suggesting as she does at many other points that Malina is by no means to be associated with oppressive patriarchs and that she deeply values what he has tried to do for her. When she is possessed by despair and self-pity and tells herself the lie that Ivan, who clearly does not love her, was the "one single beautiful human being" who might have saved her, Malina urges her to "stop falling down all the time. Get up. Go out, have fun . . . do something, anything." Supposing that she is made to be the grateful consort of a man like Ivan, made to be a mild, uncomplaining partner and the obedient caretaker of two darling children, she is corrected by Malina, urged to "learn a new style of struggle," to accept that if she is ever to be at one with herself, she will renounce the idea that she is a "normal" woman with "normal drives" and a fate that resembles that of women with whom she has virtually nothing in common.

That Malina himself should be seen as a tormentor is entirely understandable when particular lines are isolated or ripped from their proper context. Even the woman is occasionally afraid of him, though most often she expects from him—and receives—encouragement, protection, and a species of tough love not at all reducible to popular clichés. In fact, for all of her fear and agitation, the woman understands much better than many of Bachmann's readers what Malina means when he says that "you can only be of use to yourself by hurting yourself," or when 197 she imagines him saying of Ivan "Kill him! Kill him!" Whether or not Bachmann intended us to regard Malina as the narrator's alter ego—the suggestion has been widely entertained—he exists unmistakably in the novel as a substantial being with physical traits, speech patterns, and a disposition altogether distinct from hers. And the fact that he is a male figure endowed, for better or worse, with what the narrator takes to be distinctly male characteristics—"steadfast and composed," one who understands "without my having to explain it," a man with "nothing to settle"—cannot but suggest that, for Bachmann, the woman's essential failure is her inability to break out of the prison of her own narrowly constructed female identity.

Such an idea will hardly find favor with readers bent upon wringing a partisan "message" from *Malina*, readers who want to find in Bachmann what Ruth Franklin has called the "particularly virulent sort of radical feminism" epitomized by Jelinek. But again, *Malina* is not a polemical novel. If we say that Bachmann's narrator *allows* herself to be destroyed, *permits* her mentor Malina to help her destroy what is inauthentic within her, *needs* him to emerge within her as the strength to deny what she cannot truly want for herself, do we thereby betray or violate a "truth" about "patriarchy" and gender relations too sacred to be challenged? Do we thereby compromise our sense of Bachmann as a writer who had the nerve to get to the very bottom of a woman's experience without fear of melodramatic exaggeration?

To contend that no virulent formulation we can pull from *Malina* begins to capture the spirit and meaning of this novel is to contend, simply, that Bachmann invests everything she writes with a scrupulous uncertainty and misgiving. The air of excess and extremity that circulates in her pages should not distract us from the essential seriousness of her desire to understand what baffles and pains her. To read her as if she had a program to propose or a constituency to represent is fatally to misread, and lose, a major writer.

16

RUBBLE AND ICE

W. G. SEBALD

The work of W. G. Sebald is by now a part of the air we breathe. It seems to many writers and readers "noble" and "irrefutable." It possesses, apparently, a "preternatural authority," and demonstrates "that literature can be, literally, indispensable." To one of our best novelists the fiction offers a "truth" that is "exalting," while a distinguished poet regards Sebald as a "thrilling" writer who "makes narration a state of investigative bliss." James Wood, in what is surely the best of all the essays I have yet seen on Sebald, makes the case for his language as "an extraordinary, almost antiquarian edifice, full of the daintiest lusters." If a few souls whisper among themselves that the writing is occasionally "leaden," or that there reigns in Sebald "an arbitrarily associative aesthetic," or that the extremity of despair on display is frequently laughable, these objections would seem not to have won over many readers. Sebald is among the most admired of contemporary writers, and his work is routinely taken to remind us, as Susan Sontag writes, that "literary greatness" is "still possible."

No doubt, Sebald can be a thrilling writer. We admire in him the delicate shifting from memory to hallucination, from dense physical immediacy to difficult, obstructed speculation. We respond sharply to what one reviewer calls "the long tide surge" of the prose, its measured, inexorable movement, "almost unbroken by paragraphs, in long seeming digressions that slowly pull tight like a noose." To respond to these and other comparable features of Sebald's prose is to respond to the writing "for its own sake," as Christopher Hitchens put it in a 2001 obituary tribute, to its cadenced loops and recurrences, to what Wood calls the mingling "of melodrama and extremism running alongside a soft mutedness." But we do not mourn Sebald principally because we love his writing "for its own sake." If he was, as many now contend, a major writer, there was more to him than those sentences and effects, more than the "chaste lyricism" and "formal innovation" so often remarked upon.

In fact, for all of her enthusiasm about Sebald's prose, Sontag frankly concedes that Sebald's fiction is in pursuit of "the truth" about the lives it studies. "I know of no book," she writes of *The Emigrants*, "which conveys more about that complex fate, being a European at the end of European civilization." Others take *The Emigrants* and the later novel *Austerlitz* to be books *about* the Holocaust, and many follow Sontag in commending "the grandeur" of Sebald's "subject." A. S. Byatt believes that *The Emigrants* is a book "about the vanished lives of wartime Jews," and others describe Sebald's work in general as an achievement of "the historical imagination." With the publication of *Austerlitz*, says Richard Eder, Sebald takes his place "with Primo Levi as the prime speaker of the Holocaust." Whatever the sense of him as a writer wrapped in "fog bound . . . half-remembered images and ghosts," Sebald is admired not merely for the sumptuousness and occlusions of his prose but for his effort to get at something real. He is, to be sure, a writer who operates "on the soft verges of dread," but he wishes us to believe, as Anthony Lane writes, that "there is a world elsewhere," and that the fate of human beings in history is of primary importance to him.

Of Sebald's four completed novels, *Austerlitz* surely seems the most insistently situated, though, as in his other books, there is a good deal of travel and place shifting. The two principal characters are always taking a train or about to take a train. They see each other in several different cities. But the action in the novel is focused. The narrator, who speaks as if he were Sebald himself, is fascinated with—obsessed with—a man named Jacques Austerlitz, whom he meets by chance one day in the late 1960s. In a series of meetings covering more than twenty years, Austerlitz tells the narrator his story, and it is his story that dominates the novel. The story involves the efforts of a damaged man to learn the truth of his origins, to work his way back through repressed memories to some substantial image of his own parents and their fate. There is a marked affinity between the narrator and Austerlitz, both of whom suffer from the world being too much with them and are susceptible to breakdown. But it is the narrator's obsession with Austerlitz that drives the novel, presumably because the narrator sees in Austerlitz's quest an emblem. If Austerlitz can discover the "truth" of his own origins, some larger "truth" about history and about all of us will thereby come clear.

That faith would appear at least to inform the novel, though it is not faith as such that binds the narrator to Austerlitz. It has been said that "the spirit of ruined Europe" speaks through Sebald, and it is clearly that spirit that resonates for the narrator in the words of Austerlitz, which he carries around in his head even through the long years in which the two men do not meet.

From the age of five, Austerlitz had been brought up in a Welsh vicarage, the child of predictably dour "parents," described as "a Calvinist preacher" and a "timid-natured Englishwoman." The house of this Welsh childhood was, not surprisingly, "unhappy . . . which stood in isolation on a hill" and featured a variety of "locked doors," "sparse" furnishings, and "curtains drawn even during the day." Austerlitz describes himself in those years in a language heavily saturated with words like "twilight," "extinguished," "captivity," "numb with weariness," and "oppressed." The father's calendar was, of course, "grey" and "threadbare," and his sermons typically "succeeded in filling the hearts of his congregation with such sentiments of remorse that at the end of the service quite a number of them went home looking white as a sheet." We do not hear about the others, the ones who did not fill with "sentiments of remorse," but we do learn that the father himself after his standard Sunday success "was in a comparatively jovial mood," by no means long lasting, but notable. Other special childhood memories narrated by Austerlitz include a visit to a newly bombed-out site where "the ruins were still smoldering" and the bodies of the dead were assembled on the grass, "dressed in their Sunday best," identified by the father as those "who had sinned against the Lord's commandment to keep the Sabbath day holy."

More especially compelling—or gruesome—are the images of the father's childhood village, now entirely submerged "beneath the waters of the Vyrnwy reservoir," so that the child imagines "all the others—his parents, his brothers and sisters, his relations, his neighbors, all the other villagers—still down in the depths, sitting in their houses and walking along the road, but unable to speak and with their eyes open far too wide." When, later, the father shows him a photograph of a "girl sitting in a chair in the garden with her little dog on her lap"—it is reproduced in the text, one of the many black-and-white images in the book—the photo is said to have become "as familiar to me as if I were living with them down at the bottom of the lake."

I dwell on this aspect of Austerlitz's biography only in part because it is vividly evoked in the novel. What is important about this childhood portrait is that it identifies a susceptibility. This is not a portrait of any childhood. The notable features are marked by their awfulness. People here are "slowly being killed by the chill in their hearts," and their surroundings inexorably contribute to their sense of encroaching darkness and "unhappiness building up." The few paltry references to an inspiring schoolmaster or a promising "bright light" of optimism can do little to obstruct the downward drift of the narrative. When a childhood friend shows Austerlitz his "special parrot," it naturally displays "a pale face that you might have thought was marked by deep grief."

This is, all of it, convincing, as in a tone poem where everything is artificially tinted and you do not incline, or at least not immediately, to ask whether in fact reality can be consistently colored in this way. You accept that for the duration of the piece, these are the colors that will be worn, and you allow yourself to luxuriate in their gradations and subtle alterations without troubling yourself about meaning or truth. The "truth" of the work is in its integrity as a made thing that refuses to be subordinated to meaning or to be diverted from its narrow path by a concern for verisimilitude.

Still, at some point in an encounter with this writing, you may well ask yourself if this is all that is wanted, however grateful you are for that which is given. James Wood, in an essay entitled "What Chekhov Meant by Life," recalls the playwright's objection to Ibsen. He "doesn't know life," Chekhov once told Stanislavsky. "In life it simply isn't like that." Like what exactly? Wood, with characteristic brilliance, explains. "Surely," he writes:

> Chekhov's objection to Ibsen was founded in the feeling that Ibsen is like a man who laughs at his own jokes. He relishes the *dramatic* "ironies" of the situation; indeed, he can think only in dramatic ironies, like someone who can write only on one kind of wide-margin paper. Ibsen's people are too comprehensible . . . he is always tying the moral shoelaces of his characters, making everything neat, presentable, knowable. The secrets of his characters are knowable secrets.

And if we ask what this may suggest about the overdetermination that so entirely colors the narrative of Austerlitz's childhood, may we not just say that the life presented "simply" isn't "like" life? May we not declare that Sebald, like the Ibsen that Chekhov describes, is always "ordering life" into "trim acts," so that his readers will "obediently" relish what is in this version always "knowable" and even predictable? Of course it may be said—it is routinely said—that Sebald obscures rather than clarifies, that his meander is rarely a straight line, that his writing, like Chekhov's, is full of "enigmas" and "milky complication," that his thought is wonderfully pregnant and "reticent." But the early pages of *Austerlitz* devoted to the troubled quester's childhood contain but one kind of enigmatic pregnancy, and the reticences insistently point to an entirely knowable source for the character's desperate attempt to break past his "inhibitions." We believe him when he says that "an agency greater than or superior to my own capacity for thought . . . has always preserved me from my own secret," but the agency is by no means obscure to us, and the secret itself is a good deal less mysterious and impenetrable than the character and perhaps Sebald himself would wish it to be. For all of the apparent drift and obscurity, there are a great many straight lines in Sebald, and whatever the insistence upon what is essentially unsayable, *Austerlitz* insistently clarifies and efficiently extorts from the reader an obedient confirmation and approval.

We confirm, among other things, that a childhood of a particular kind will tend to produce a "troubled" person. We also confirm that the very awfulness of a life or a childhood may be "ironically" hilarious in its extremity. But we may also confirm that "reality" may legitimately be evoked with the inexorable logic of an artificially constructed nightmare or hallucination, so long as the artificiality is somehow acknowledged and "reality" itself is set within brackets. We want to be assured that the author understands that what he is doing is not describing reality as it ostensibly exists in the world. We want the author's freedom to be, as it were, a responsible freedom, so that his refusals to toe the line of the ordinary will not seem arbitrary or frivolous.

Of course, there is nothing that feels frivolous in Sebald. Not even his willful digressions have an air of blithe inconsequence. But we are not, all the same, inclined to confirm that Sebald's creations have about them the freedom we most admire in fiction. Would we say of any of his characters what Wood says of Chekhov's people, that "they forget to act *as purposeful fictional characters*"? Do they ever "mislay their scripts" or "stop being actors" like "Ibsen's envoys"? Certainly there is no moment in the narrative of Austerlitz's childhood when anyone mislays the determining script or fails to be "purposeful," that is, to underline with perfect predictability the certifiable tenor of the author's imagination. No one in this narrative is free to go his own way. We do get, as in Chekhov,

W. G. SEBALD

what Wood calls "the stream of the mind," but it is rarely "accidental," and it does not "beautifully" or darkly allow "forgetfulness into fiction." Austerlitz may believe he has forgotten where he came from, but Sebald has not forgotten, and does not at any moment allow us to suppose that what has been suppressed will long remain hidden. The aura of secrets and probing and obstructed consciousness is underwritten by a secure and purposeful movement. The "mental journeys," as Wood describes them in Chekhov, in Sebald always have a destination, whatever the ostensible surprise the characters themselves are often made to express when they open their heavy-lidded eyes and take in the prospect. In *Austerlitz* more than in the other novels, the destination has not only a shape and an implication but a name, a particular history, and a related series of identifiable aftermaths.

The bleak childhood of Austerlitz not only disposes him to suspect that the secrets he is after will be dark, but that his way to them will be arduous. Thus it is not surprising that the novel should assume the shape of a quest narrative, in which obstacles are overcome, deductions are reached, and speculation is liberated to work upon gradually accumulating evidence. Neither is it surprising, given the years in which the childhood is set—the boy comes to England in 1939—and the fact that Sebald had earlier written *The Emigrants*, that the secrets should have something to do with things German. To be sure, even in Liverpool the passing cabs are black, and a newspaper story about a grieving man in Halifax has him ending his life in gruesome fashion "by means of a guillotine which he had built himself." There are everywhere the dying and the sick, and on excursions in the English countryside one is bound to see "houses with their roofs falling in, houses knee-deep in rubble, refuse and detritus." But the "morbid and intractable," however pervasive, seem in this novel simultaneously a reflection of "the way things are" and of a particular eruption that took place in the countries dominated by Hitler's Germany.

Austerlitz's reluctance to concern himself with the events of his own time is pronounced. He regards his life as "a constant process of obliteration," so that his determined efforts to discover where he came from and to learn the fates of the biological parents who saved his life by sending him to England do seem quite remarkable. We are astonished, of course, by Austerlitz's insistence that he understood "for the first time . . . the history of the persecution" only when he visited the Terezin concentration camp forty years after the end of World War II. And we are somewhat astonished as well by the fact that what Sebald has him discover is utterly familiar. The pages devoted to Terezin in particular read like an eloquent Sebaldian recitation of facts readily available to any tourist on a visit to Terezin, "a world made by reason and regulated in all conceivable aspects," complete with "pieces of luggage brought . . . by the internees" and, in numerous display cases, "balance sheets . . . endless rows of numbers and figures, which must have served to reassure the administrators that nothing ever escaped their notice."

Of course it is not *any* tourist brochure that will evoke the bus ride back to Prague as Sebald does, "as if we were descending a kind of ramp into a labyrinth through which we moved very slowly, now this way and now that, until I have lost all sense of direction." The power of Austerlitz's recitation is secured by the somber and suggestive language, and also by the oddly literal but no less haunting black-and-white photographs of Terezin doors, walls, numbered trash cans, filing cabinets, and random objects, including a "stuffed squirrel . . . which had its beady button eye implacably fixed on me, and whose Czech name—*Veverka*—I now recalled like the name of a long-lost friend." However little we can be surprised or enlightened as Austerlitz slowly discovers what he might, for the most part, have learned many years earlier, we are surely fascinated by the spectacle of his slow awakening. Equally fascinating is Sebald's way of making the familiar facts about the Holocaust so entirely compatible with everything else in the novel.

For, what, after all, does Austerlitz discover? That his mother, like his father a Czech Jew, was sent to Terezin and was later killed in another camp. That the treatment of prisoners in the camps was brutal, and that many died of disease and malnutrition. That diabolically clever deceptions were used to get the Jews into places like Terezin, and that in France, Belgium, and other countries ordinary people participated in the persecution and extermination of people like his parents. Such "revelations" are unearthed over the course of many pages in Sebald's novel, and if there is nothing new in any of this, considered merely as facts, there are many individualizing particulars. Some of these have to do with Austerlitz's alternating resistance and determination, his susceptibility and consequent tendency to see meaning and confirmation everywhere he turns. Thus, at a time when he was immersed in studies of the distant past at the Bibliotheque Nationale, he could not help dwelling on "the library's nervous system" and wondering whether, watching a film about the library, he "was on the Islands of the Blest or,

205

on the contrary, in a penal colony." Similarly, walking in Paris with a friend named Marie, he sees "a family of fallow deer gathered together . . . near the perimeter fence of a dusty enclosure where no grass grew, a living picture of mutual trust and harmony which also had about it an air of constant vigilance and alarm." And indeed, the accompanying photograph of those very deer, quite as Sebald's language suggests, does express that combination of harmony and vigilance, mutual trust and alarm. And it is impossible, moreover, not to feel that those deer, and the library, and ever so many other particulars that rise to and fall from our drifting consciousness as we follow Sebald, have everything to do with the facts that Austerlitz is so assiduous to unearth.

But are they connected? So we may wish to ask. And ought they to be connected? And what may be gained by connecting them? If we begin by declaring *Austerlitz* a novel of consciousness, then we answer all three questions at once. Austerlitz sees things in a distinctive way which, apparently, he shares with our narrator and, to some degree, with Sebald himself. Experience prepares all of us to see things as we see them, so that, in accordance with the appropriate logic, no objection is possible to any given perspective. If Austerlitz visits Terezin as an adult and sees things that both open his eyes to a "reality" he had long avoided and at the same time confirm everything in his previous experience, that is certainly one legitimate way of "understanding." Is the chill in the hearts of selected Welsh citizens in the 1940s at all helpful to us if we wish to understand the cool efficiency and apparently untroubled brutality of the murderers of Jews? It may be helpful or it may not, but either way, it is potentially interesting to consider that the linkage is compelling to a certain kind of intelligence. Does a dream of newspapers consisting "almost entirely of death announcements" tell us that Austerlitz's susceptibility to "an abysmal sense of distress" must surely account for and thereby invalidate his sense of reality, undermining even the authenticity of his recorded visits to Terezin? But again, if we proceed from the assumption that Sebald is principally interested in the operations of consciousness, then validity and authenticity must be assessed largely in terms of consciousness. Austerlitz persuasively takes in things—all things—in a vivid and unmistakable way. That is all we know and all we need to know.

The difficulty with this approach to an ambitious novel is that it does not quite take the novel seriously. We are not, or not quite, content to declare that a novel like *Austerlitz* is simply the record of a troubled consciousness. We do not wish to read as if our sole or primary objective were simply to see what this wretched fellow makes of things. His brilliantly learned forays into arcana of one sort or another, like the comparable forays of our narrator, are always interesting and sometimes oddly affecting, but the material dredged up is always harnessed to the larger, unfolding sense of things, and implicated in the saturating malaise. There is nothing sudden in Sebald; everything is allowed to slowly gather and simmer. But the wide plane of his intelligence tends always to narrow, so that what had seemed far flung and eccentric is recalled to the overarching, insistent purpose to which Sebald assigns everything. In the face of this overdetermining insistence, it is difficult not to conclude that consciousness is all, or that Sebald's purpose in the novel is simply to confirm what he already knows in his bones. If this conclusion fatally prevents our taking seriously the quest or investigation apparently central to this novel, and thus prevents our doing more than appreciating Sebald's writing "for its own sake," then we must think *Austerlitz* rather less of an achievement than we would like.

207

If we ask, again, what may be gained by connecting things as Austerlitz and Sebald connect them, then of course we are compelled to consider the meaning of connection where such materials and ideas are at issue. In other writers—Saul Bellow comes readily to mind—connection, as between one thing and another, always feels provisional. There is no sense of a fixed program driving things together, and if one idea is made to stand next to another, they are likely soon to be separated by unpredictable gusts of writerly intelligence. The very instinct to put things together is informed by a desire to tell them apart or, to put it another way, to see what each thing and idea in itself really is. Sebald does not at all appear to operate from such a desire. In his work, connection is the expression of a will to make things submit to laws that are felt to be inscribed in the fabric of the universe. Connection, as it were, demonstrates that nothing is entirely unknowable, however much we may regard an event, emotion, or idea as unsayable. The panic of the central figures in Sebald is reflected in their need to make things connect and their fear that the fixed pattern thereby revealed will drive them yet deeper into despair.

Of course, there is a potentially hopeful meaning associated with connection. That meaning is captured in what may be called a theory of history. *Austerlitz* is informed by such a theory. Where things recur, patterns multiply, and vagrant particulars merge, there is usually a

W. G. SEBALD

theory or a master narrative. Great novels are sometimes informed by a theory, and so too are tenth-rate novels. For every *Doctor Faustus* there are untold numbers of novels organized around some revealed truth or master-key intended to unlock the secrets of history. Even where there is an apparent diversity of outlook, there may be an informing theory to make of history a coherent, comprehensible, unstoppable motion. We object to that coherence when it seems to us specious, when the events gathered together "theoretically" do not in fact cohere, where imaginative violence is done to reality in an effort to uphold a theory. But where a theory of history is respectful of the variety it is asked to encompass, we may find it acceptable, perhaps even essential.

In *Austerlitz*, Sebald's theoretical ambitions are very much in evidence. Though his narrator is skeptical about "reasons," he early refers to "the fixed, inquiring gaze found in certain painters and philosophers who seek to penetrate the darkness which surrounds us purely by means of looking and thinking." That this procedure requires a theory is asserted throughout the novel. Not only are there references to presiding figures (the barmaid early on is casually described as "the goddess of time past") and suggestively thematic tokens (the clock's hand is said to move like "a sword of justice"), but again and again in *Austerlitz* there are earnest, occasionally playful reflections intended to generalize about what might otherwise seem a bewildering diversity of things. When Austerlitz launches into a lengthy discourse on model towns or workers, he concludes by noting that "our best-laid plans . . . always turn into the exact opposite when they are put into practice." Chance remarks are typically pregnant with some idea that will at once or gradually clarify whole areas of experience. Even on her deathbed, young Austerlitz's adoptive mother whispers "what was it that so darkened our world?" so that we are confronted with the prospect of something vast in the design of things that we must understand if we are to deal with the darkness.

Perhaps all of this amounts to something less than a theory and more like a worldview. "In any project we design," Austerlitz says, "the absolute perfection of the concept . . . in practice . . . must coincide with its chronic dysfunction." The observation is clearly self-canceling, the "theory," such as it is, advanced to deny its own potential efficacy. This is a constant element in the novel, as if Sebald were aware that the insistent pointing and merging and purposefulness were, all of it, helpless in the end to make a compelling case. "The absolute perfection of the concept" would thus be worth remarking, but not nearly the persuasive sufficiency a theorist would presume to establish. We may see, as the novelist William Gaddis once wrote, "how all the goddamn pieces fit together," but we will not believe that the informing concept accurately or believably accounts for this stunning, artificially worked-up coherence.

In what is a telling moment early in the novel, Austerlitz remarks that "the frequent result . . . of resorting to measures of fortification marked by . . . paranoid elaboration was that you drew attention to your weakest point, practically inviting the enemy to attack it." The passage goes on at some length to uncover "the whole insanity of fortification and siege-craft." In the 1832 battle of Antwerp, Austerlitz explains to a characteristically rapt narrator, fortifications were at once revealed to be hopeless, just as we now "know by instinct that outsized buildings cast the shadow of their own destruction before them, and are designed from the first with an eye to their later existence as ruins." We read such a passage with a combination of curiosity and resistance. The antiquarian interest it invites is unmistakable, and we respond readily enough by allowing ourselves to savor the insights lavished on the battle of Antwerp. But we know too that the business about "outsized buildings" being "designed from the first with an eye to their later existence as ruins" is more than a bit much to swallow even as a "metaphysical" notion, and that it is best read as a characteristic expression of the "paranoid elaboration" to which Sebald is infinitely susceptible. This is not a small thing in Sebald. Paranoia is the dominant weather of his imagination. He sees things as if they were swathed in or overhung by ominous black clouds. This way of seeing can seem amusing, even to Sebald, in the way that a tendency marked by exaggeration and fixity can lend itself to parody or self-parody. The fatalism inscribed in the passage above, on the battle of Antwerp and on "outsized buildings," is itself an instance of that self-parody. For is not the theoretical ambition informing the passage outsize and grandiose, given the eccentric substance of the central observation? And is it not Sebald's wish to signal his amusement at this lame effort at theory by suggesting that paranoid elaboration often lies at the heart of such enterprises?

In this sense, inviting a reader to resist or attack what is offered, Sebald disarms criticism by conferring upon his own creation the status of a merely "paranoid elaboration." To be sure, there is or may be pleasure in observing the apparent complexity or ingenuity involved in such a creation. It may well contain multitudes, and if we note that the informing paranoia flattens things to a certain meaningful sameness in

209

W. G. SEBALD

order to contain them, the procedure may yet seem worthy, simply as an exercise of the creative imagination. Again, this is hardly the level at which we should wish to appreciate a writer of Sebald's brilliance, and yet it is not always easy to know what more we may do to get at the nature of his achievement.

It is tempting to say that because the principal characters in Sebald so often resemble one another, these figures are not really credible as people. More than one critic has said as much, remarking especially on the resemblances between Austerlitz and the narrator in this last of Sebald's novels. But Austerlitz, like a number of characters in the other books, is very much a living figure. He is capable, as Sebald places him before us, of occasional surprises, and if his development is more or less settled, his disposition unchangeable, he is more than the sum of the fixities ascribed to him. His very obsessions, like those of the narrator, bristle with a peculiar air of agitation. We do not feel that Sebald is intent upon making the "pedagogical" statements that James Wood, for one, takes to be utterly disabling in standard works of paranoid fiction. Paranoid novelists, Wood argues, "can employ only characters who are loyal to [the novelists] and [their] agenda." With Sebald, there is, to be sure, paranoia, and there can be, moreover, "only characters" who can be harnessed to the singular purpose at hand. But the "agenda" as such is not promulgated with "pedagogical" earnestness. We do surely find in Sebald, quite as Wood says of paranoid fiction, "that anything can be connected with anything," and that tendency does often seem too much like "a dogmatic occultism." But if Sebald cannot "stop collecting connections" and suggesting that they do somehow add up, he manages his paranoia with some sense that it is disabling not only to his miserably unhappy characters but, in some degree at least, to his own imaginative faculties.

Which brings us to the question raised earlier in citations from readers who find in *Austerlitz* not merely beauty but truth. Is it possible, we must ask, that an essentially paranoid imagination can yet elaborate a serious theory of history and a substantial account of events that did actually take place or that might conceivably take place in an actual world? Can a book like *Austerlitz* legitimately be said to convey "more about that complex fate, being a European at the end of European civilization," than other contemporary fictions?

There are several ways to come at such a question. One proceeds from the view that the theory of history elaborated in *Austerlitz* is in fact no such thing. Paranoia is not a theory of history but a reflex. If Sebald believes that everything inevitably confirms everything else, and that anomalous particulars only apparently fall outside the revealed pattern everywhere inscribed in the novel, then of course he is not really looking at things *as they are* but forcing them to confirm what he already knows. To his credit, Sebald never puts on an objective air, not even when he is ostensibly looking directly at specimens in a display case or a laboratory. Neither does he offer his historical observations as if they were ratified by an existing consensus. Always Sebald permits us to beware of the susceptibility, eccentricity, or derangement of the perceiving intelligence. If we choose to believe in the validity of what we are told, we do so in spite of this acute awareness.

In *Austerlitz*, the ostensible theory of history, if indeed that is what Sebald intended, must account for the Holocaust. That would seem to be its primary assignment, given that the novel circles insistently around that enormity almost from beginning to end. Of course nothing in history can be exhaustively or definitively accounted for, explained, or narrated. And yet we do suppose that novels can sometimes account for some aspect of history, some period or movement, as Arthur Koestler accounted for the implacable brutality of Stalinism in *Darkness at Noon*, or as V. S. Naipaul captured the peculiar combination of change and stagnation so central to postcolonial independence movements in Africa and the Caribbean in novels like *A Bend in the River* and *Guerrillas*. Koestler's work is compromised by its seeming to operate from what Irving Howe once called a "self-confirming hypothesis," and that, surely, is a feature of everything Sebald has written. And yet Koestler's work continues to provide a credible accounting, however crude the dualism that informs the novel.

Austerlitz does not presume to account for the Holocaust by going to the ostensive political or historical origins of "the final solution." No effort is made to show that what happened to people like Austerlitz's parents was related to a long, gradually evolving history of European anti-Semitism. There are no accounts in the novel of the changing fortunes of European Jews, no references to theories of race or debates about the relative merits of assimilation and segregation. In Sebald's novel, the Holocaust is a series of events *in* history but without a particular history to account for them. We do not feel that Austerlitz's parents just happened to find that the only secure way to save their son was to send him away. Nor do we feel, as we are invited to think about Terezin,

W. G. SEBALD

that there just happened to be a time when such a place improbably held 60,000 people brought there for no reason other than that they happened—most of them—to be Jews. Sebald evokes these facts of history with every intention of making them feel like the culmination of something momentous that somehow gathered *in the past*, though he apparently has no wish to identify the particular factors in the past that might account for what happened. Perhaps he believed that any such identification of factors would inevitably be misleading. In any case, the factors are not substantially present in *Austerlitz*.

What is present is an aura of terrible sadness. That sadness is the only feature of the novel that may be called genuinely "irrefutable." It cannot be answered or compromised away. It cannot be corrected by "facts" or lifted by a decisive change of mood. If in the novel the sadness derives from or is associated with a neurotic susceptibility established without immediate reference to the Holocaust, the essential gravity of the pervasive sadness and the sense of consequence it assumes have everything to do with the novel's insistence that the events of the Holocaust actually occurred. However familiar the facts the novel rehearses—the deportations, the ghettos, the camps—the sadness of this novel never seems familiar. *Austerlitz* responds to the familiar facts very much in its own way, and its central character comes to those facts very much in his own peculiar way.

There is nothing political in *Austerlitz*, no element of political analysis, no sense of a future that might reflect changes in the way human beings conduct their affairs. Will itself seems almost entirely irrelevant to what matters most in the novel, for where there is will, there is the possibility of meaningful intervention, resistance, opposition. That possibility Sebald does not wish to summon or consider. He does not ask what might have been done or what might be done. The will summoned by Austerlitz to investigate his origins and find out what became of his parents is entirely a personal matter as we understand it in this novel, an anomalous reflex. It does not relate to some general demand for human justice. It is at most an expression of something very deep in the character, something which Sebald does not generalize, thematize, or celebrate. It is, this quality of will in Austerlitz, a frail, singular thing that does not hold within it any discernible promise. It is not a harbinger or token of qualities that may be mobilized in the name of a political ideal. Austerlitz had to pursue the truth about his parents quite as others had to hunt them down or expropriate their property. The big "truth" the novel steadily unfolds is that nothing can be done to alter the things that matter. Those who explain things politically must, according to this logic, convince themselves that we can make things happen because we want them to happen. Sebald does not debate the merits of the political imagination because, as a novelist, he has no interest in it. None at all.

But is it possible, then, to understand the Holocaust without recourse to politics? Is the sadness of *Austerlitz* a sufficient—what to call it?—emblem, token, of ultimate meaning? And is it something ultimate that is wanted when a determinate series of *events in history* is at issue? Again, Sebald does not purport to account in some ultimate or comprehensive way for the Holocaust. He does not deliberately avoid politics because, again, it clearly seems to him irrelevant given the magnitude of the experience he is evoking. The Holocaust in his telling is not an object lesson or an occasion for retributive fury or breast beating. The novel does not ask *why*, nor consider what might be a redemptive aftermath. More to the point, it does not reflect upon or ask its reader to reflect upon the theme of responsibility. It does not hold the perpetrators or the merely complicit before the mirror of narrative and demand that they acknowledge guilt or somehow point the way to an alternative vision. If there is in Sebald's narrative an unmistakable sense of crimes committed and of untold sufferings needlessly, wantonly inflicted, there is no sense of a corresponding resolve that might attend such a witnessing.

If we try to take seriously the idea that "Sebald stands with Primo Levi as the prime speaker of the Holocaust," we quickly conclude that the idea is ludicrous. To be sure, the Holocaust is represented in *Austerlitz* as an event without end, an event whose consequences reach into the very heart of European civilization. But Levi was, after all, an anatomist of the camps, interested both in the minute particulars of the Nazi apparatus and in the essential spirit of the atrocities visited upon the European Jews. He was, unlike Sebald, deeply committed to exploring such subjects as crime and complicity, collective and individual responsibility, resistance and the failure to resist. One intends no disrespect in saying that Sebald, in ignoring those subjects, among others, could not possibly be a "prime speaker of the Holocaust."

There is something valuable in Sebald's suggestion, embodied in this haunting novel, that certain things cannot ever end, that they must go on and on in the very fiber of the lives they have marked. This is not, in Sebald, an assertion of fact. It is not even an insight. It is a felt whisper of "the truth" of things that rises like the breath of anguish *there*, and there again, throughout a novel in which anguish is always at hand. It is not a truth with which a reader can argue. It cannot be judged, as if evidence could be invoked to refute or support it. Terrible things happen, the novel says, in the several ways that such a work has of saying what it wishes us to believe. Human beings, as they must, allow those terrible things to happen, and suffer, as they must, and erect edifices of one sort or another to defend themselves against pain and grief, but to no avail, as we know. The Holocaust was one of those terrible things that happened, perhaps in some ways the worst of such things, but in the end different from all the others—so far as we can tell—principally in the effect it had and continues to have on people who were in a position to be affected by it, as W. G. Sebald, a German writer born in 1944, had inevitably to be affected by it.

Is this a worldview? Does it tell us what it means to be a European "at the end of European civilization"? Do we take it that "the end of European civilization" was in some way a consequence of the Holocaust? In fact, Sebald himself does not at all suggest that the Holocaust was the primary factor in the inexorable devolution of his civilization. It was not the Holocaust that caused the painter Fragonard hundreds of years earlier to dissect "over three thousand bodies and parts of bodies in the course of his career" and thereby to provide for Sebald and for us one of many emblems of a fascination with death and a corresponding belief in the aesthetic "miracle" that is sometimes made from this fascination. It is not the Holocaust that causes all manner of people to be mesmerized by the "slow sound of a funeral march" or to feel that "everything was fading before our eyes, and that many of the loveliest of colors [have] already disappeared, or existed only where no one saw them." The Holocaust in Sebald belongs to a larger perspective in which things inevitably darken and deteriorate. In *The Rings of Saturn* we read, in a passage that has nothing whatever to do with the Holocaust, that "too many buildings have fallen down, too much rubble has been heaped up, the moraines and deposits are insuperable." In *The Emigrants* we read again and again of "the insatiable urge for destruction," an urge not invariably associated with the Holocaust. *Vertigo* is a work of profound disquiet in which the narrator wonders whether in fact he is in the land of the living, a work in which that same narrator dwells for a time on the figure of Dante and his fear of being burned at the stake.

If we are to think seriously, then, about "the end of European civilization," we must not think of the Holocaust as a cause—not, surely, if we follow Sebald. More significantly, the work of this writer does not reliably permit us to understand those very words, "end of European civilization." For if the signs of an ending, a deterioration, a coming on of barbarism, have been with us—in Europe, in the West—for many hundreds of years, surely from the time of Dante, why then one might as well say that the signs have been with us always, in which case it would hardly be reasonable to credit Sebald for having rightly called our attention to a phenomenon that is not properly to be understood as an ending at all. The sadness of *Austerlitz* would then reflect not the end of a civilization in the dungeons and gas chambers erected by the Third Reich, but the sense of a continuing, neverending "annihilation" that is intrinsic to "civilization" itself, in the face of which we are helpless.

The perspective is, to say the least, bleak, and it does surely reflect, as we have said, a disposition. No one would say that in Sebald we miss entirely what Seamus Heaney calls "the complicating drag of the contingent," though there is rarely so much as a nod toward "the middle state of human life." There is in Sebald what Heaney calls "the interesting impairment of specific personal gravity" so notable in the work of Czeslaw Milosz, though in Sebald the impairment is of one kind only, the "personal" so entirely underprized and underrealized as to seem thin, paltry. "It was as if I were buried under snow and ice," says Henry Selwyn in *The Emigrants*, and in truth, that is what the "personal" often seems in Sebald, something chill and inaccessible, though almost real, beckoning, if only there were a way to reach it, to open it up, to breathe a little more life into it.

James Wood contends that the facts in Sebald "seem never to have belonged to the actual world, and seem only to have found their proper life within Sebald's prose." Even the sentences in Sebald, Wood writes, often do not "really refer to anything outside language." This is a radical and deeply illuminating way to think about such a writer, though it troubles me to think of Sebald exclusively in such terms. For one thing, a novel like *Austerlitz* does not invite us to read it as if its sentences referred to nothing "outside language." For another, there are a great many facts in the novel that do certifiably belong "to the actual world" and continue to belong to the common world we inhabit. It is important to note, of course, that Wood's observations were originally published before the appearance of *Austerlitz*, and do more aptly describe the earlier novels, where Sebald's "reticence," "opacity," and reliance upon a "terrible abundance of [defining] lacunae" do allow us somewhat to accept that the "actual world" is not principally what Sebald is evoking in his fiction.

Still, this notion is troubling. Perhaps it is bound to trouble only a reader whose commitment to the "actual world" is greater than Sebald's, or a reader more inclined than Wood to believe that the novel itself is bound to engage with facts that seem at least "to have belonged to the actual world." Wood writes in another essay, an attack on paranoid fiction, that "fiction's task is to show where connections seem to end," which can only mean that fiction should do more than give us facts *only* properly belonging to prose itself.

We cannot, in the end, complain of Sebald that his fictions are not more cheerful, hopeful, or emphatic than they are. The works are, as such works are bound to be, an expression of temperament, and their music is saturated with a quality of elegy and lamentation we cannot but find affecting. If we say of them nonetheless that they are limited by their temperament or outlook, that they are *unduly* pessimistic, that is because they seem to us to leave out more than they should. A great novelist is not required to love the world, but he is required to see the world. The creative imagination, Adam Zagajewski has written, must not lose "sight of the common world," which cannot be "dissolved in art." Sebald cannot be asked to join with the great Polish poet in marveling "at the generosity of human nature," but we may wish that his novels gave us a somewhat broader view of the human spectrum, so that his pessimism would seem less settled, less reflexive, and so that the darkness in the novels would seem to have been tested by some genuine engagement with—Zagajewski's language is precise—"the calm and courage of an ordinary life."

SELECTED BIBLIOGRAPHY

1

Roth, Philip. *American Pastoral*. New York: Houghton Mifflin, 1997.

2

Deane, Seamus. *Reading in the Dark*. New York: Knopf, 1997.

3

Ginzburg, Natalia. *All Our Yesterdays*. Translated by Angus Davidson. New York: Arcade, 1985.
——. *The City and the House*. Translated by Dick Davis. New York: Arcade, 1986.
——. *It's Hard to Talk About Yourself*. Edited by Cesare Garboli and Lisa Ginzburg. Translated by Louise Quirke. Chicago: University of Chicago Press, 2003.

4

Desai, Anita. *Baumgartner's Bombay*. New York: Knopf, 1989.
——. *Clear Light of Day*. New York: HarperCollins, 1980.

5

Updike, John. *Toward the End of Time*. New York: Knopf, 1997.

6

Vargas Llosa, Mario. *The Real Life of Alejandro Mayta*. Translated by Alfred MacAdam. New York: Farrar Straus and Giroux, 1986.

7

Manea, Norman. *The Hooligan's Return*. Translated by Angela Jianu. New York: Farrar Straus and Giroux, 2003.

8

Schneider, Peter. *Couplings*. Translated by Philip Boehm. New York: Farrar Straus and Giroux, 1996.

————. *Eduard's Homecoming.* Translated by John Brownjohn. New York: Farrar Straus and Giroux, 2000.

————. *The German Comedy.* Translated by Philip Boehm and Leigh Hafrey. New York: Farrar Straus and Giroux, 1991.

9

Jaeggy, Fleur. *Last Vanities.* Translated by Tim Parks. New York: New Directions, 1998.

————. *Sweet Days of Discipline.* Translated by Tim Parks. New York: New Directions, 1993.

10

Gordimer, Nadine. *My Son's Story.* New York: Farrar Straus and Giroux, 1990.

11

Coetzee, J. M. *Waiting for the Barbarians.* New York: Penguin, 1982.

Kafka, Franz. "In the Penal Colony." Translated by Willa and Edwin Muir. In *Selected Stories.* New York: The Modern Library, 1952.

Naipaul, V. S. *In a Free State.* New York: Knopf, 1977.

12

Barker, Pat. *The Eye in the Door.* New York: E. P. Dutton, 1994.

————. *The Ghost Road.* New York: Penguin, 1995.

————. *Regeneration.* New York: E. P. Dutton, 1992.

13

Krasznahorkai, Laszlo. *The Melancholy of Resistance.* Translated by George Szirtes. New York: New Directions, 2000.

14

Roa Bastos, Augusto. *I The Supreme.* Translated by Helen Lane. New York: Knopf, 1986.

15

Bachmann, Ingeborg. *Letters to Felician.* Edited by Damion Searls. Berkeley, Calif.: Green Integer, 2004.

————. *Malina.* Translated by Philip Boehm, with an afterword by Mark Anderson. New York: Holmes and Meier, 1990.

16

Sebald, W. G. *Austerlitz.* Translated by Anthea Bell. New York: Random House, 2001.

218